The Lost Houses of Ireland

Randal MacDonnell

The Lost Houses of Ireland

WEIDENFELD & NICOLSON

Contents

Introduction

BETWEEN 1947 AND 1961, the *Irish Tatler and Sketch* published a series of some 60 illustrated articles on Irish country houses, but few of the original photographs have survived. Most people did not keep old copies of the Irish magazine, but complete collections were assembled at the National Library of Ireland and at Trinity College, Dublin. Unfortunately, about 20 years ago, somebody took a razor blade to the architectural articles in the magazines held by these two institutions and there now remains only a single run of the publication between them.

It was, therefore, important to re-publish these photographs while this was still possible. It was decided to concentrate on houses that had not properly appeared in book form before and those that have been demolished so can never be photographed again. Those that survive may still be described as 'Lost Houses', in so much as they are now golf clubs, hotels, old people's homes or schools (one is even a prison). Devoid of their original furnishings and pictures and stripped of their demesnes, they will never be family homes again.

The Irish gentry and nobility for whom they were built were an eccentric crew, whose extravagant and wilful behaviour not only bemused their British counterparts but also eventually led to their own downfall. An example of this sort of conduct was that of Sir Robert Tilson (afterwards the 1st Lord Muskerry) who built Upper Dromore House at the cost of some £30,000. He occupied his new home for only a single night before he tore it down in order to recover some of the costs of its construction from the salvaged materials.

Alcohol, so long associated with the Irish nation, was no stranger to the inhabitants of these houses. In 1836, Sir William Gregory described a visit to the Handcock seat at Carantrila. After a drunken evening, he arrived downstairs at noon the following day only to be confronted by an aged retainer who told him 'the divil a mouthful you'll get before three o'clock, so you had much better go to bed again.' Lady Fingall recalled that the guests at Danesfield blasted the sideboard to pieces and at Colganstown, the plaster birds by Robert West were decapitated and liberally peppered with shot by the intoxicated guests as an after-dinner entertainment.

This addiction to strong drink was endemic in the population from the highest to the lowest. On a modest stipend, the Reverend Mr Robert King of Ballylin kept a cellar of over 1300 bottles of fine wines. The servant class did nothing to set an example to their betters. The politician Isaac Butt had a butler who was partial to drink, but Butt persuaded him to make a formal promise to stop. The butler was so proud of this pledge that he had the certificate framed and hung up in the place of honour in his pantry. About a week later, Mr Butt found his butler drunk in a chair, with the credential hanging over his head!

Music was another feature of the Irish country house. The gentry followed in the tradition of the Gaelic aristocracy of the country and encouraged native musicians. The harpers Toirdhealbhach Ó Cearbhalláin (Turlough Ó Carolan), Art Ó Néill and Donnchadh Ó Hámsaigh (Dennis Hempson) were all habitués of these houses. At Charleville, near Enniskerry, County Wicklow, the Monck family were entertained by 'Dargle-John' or 'John-in-the-box' (a cripple who travelled throughout the county providing fiddle music to the gentry) and on the other side of Ireland, the Martin family had the services of 'Pete-een bawn', an albino fiddler who played from his perch on the windowsill, the dancing only interrupted by the quaffing of whiskey, which was available from a hip bath.

There was, however, another side to the coin. The majority of the Irish people lived outside these great houses and their lot was very different indeed.

Visitors to the country were appalled by what they saw: 'The poverty of the people as I passed through the country has made my heart ache', wrote Mrs Delaney, the English wife of an Irish Dean. She added, 'I never saw greater appearance of misery'. Her friend Jonathan Swift wrote in 1732 'There is not an acre of land in Ireland turned to half its advantage, yet it is better improved than the people … Whoever travels this country and observes the face of nature, or the faces and habits and dwellings of the natives, will hardly think himself in a land where law, religion or common humanity is professed.'

By the 19th century, hardly anything had changed. Sir Jonah Barrington (in retrospect) described his grandfather's tenants as loyal 'though to a man Papists, and at that time nearly in a state of slavery' and the Victorian Royal Commission on The State Of The Law and Practice In Respect Of The Occupation Of Land In Ireland Land Tenure In Ireland – The Devon Commission – reported, 'It will be seen in the Evidence, that in many districts their only food is the potato, their only beverage water, that their cabins are seldom a protection against the weather, that a bed or a blanket is a rare luxury, and that nearly in all, their pig and manure heap constitute their only property.' This was a shameful state of affairs and an understanding of these houses (and of how their owners were perceived by the majority of country people) needs to take these facts in consideration.

The writing was on the wall for the landed classes, but they failed to see it. The descendants of the Volunteers of the 18th century, seduced by the lure and glamour of Empire in the 19th century, left the popular representation of the Irish people to a new breed of politician. As a class, the Ascendancy opposed the wishes of the nation for self-determination, and took comfort in the jolly tales by Somerville and Ross of the fictional Resident Magistrate, Major Yeats, and his dealings with the stage-Irish characters that he encountered, believing that they were well regarded by their tenants. It took the Land War and later, the War of Independence to open their eyes. Their own actions, and the propaganda of their enemies, had made them truly strangers in their own country. It was not for nothing that, in Bowenscourt, Elizabeth Bowen, more perceptive than most of the gentry, described closing the front door of her house each night as though she was 'shutting Ireland out.'

Nowadays when a great Irish house is sold, it usually reappears for sale within a decade. Most of the properties in this book were owned for over three centuries by the same families and were at the centre of Irish life. It was their proprietors, the Irish landed gentry, who, although mostly alienated from the majority of the population by language, religion and political sympathies, held the social and political power of the country in their hands. In fact, the owners of the 25 houses described here controlled between them more than half a million acres of Ireland, together with the livelihoods, through their rent rolls, of tens of thousands of Irish men, women and children. Today, almost in the blinking of an eye, all of this has gone forever.

The purpose of this book is to reproduce a unique and historic photographic record of 25 of the once great houses of Ireland and to place them, and the families who lived in them, in their historical, cultural and social context. The notes, which start on page 214, expand on some of the people and events mentioned in the text.

Randal MacDonnell, Dublin, 2002

Pages 2 and 3, left to right
The entrance front, Gormanston Castle.
The drawing room, French Park.
The 'nunnery' at Shelton Abbey.
The long gallery, Mount Juliet.
The entrance and garden front, Rockingham.
The entrance hall, Clonalis.

Previous page
The entrance hall, Borris House.

A NOTE ON NAMES IN IRELAND

The following explains how and why Norman English and later anglicized surnames came to Ireland. ('Ó' means 'descendent of'; 'mac' is the Irish for 'son of' and 'fitz' is the Norman equivalent.)

In 1152 Diarmuid mac Murchadha (1110–77), King of Leinster, became involved in a feud, when he abducted Derbhorgaill, the wife of Tighearnán Ó Ruairc (King of Bréifni from 1124 to 1172). Ó Ruairc had his revenge in 1166. In that year, he defeated Diarmuid mac Murchadha, and his ally, the High King, Ruaidhrí Ó Conchobhair, banished Diarmuid from Ireland.

Diarmuid went to King Henry II of England for help and Henry gave him permission to enlist a force to invade Ireland in 1170. This force was led by Richard fitz Gilbert de Clare, 2nd Earl of Pembroke and known as Strongbow, as well as other Norman barons from Wales. Strongbow later married Aoife, Diarmuid mac Murchadha's daughter. Through Strongbow, King Henry claimed the fief of the interior of Leinster.

Henry II was given Ireland to hold as a papal fief in 1155 by the only English pope, Pope Adrian IV (formerly Nicholas Breakspear). This allowed the English king to claim to be Lord of Ireland. Ruaidhrí Ó Conchobhair (c.1116–98) was the last de facto High King of Ireland. He became King of Connacht in 1156 and seized the High Kingship in 1166. His quarrel with Diarmuid mac Murchadha, mentioned above, led to Ruaidhrí's submission as vassal to King Henry II under the terms of the Treaty of Windsor in 1175.

Until surnames were adopted and a foreign language had been imposed on Ireland, no one, including the Normans, anglicized their names. In fact, the Normans often gaelicized their names. The houses in this book feature a number of indigenous Irish names, but seven of these are particularly important. Easiest of the anglicizations to discern are the following:

Ó RUAIRC, subsequently anglicized as O'Rorke (sometimes O'Rourke). The Ó Ruaircs were formerly kings of Breffni c.1128–1605.

Ó NÉILL became O'Neill. Formerly high kings of Ireland from at least 440, they held several other kingships and were kings of Tír Éoghain until 1616.

Ó BRIAIN became O'Brien. The Ó Brians were kings of Thomond until 1657.

Ó MHÁILLE became Ó Malley. They were a fairly powerful west of Ireland clan and once lords of Umhall Uachtaracht.

Less easy are:

Ó FLAITHBHEARTAIGH which became O'Flaherty, another fairly powerful native west of Ireland clan. They were lords of Muintir Murchadha and, until the end of the 16th century, Iar Connacht.

Ó CONCHOBHAIR DONN was subsequently anglicized as O'Conor don (Donn means the dark haired). This branch of the clann Ó Conchobhair were kings of Connacht from about 1183 to 1654 and also sometimes High Kings of Ireland.

The most confusing of the Irish names after the adoption of standardized surnames is mac Murchadha:

MAC MURCHADHA was later anglicized as MacMurrough. This became more complicated because one progenitor of the family was called Domhnal Caomhánach (gentle Donal). The adjective Caománach led to the anglicization of their name as Kavanagh, but both were sometimes combined as is the style of the head of the family mac Murchadha Caomhánach, which was anglicized as MacMurrough Kavanagh. They were kings of Leinster until 1603 and also kings of Uí Chinnsealaigh.

Ballynegall
near Mullingar,
County Westmeath

A handsome Regency house
surrounded by fine parkland,
Ballynegall was designed by
the renowned Irish architect,
Francis Johnston.

Ballynegall was situated at Crooked Wood, near Mullingar. The house, designed by architect Francis Johnston, was commissioned in 1808 and eventually demolished in 1981. In 1849, Mr James Fraser wrote of the demesne, 'The handsome Greek mansion accords with the rich and beautiful park around; while the schools and neat church in the demesne, together with the comfortable houses for the tradesmen and labourers, show the good taste and liberality of the proprietor.'

THE HOUSE AT BALLYNEGALL consisted of two storeys over a basement. It had six bays, with a two-bay breakfront, a single-storey Ionic portico and a parapet with a dentil cornice. On the garden side was a bow containing the dining room and flanked by one-bay Wyatt windows. The wings were built in about 1840, and a stone balustrade swept around the house framing the area beneath. The Ionic portico led into an entrance hall, which had restrained and elegant neo-classical plasterwork. In this room, two columns, flanked by their pilasters, matched those on the entrance portico. Behind the entrance hall was a staircase hall also designed by the architect Francis Johnston. The Portland stone stairs rose the full height of the house and had 104 brass banisters on their treads; the mahogany handrail was inlaid with a brass strip along its entire length.

Inside, to the right of the hall passage, was a drawing room with pink walls, and gold and green predominating on mould-ings and other decoration. The splendid plasterwork on the ceiling was by Michael Stapleton of Dublin, who was the finest stuccodore working in Ireland at the end of the 18th century. Two large giltwood console tables and mirrors and a beautiful Regency white marble chimneypiece, with its shelf supported by two caryatids, dom-inated the room. At the end of the drawing room was a conservatory, which looked out over the Ballynegall gardens towards the woods of Knockdrin Castle.

The dining room, which was painted green with gold ornamental paper appliqués and had red curtains at the windows, looked

Previous page
The entrance hall with its imposing Ionic columns, matching those on the entrance portico, and elegant neoclassical plasterwork.

These pages
1 The drawing room with ceiling plasterwork by Michael Stapleton, a fine 18th-century stuccodore.
2 The imposing entrance front of Ballynegall.
3 One of a pair of console tables and pier glasses in the drawing room.

Ballynegall
near Mullingar,
County Westmeath

Ballynegall
near Mullingar,
County Westmeath

out over gently rising land to an artificial lake of some 32 acres in the near distance. The room was curved on the garden side and had a balcony, which was built to prevent guests who had drunk 'not wisely but too well' falling down into the area beneath while admiring the view at the end of an evening. The dining table could seat 36 and the room also contained a sideboard attributed to Francis Johnston. In the fine library was a long, pedimented mahogany bookcase which contained a collection of books made by James Middleton Berry, one owner of Ballynegall. A billiard room and a smoking room completed the ensemble of reception rooms in the house. In the bedrooms, the four-posters still had their original blankets which dated from the early 19th century and were an astonishing weight.

The gate lodge was a miniature version of the garden front of the house, with a curved bow and a tripartite window, here flanked by niches for urns or statuary. The gardens were spectacular. Mimosa and Japanese tree ferns were everywhere, and there was once a datura plant. There is a legend that the scent of this plant is so strong that anybody who inhales it will fall asleep and never wake (the dénouement of Meyerbeer's opera *L'Africaine* takes advantage of this myth with great effect). Whatever the truth of the legend, the plant has powerful anti-cholinergic properties with extremely strong side effects, such as disorientation,

apparent astral travel, tactile hallucinations and intoxication.

The history of the house goes back to the time when, following the Norman invasion of Ireland, the principal barons got their hands on large tracts of Irish land. One of the most successful was Hugh de Lacy, who obtained thousands of acres in County Westmeath. He gave the land of Baile na nGall (or 'The Town of the Foreigners') to his followers, the Tuites, and it remained in their possession until 1720 when they sold it to Colonel Arthur Reynell, who renamed the old house on the land Castle Reynell.

The Reynells lived at Castle Reynell until 1803 when they sold it to a Mr James Gibbons. This gentleman died shortly afterwards and his son, also named James, pulled down the old Castle of the Tuites and, in 1808, engaged Francis Johnston, the architect of the General Post Office in Dublin (as well as two of the most important mansions in the country, Charleville Castle in County Offaly and Townley Hall in County Louth) to build him a new house. This residence incorporated much of the stonework from the destroyed Castle. James Norris Brewer, author of *The Beauties of Ireland*, wrote, 'In 1826, by this gentleman a splendid mansion has been erected, after the designs of Mr Francis Johnston, at the expense, as we believe, of more than thirty thousand pounds. The demesne constitutes one of the finest, and most extensive planted estates in the county'. James Gibbons also engaged Alexander McLeish to lay out his gardens (McLeish had already worked at the neighbouring estate of Knockdrin Castle).

Mr Gibbons changed the name of the place back to Ballynegall and left it to his nephew-by-marriage, James Middleton Berry. Berry in turn left the house to his cousin, Thomas Smyth of Benison Lodge in the same county. This

Ballynegall

near Mullingar,
County Westmeath

Thomas Smyth was the great-grandfather of the owner of the property at the time that the pictures shown here were taken.

The Smith family (they 'gentrified' their surname in about 1800) were descended from William Smith of Rossdale Abbey in Yorkshire who moved to Ireland (as did so many Englishmen in the early 17th century). He settled initially in Dundrum, County Down, which was being settled by 'civilized' Protestants, along with the rest of the confiscated lands of Ulster, in the wake of the departure from Ireland of the last great Gaelic lords. The Smith family ended up, for the most part, in County Westmeath. They owned, in addition to Ballynegall, the demesne of Drumcree, Barbavilla, Benison Lodge, Gaybrook and Glananea (the last two are included in this book). The Ballynegall Smiths descended from Thomas, the younger brother of the Bishop of Raphoe, who founded the Gaybrook branch of this relatively undistinguished family.

In 1962 Major Thomas Smyth, the last of the family to live at Ballynegall, sold the house to an architect, Mr David Cronin and his brother-in-law, Mr Michael MacDonald. These gentlemen were described in a magazine article as 'experts in unrelated professions', Mr MacDonald having a degree in agriculture. The farm was extended to 80 acres, 32 of which had been the beautiful artificial lake. The lake was drained and the reason given for this vandalism was that 'Mr MacDonald has an appreciation of Irish soil and deplores waste.' Photographs of Eamon de Valera and John F. Kennedy replaced the family portraits on the library walls. The house was eventually stripped and, in 1981, demolished. Its contents were dispersed and its portico dismantled and removed to Straffan House in County Kildare.

A late 18th-century house, Bermingham was
built for the de Bermingham family, the Lords
Athenry, and was afterwards the home of the
O'Rorke and Cusack-Smith families.

Bermingham House *near Tuam, County Galway*

Bermingham House, some two miles east of Tuam in County Galway, is a plain, square 18th-century house of two storeys. Five bays deep, it has a three-bay entrance front and widely spaced windows. The interior has mid- to late 18th-century plasterwork cornices and pedimented door cases, one of which is placed between the entrance hall and the staircase hall. The land was originally the seat of the de Berminghams (the Lords Athenry), the first of whom had been the Lord of Birmingham in Warwickshire and had arrived in Ireland by 1175. His son was one of the ten Norman-Irish and 22 Gaelic-Irish leaders, who in 1243 received estates from Henry III as a reward for their loyalty; his grandson, Meiler de Bermingham, founded the Abbey of Athenry.

RICHARD DE BERMINGHAM ('Richard of the battles'), the head of the family in 1316, won the Battle of Athenry, which saw the defeat of Edward Bruce and the death of Feidhlim Ó Conchobhair, King of Connacht. The Annals of Clonmacnoise record that Feidhlim had initially joined with Richard de Burgo, Earl of Ulster, but that Bruce had persuaded him to leave the 'Red Earl' and to change sides. It would prove to be a fatal decision (and not just for King Feidhlim), since this victory was the turning point in the Normans' sub-jugation of the native Irish, a process that was completed in 1318 when another Bermingham, John, crushed the Irish at the Battle of Dundalk. For this victory, in which Edward Bruce was killed, John Bermingham was created Earl of Louth. The English of Oriel murdered him a few years afterwards and his peerage became extinct. (It was to be re-created for his collateral heirs in the 18th century.)

In the 15th century, the Lords Athenry appear to have gone native, as did so many of the Norman invaders, and they became 'more Irish than the Irish themselves'. They took on Irish names – altering their surname to Mac Feorais (from Fitz Piers) after the progenitor of the family in Ireland – and they seem to have adopted something like the position of a gaelic lord. The 6th Baron was Thomas Óg, whose succession to the title was disputed by his uncle, Richard, on the perfectly sound Gaelic principle that the family's followers had elected him to the rank. Unfortunately for Thomas's aspirations, the Crown refused to accept this novel method of succession to an Irish peerage. (In the end, Richard's descendants would inherit the title – in the more conventional way.)

The 7th Baron was one of those who travelled to Greenwich in order to pay homage to Henry VII in 1489. At this time he was ranked third among the Barons of Ireland (the Lords Kingsale and Gormanston came fourth and fifth in the pecking order). Sir Henry Sidney, the Lord Deputy of Ireland, described the 9th Lord, in 1572, as being 'as poore a Baron as lyveth and yet agreed on to be the auntientest Baron of this lande.'

The 12th Lord became a Dominican friar. He attempted to, and apparently did, give away his peerage in a deed dated 1645. This was an unusual but not unique occurance in the Irish peerage. The 5th Viscount Buttevant had been passed over in both his peerage and estates because, although of sound mind, he was deaf and dumb.

Incidentally, the viscountcies of Buttevant and Fermoy were never created as viscountcies by the Crown but simply assumed by their respective families. The editor of *The Complete Peerage* remarked that this was an 'audacious and successful assumption of a higher title, which could hardly have occurred any-where but in Ireland.'

The 14th Baron conformed to the Established Church and took his seat in the House of Lords in 1713. Bermingham House was probably built by his son in the 1730s. The 15th Baron was created Earl of Louth and died in 1799, when his earldom became extinct and the barony fell into abeyance. It was claimed the following year by a remote cousin and, in 1836, the Attorney General confirmed to William IV that the nephew of the claimant from 1800 had indeed made out his claim to the peerage. However, nothing seems to have been done and the known legitimate line of the family died out shortly afterwards. (There are, how-ever, illegitimate descendants alive of the gentleman who claimed the title in 1800.) Had the Athenry Peerage survived, its holder would supersede Lord Kingsale in his position as Premier Baron of Ireland.

Bermingham House
near Tuam, County Galway

1 A portrait, still on the wall of the dining room at Bermingham, of John Dennis, noted hunter, steeplechaser and shot, on his grey.
2 The Cusack-Smith coat of arms.
3 The redoubtable Lady Cusack-Smith at her embroidery. She was born Mollie O'Rorke, the daughter of Charles Trench O'Rorke of Bermingham House.

Bermingham House
near Tuam, County Galway

At the beginning of the 19th century, the Dennis family (one of whom, John Dennis of Carraroe, who was born in Fiddane, County Galway, was a noted hunter, steeplechaser and shot) bought Bermingham House. In 1839, the newly established County Galway Foxhounds (under the chairmanship of Sir Michael Bellew) asked John Dennis to be their first Master and Huntsman, for which service he was given the sum of £420, paid in three installments. He did not, as has been subsequently claimed, found this Hunt, which soon was universally known as 'the Galway Blazers'. As a result of his new position, he presided over the first 'Blazers' Hunt Ball, which took place in 1841. A comment in the local newspaper set the scene appropriately: 'Miss X looked radiant in a dress of white Satin Princess draped with chiffon, and trimmed with silver lace and bugla tassels.'

Anthony Trollope portrayed John Dennis under the disguise of 'Black Jack Daly' – 'There was nothing which a horse could do with a man on his back which Black Jack could not make him do... he was unmarried, his hounds were his children, and he could have taught no wife to assist him in looking after them with the constant attention and tender care which was given them by Barney Smith his huntsman'. Dennis served as Master of the Blazers for 11 seasons and retired in 1850. He died 18 years later and, although he may be gone, he is definitely not forgotten. His portrait, showing him seated on his famous grey with three hounds looking up at him, still hangs in the dining room at Bermingham House.

The Bermingham estate passed to the descendants of his sister, who had married John O'Rorke of Menlough. Her grandson, Charles Trench O'Rorke, married a lady who was half French, and their daughter, Mollie O'Rorke, was one of the most colourful characters that the Irish gentry ever produced. After boarding school in Devon (which she loathed), Mollie spent a year studying painting and drawing and became a friend of Augustus John, who painted her as *The Tulip of Tuam*. This, perhaps, explains the presence at Bermingham of paintings by Irish artists such as Jack B. Yeats, Louis le Brocquy and Evie Hone – all purchased before they became famous. After art, came singing. She studied for another year with Gabriel Lapière, who had been Dame Nelly Melba's accompanist. Mollie intended to have an operatic career but her father became ill and, as she said, 'I adored him really and I thought I'd better come home. My father and I were like brother and sister.' Mollie didn't quite give up on singing altogether and when asked what she liked, she would reply, 'Oh, all the rebel songs.'

After an argument with her father (over a horse), Mollie packed up again and went to England, where she opened her own fashion establishment. She later took on a Russian partner and together they opened a branch in Brussels, but she gave it all up after four years, when she decided that *haute couture* wasn't for her. Apart from any other considerations, she kept putting the buttons on the wrong side and, as for cutting, she commented, 'Jesus – you have to be a genius to follow a pattern.'

Mollie married Sir Dermot Cusack-Smith in 1946. According to his wife, Sir Dermot was a heavy drinker. She once told a friend, Baron Thierry Terrier de Palente, that she had discovered this fact on her honeymoon, as the mosquitoes, which frequented their bedroom in Naples, passed by her every night in order to gorge on the blood of the baronet. 'They were drawn by the smell and taste of the sugar in his blood, you see, my dear.'

The Smiths, Sir Dermot's family, claimed to be descended from a mayor of Dublin in the 12th century. They actually descended from a Joseph Smith, of unknown parentage, from County Carlow, whose great-grandson, the Right Honourable Michael Smith, was made a baron of the Exchequer in 1793. He was created a baronet in 1799 and at the Act of Union he was made Master of the Rolls and a Privy Councillor for Ireland. He married Mary-Anne, the daughter of James Cusac of Dublin (which was the spelling of the surname that was used in 1799 when he was granted supporters to his coat of arms).

Michael's son added his mother's surname to his own and quartered her Arms with his. When his father received the baronetcy, he also requested (and received) a grant of supporters – in the form of a merman with a trident and a mermaid with a mirror. The 2nd Baronet also rose to become a baron of the Exchequer. Caroline, the daughter of Sir William, the 3rd Baronet, married James Middleton Berry of Ballynegall. (Sir William was the judge who attempted unsuccessfully in the courts to end the career of Irish political leader Daniel O'Connell.) It was the failure of Caroline's union to produce children that led the Smyths to inherit that property.

The heir was a curious gentleman. Sir William Cusack-Smith (the family had changed the spelling) lived for 97 years from 1822 until 1919. From his entry in *Burke's Peerage* it appears that during his long life he actually did nothing at all of any note. His uncle, on the other hand, was the Member of Parliament for Rippon in Yorkshire between 1843 and 1846 and eventually became the Master of the Rolls in Ireland and it was his grandson who in 1919 became the 5th Baronet. He received the KCMG for his services to the Crown which included stints as Consul to Samoa and Chile between 1890 and 1905. His son was Sir Dermot Cusack-Smith (the 6th Baronet) who married, as

his second wife, Mollie O'Rorke of Bermingham House. Apart from other considerations, they both shared a passionate love of hunting.

In 1939, Lady Cusack-Smith had become the first Lady Master of the Galway Blazers and she also had her own pack, the Bermingham and North Galway, which she founded and of which she was Master for 34 seasons. Unfortunately, after a lifetime of service to hunting in Ireland, it all ended rather unpleasantly when, in 1985, various internal conflicts and rivalries caused members of the Bermingham and North Galway Hunt to break away and set up their own rival hunt. During her time as mistress of the house, Mollie did her best to make the Bermingham estate self-sufficient, even going so far as to take in paying guests. Her brochure informed prospective guests that this was 'The home of Lady Cusack-Smith MFH who is ready to receive you and to do everything in her power to entertain you…' She went on to offer 'Reliable horses; dinner parties; dancing and wonderful food.' She concluded 'State your wishes and they will materialise' – and all of this at a rate of £10 a day, inclusive of drinks.

Mollie also established one of the great traditions in the Irish social calendar, the Bermingham Hunt Ball. This was always held in the house on the second Friday after Christmas. At 10 pm exactly, Lady Mollie would blow her hunting horn to inform the first 50 of her 100 guests that supper was ready. She could be persuasive. On one occasion, when she thought that it was time for her guests to depart, she said so – firmly. She was tired, and her state of health was not improved when a guest came up and said, 'Good night, Lady Mollie'. 'I told you to leave' she said, a trifle crossly. Fifteen minutes later, this gentleman (who obviously had a death wish) came back with his girlfriend. 'I said get out' she shouted and hit him with the horn. It had been snowing outside and the floor was wet. The guest slipped and fell and, unable to regain his feet, crawled to the door, aided by the occasional kick from Mollie and the encouraging shout of 'Get out you swine!' Most people left at that point, without bidding her adieu.

Cultured and stylish, Lady Mollie was, as may be gathered, forceful in both her opinions and her speech. Perhaps the best known, and certainly the most repeated, story about her activities in the hunting field is the one that tells how,

Bermingham House
near Tuam, County Galway

on one occasion, she found herself without a mount and was obliged to borrow one from a member of the hunt. The chase that day was fierce and her Ladyship led the field. Never one to take prisoners where the sport was concerned, she returned exhausted with the hunter at the end of the day only to be confronted by the irate owner. It was obvious to anyone (except, perhaps, to Lady Cusack-Smith) that the poor horse had never been ridden quite so energetically before. 'Madame,' said the infuriated owner, 'How dare you treat an animal like that! Just take a look at it! Its legs are shaking; it is frothing at the mouth and it is sweating all over!' 'Well,' Mollie replied, 'what would you expect? If you too had been between my thighs for the past three hours, your legs would be shaking, your mouth would be frothing and you would most certainly be sweating all over!' In fairness, it must be said that she then proceeded to buy the horse.

On another occasion, the Honourable Desmond Guinness saw her in action. He recalled, 'She is a proper lady but could swear like trooper. She let loose at a man who had been throwing stones at her and her horse. When I asked her why she hadn't moved earlier she just told me she was broadening her vocabulary.'

Hunting was Mollie's life, and she kept a pack of 27 couple. She recalled with some pride, 'While I was master of the Blazers, I did the best I could and we showed some good sport. My mother once asked the secretary whether or not I was any good and he said the best ever.' Celebrities rushed to hunt with Mollie and film director John Huston, who lived at nearby St Clerans, was joint Master in the late 1960s. Mollie commented that he was 'more a figure-head than anything else'.

Mollie's taste in interior decoration was eclectic. She had the entrance hall and study of Bermingham painted deep green; the dining room was pink and the staircase hall was pale blue. She upholstered a chaise longue in turquoise tweed, commenting 'my Steward and I put springs in that and then widened it, as it was very uncomfortable.' Shortly after that, the steward retired at the age of 80, 'he needed the rest' Mollie said. Garech Browne recalls her ripping up the stone flags in the entrance hall and replacing them with ones of Connemara marble so that, as she said, she would 'not have to paint them every year'.

From the entrance gates with their inviting sign, which read 'No carcasses, no dumping', a long potholed avenue leads to the house, which Mollie had painted hunting pink. She commented, 'my father hated coloured houses. If he saw this he would turn in his grave.' There, in the middle of a demesne with its original 1500 acres somewhat depleted, Mollie's daughter, Oonagh Mary, now lives with her family.

Mollie herself died in 1998, aged 90, the last of a generation of extraordinary Irishwomen, whose like we shall not look on again. Asked by a reporter in Canada what constituted a proper Irish lady, the dramatist Brendan Behan recalled that at the 21st birthday party of the Honourable Garech Browne at Jammets restaurant in Dublin, Lady Cusack-Smith had lifted her napkin and blown her nose into it. Perhaps with the innocent intention of stirring things up a bit, Behan called over the (very correct) head waiter and pointed this out to him. 'Ah indeed, and what else would you expect?' replied the man, 'For isn't she a real lady?'

The O'Rorke family motto is *Nil admirari* – 'Nothing amazes'. Whoever chose that for the family had obviously not considered that Mollie might become a member.

A pole screen featuring the O'Rorke coat of arms. On this is the family motto *Nil admirari*, which means 'Nothing amazes'.

Bermingham House
near Tuam, County Galway

Blarney Castle *Blarney, County Cork*

Blarney is the 15th-century stronghold of the Mac
Carthaigh Múscraighe (MacCarthys of Muskerry).
In the demesne is a late 19th-century house
lived in by the Colthurst family, the present
owners of the estate.

A stone that whoever kisses

O he never misses to grow eloquent.

This doggerel was published by 19th-century Irish writer Father Prout in his *Reliques* of 1860. The rhyme continues:

Tis he may clamber

To a lady's chamber,

Or become a member

Of sweet parliament.

The subject of this verse is the block of stone that is located at the top of Blarney Castle in County Cork, and which is known the world over as 'The Blarney Stone'.

2

THERE IS A STORY, which has been 'authenticated' by Crofton Croker, the early 19th-century antiquarian, that Cormac mac Diarmada, Chief of the Mac Carthaigh Mhúscraighe (Lord of Muskerry) was instructed by Queen Elizabeth I's agents that he must renounce his Irish practices and become a good and loyal English subject. He procrastinated and made promises 'with soft words and fair speech', time and time again until Elizabeth burst out with the famous words, 'This is all Blarney; what he says he never means!'

Of course, Ireland being what it is, there have to be at least two or three other stories to explain the power that the stone allegedly possesses. One is that a MacCarthy lord, having helped Edward Bruce in his doomed attempt to win the Irish Crown in 1315, was rewarded with a piece of the Stone of Scone and fixed it on the battlements. If this were true (which it is not) it would mean that a piece of the stone had returned to Ireland, because another tradition relates that Hibernian Dalriads had brought this relic to Scotland from Ireland almost a thousand years before.

But the Blarney Stone's travels do not stop there, since there is yet another story that it originally came from the Middle East and was, in fact, the pillow that Jacob's head was resting upon when he had his famous dream. Of such things are legends made. Yet another tale recounts that an old woman, who was saved from drowning by a king of Munster, rewarded him with a spell. He would only have to kiss a certain stone at the top of his castle in order to achieve such eloquence that all men would obey his commands.

Certainly, by the 19th century, the legend of the Blarney Stone was firmly established (and the tourist economy in County Cork has blessed it ever since). Sir John Carr wrote, 'About four miles before we reached Cork, my *compagnon-de-voyage* pointed out to me Blarney-castle, upon a turret of which there is a stone nearly inaccessible, which possesses, it is said, the rare virtue of making those for ever happy who touch it.' And, in 1817, novelist and dramatist Ann Plumptre stated that 'The virtue I have always heard ascribed to it is, that whoever kisses it may allow himself to run into fiction as much as he pleases… the virtue of the Blarney stone is, that after kissing it, how muchsoever the

Previous page
The old castle seen from the parkland. The Blarney Stone is just above the top window of the tower.

These pages
1   An 1817 engraving of the old castle showing the now ruined gothick house that James St John Jefferyes added on to the keep in 1745.
2   The famous Blarney Stone, situated high up in the castle battlements. Legend has it that whoever kisses the stone is given the gift of flattery.

Blarney Castle
Blarney, County Cork

1 The late-Victorian house seen from the battlements of the old castle. This house, begun in 1872, is a somewhat severe construction in the Scots-Baronial style.
2 The interior of the old Blarney Castle built in 1446 by Cormac Láidir MacCarthy.
3 The old castle, with the ruin of the 1745 gothick addition on the left.

Blarney Castle
Blarney, County Cork

kisser may indulge in fiction he is certain of being believed; and if afterwards he should plunge into the Shannon, all may be done without danger of a blush.'

Another 19th-century traveller related that 'the military and historical recollections connected with Blarney are doubtless of sufficient importance to give an interest to the place; but to a curious superstition it is perhaps more indebted for celebrity. A stone in the highest part of the castle wall is pointed out to visitors, which is supposed to give to whoever kisses it the peculiar privilege of deviating from veracity with unblushing countenance whenever it may be convenient.' In 1825, Sir Walter Scott visited Blarney in the company of Maria Edgeworth and his son-in-law, John Gibson Lockhart, who wrote, 'Sir Walter climbed up to the top of the castle and kissed, with due faith and devotion, the famous Blarney Stone, one salute of which is said to emancipate the pilgrim from al future visitations of *mauvaise honte*.'

The old Blarney Castle was built at Blarney (An Bhlárna) in 1446 (thus giving the lie to the Edward Bruce story) by Cormac Láidir 'the strong') MacCarthy, an ancestor of Cormac mac Diarmada. The family, as Barons of Blarney, Viscounts of Muskerry and Mountcashel and Earls of Clancarty, dominated this area until they left Ireland in the aftermath of the Battle of the Boyne in 1690. The old castle comprises a tall tower and keep with good machicolations – projecting parapets with openings through which missiles can be dropped. The solid base and good-sized rooms give an idea of what such a castle looked like in the 15th and 16th centuries in Ireland and the great rectangular tower is one of the biggest in Ireland.

The castle was built in two stages. First there was a tower some 20 feet square and four storeys high that contained a few rooms. About 40 years later Cormac Láidir added a large tower, measuring about 60 feet by 39 feet, beside the original structure, thus creating an L-shaped castle. The walls of the later addition are 12 feet thick, but reduce a little as they rise up, and the chamber on the second storey of the later building has a vaulted roof. The massive corbelling, machicolations and Irish 'stepped' battlements were added about a century later.

Charles I created Cormac (Charles) MacCarthy (the son of Cormac mac Diarmada) Baron of Blarney and Viscount Muskerry in 1628 and the 2nd Viscount, Donnchadh (or Donough), became the 1st Earl of Clancarty in 1658. The Honourable Justin MacCarthy, brother of the 4th Earl of Clancarty, was created Viscount Mountcashel; both brothers were supporters of James II. As a result of the Williamite victory at the Boyne, the family's titles and estates were declared forfeit in 1691.

There is a story that, before he left Ireland, the 4th Earl threw all of his silver into the lake at Blarney. An early 19th-century account relates the following tale: 'A short distance to the southwest of the castle is a lake, said to be full of a species of leech. It does not afford one good subject for the pen, as it is without islands, the margin swamp, and the adjacent trees planted without much attention to regularity. It is a very generally believed tradition that, before Blarney was surrendered to King William's forces, Lord Clancarty's silver was made up in an oaken chest, which was thrown into this lake, and has not been recovered; nor does this appear improbable, as I understand that recent attempts have in vain been made to drain it. In 1814, Mr Milliken, whose well-known song of 'The Groves of Blarney' has identified his memory, in this place, gave Mr Crofton Croker a clumsy silver ring for the finger, which had been taken out of the lake by a boy who was fishing in it.' The 4th Earl died in Hamburg in 1734, but there is a legend that he returns to the lake at Blarney from time to time in search of his missing treasure. The present MacCarthy of Muskerry lives in Australia and is the head of the Carrignavar branch of the family, who descend from Cormac mac Diarmada, Queen Elizabeth I's bête noire.

In 1692 the forfeited lands were sold to The Hollow Sword Blades Company from London. Richard Davies, the Dean of Cork, took a lease on the castle, which, together with its demesne of 3000 acres, was sold in 1701 to Sir Richard Pyne, the Lord Chief Justice of Ireland. It is said that when Davies left Blarney he took enough materials with him to build himself a new house. Whether or not this was the reason, Pyne sold on the estate, pretty well immediately, to Sir James Jefferyes, who had been the Governor of Cork since 1698.

Sir James had been a soldier of fortune, a lieutenant colonel of a foot regiment in the service of the King of Sweden and subsequently a brigadier general in the British Army. He had been the Governor of Duncannon before his time as Governor in Cork and would later be the British Resident at Danzig, as well as serving as a Member of Parliament. His first action on acquiring the property was to build a new house in front of Blarney Castle.

In about 1745, Sir James's son, James St John Jefferyes, gothicized the house beside the old keep with the additions of a central bow, a turret and a cupola; he added pointed windows in the top storey and ogee battlements in a sort of 'Batty Langley' style. He also laid out a landscape garden, known as the Rock Close, which has great boulders and smaller stones arranged to look as though they had been there since prehistoric times (there is a similar arrangement at Luggala in County Wicklow). This 18th-century house was burnt early in the 19th century, and its ruin remains beside the old castle.

Ann Plumptre, writing about Blarney in 1817, stated that 'this was formerly a very strong castle, the seat of the Earls of Clancarty, but forfeited by them, with a great deal of other property, for their adherence to James the Second. It was afterwards purchased of the crown by Sir James Jefferyes, in whose family

1 The new Blarney Castle, with its
  round corner turrets, bartizans and
  large, rectangular plate-glass windows.
2 The garden front of the new Blarney
  Castle with the croquet lawn in the
  foreground.
3 The grand entrance porch has Ionic
  columns and Corinthian pilasters on
  the window above.

Blarney Castle
Blarney, County Cork

it still remains, though the present possessor was at this time endeavouring to dispose of the estate.

'It was described in old writings as having been in Queen Elizabeth's time one of the strongest fortresses in Munster, being composed of four large piles joined in one. Of this ancient building only one tower remains, a square of perhaps twenty or twenty-five feet. To this a modern building has been added as a dwelling-house; but the place has been entirely deserted for many years, and is falling miserably to decay; indeed, the more modern part seems very likely to fall before the ancient.

'There have been delightful shrubberies, which might easily be restored. The castle stands on a rock, not very high, and below are fine meadows, with an ample stream flowing through them: there is plenty of wood, and a considerable lake a short distance from the house, which furnishes excellent trout: – in short Nature has left little for Art to apply; and yet this spot is deserted, abandoned, looking wholly neglected and forlorn. Though I kissed the Blarney stone I am not here exaggerating. The country beyond the immediate precincts of the castle is not very good; the slopes are pretty, but they are destitute of the greatest ornament to them – wood.'

In 1798, a Cork attorney, Richard Milliken, composed a poem, which contains the following lines:

> *The Groves of Blarney they look so charming,*
> *Down by the turling of sweet silent streams…*

These came from a faintly bawdy poem entitled *The Groves of Blarney* that the leading Irish poet and writer James Stephens said that he would rather have written than anything else in Irish anthology. Given the breadth and scope of Irish poetry this has to is one of the most facile comments ever made by a fine native writer. *The Groves of Blarney* was written as a burlesque on *Castle Hyde*, a poem that had been composed by a weaver named Barrett in about 1790. More lines follow:

> *Tis Lady Jeffers that owns this station*
> *Like Alexander or Queen Helen fair*
> *There's no commander in all the nation*
> *For emulation can with her compare!*
> *Such walls surround her*
> *That no nine pounder*
> *Could dare to plunder her place of strength;*
> *But Oliver Cromwell*
> *He did her pummel,*
> *And made a breech in her battlement.*

Scottish writer of doggerel, William McGonagall (1830–1902) could not have done better.

Throughout the second half of the 18th century, the family made some remarkable marriages, but did not achieve anything of note. Sir James Jefferyes was the Governor of Cork and married the sister of John Fitzgibbon, 1st Earl of Cork (the Lord Chancellor of Ireland who forced the Act of Union through parliament). George Jefferyes married Anne, daughter of the Right Honourable David la Touche of Marlay, the richest man in Ireland and the head of the great

banking dynasty. The next generation was represented in the person of St John Jefferyes who left a son, also St John, who lived in Paris and died in 1898. He never inherited the estate, which passed to his sister Louisa, who married Sir George Colthurst.

The Colthursts had arrived in Ireland from Yorkshire towards the end of Elizabeth I's reign and settled in Cork. Christopher Colthurst was murdered by the rebels in 1641 near Macroom in County Cork. By the 1730s, they were High Sheriffs of County Cork, and in 1744 John Colthurst, who had married the daughter of the 1st Earl of Kerry, Lady Charlotte Fitzmaurice, was created a baronet. It would be uncharitable to suggest that it was his father-in-law's influence that procured him this advancement. He was Member of Parliament for Doneraile from 1751 (and afterwards for Yonghal and Castle Martyr). His son Sir John Colthurst, the 2nd Baronet, was killed in a duel with Dominick Trant in 1787 and the title passed to his brother (Member of Parliament for Johnstown, County Longford and then for Castle Martyr until 1795), who married Harriet, daughter of the Right Honourable David la Touche. Sir Nicholas Colthurst, the 4th Baronet, was the Member of Parliament for the City of Cork from 1812 until 1829.

It was his son, Sir George Colthurst, the 5th Baronet, who married Louisa Jefferyes of Blarney Castle in 1846. Louisa inherited the Blarney estate in 1862, and they started to build a new house in 1872. This new building is in the Scots-Baronial style of architect John Lanyon, eldest son of Sir Charles Lanyon. It has two storeys over a raised basement (as at Humewood Castle in County Wicklow) and there is a gabled attic. There are round corner turrets and bartizans (small turrets projecting from a wall parapet or tower), as well as rectangular plate-glass windows. All in all, it is a very severe building. The entrance porch has Ionic columns and the window above it is framed with Corinthian pilasters. The entrance hall has a timbered ceiling. Stone steps lead up to the principal rooms, and there is a top-lit inner hall with a Jacobethan-style oak staircase, which is very similar to Lanyon's design for Belfast Castle of a few years earlier. There are large and small drawing rooms en suite, with

1 | 2 | 3

1 A plasterwork frieze adorns the drawing room at Blarney.
2 On the upper landing of the staircase hall is a portrait of Charles XII of Sweden. This painting is a copy of an original by David Von Krafft (1665–1724), which hangs in the National Museum in Stockholm.
3 The dining room, which features a frieze of Adamesque plasterwork.

Blarney Castle
Blarney, County Cork

friezes of Adamesque plasterwork; the decoration in the dining room is similar. The mirrors and fireplaces, as well as the neoclassical porch, came from Ardrum House, the Colthurst's ruined house at Inniscarra in County Cork. In its restored form, the billiard room went down to the basement while the kitchen came upstairs. The former dining room is now the library.

Sir George and Louisa's son and two grandsons (the 6th, 7th and 8th Baronets) did nothing at all of any consequence, save that Sir Richard Colthurst, the 8th Baronet, was High Sheriff of County Dublin between 1920 and 1921. A different character altogether was Richard's daughter, Mary, who married Major Jack Hillyard. Born in 1912, she was the terror of the reading room of the College Historical Society at Trinity College, Dublin. She was the sort of gentle eccentric who would talk for hours to any student gentlemanly (or foolish) enough to engage her in conversation and it became a habit among seasoned hands to approach Mrs Hillyard and inform her that a particular callow youth wanted to discuss something or other with her (religion and the Jesuits were always a good topic). They would then watch the young man squirm as he was trapped for what seemed to him like an age.

The 9th Baronet, Sir Richard Colthurst, is the present head of the family, and he and his wife have restored the new castle, which was in danger of going the way of the old one. His son Charles, a member of the Irish Timber Growers Association, is a solicitor in Cork. He has three daughters and a son, John, born in 1988.

The family motto *Justem ac Tenacem* (Just and Persevering) and the quartered Colthurst and Jefferyes Arms are set in the entrance façade of a house that had lain empty and left to rot for three generations, until Sir Richard Colthurst and his wife moved in, replumbed, rewired and redecorated it and, in the process, saved the building – for once a statement that does not contain a word of Blarney.

A magnificent Regency remodelling
by Sir Richard Morrison and his son,
William Vitruvius, of an early 18th-
century house, Borris is built around
the ancient tower house of the
MacMurrough Kavanagh family,
Mac Murchadha Caomhánach.

Borris House   *Borris, County Carlow*

A contemporary account of Borris House, as rebuilt in the 19th century, states that 'The Mansion stands in the best point for command of prospect, overlooking a rich tract of well wooded country terminated by a fine range of mountains, and was erected about seventy years ago… in its original form, the building was without any pretensions to architectural beauty, and in its interior arrangements not sufficiently commodious.' The author continues, 'The interior is so arranged now, as to render it not only complete in its accommodation, but grand in its ornaments and decorations, particularly the Saloon, the principal apartment, the ceiling of which is highly adorned, and supported by groins of a slight curve resting on pillars of Scagliola: in the Spandrils of the arches are Shields supported by eagles.'

2

BORRIS HOUSE was the home of Mac Murchadha Caomhánach, whose family managed to produce some of the most reviled, as well as the most inspirational, characters in this book. The villain was Diarmuid mac Murchadha, King of Leinster, who invited Richard de Clare, Earl of Pembroke, known as Strong-bow, to assist him and thus brought the Normans to Ireland. An event whose repercussions are felt every time one Irishman decides to kill or maim another in the name of their particular view of what is important to the country. The hero is Arthur MacMurrough Kavanagh MP – of whom more anon.

The family descend from Diarmuid mac Murchadha's son, Donal Caomhánach. In the late 14th century, Art mac Murchadha was one of the Irish kings who were offered the honour of knighthood by Richard II (the others being Ó Néill, Ó Briain and Ó Conchobhair). The name MacMurrough was the title of the elected lord, and the branches of Polmonty, Coolnaleen and Clonmullen held it at various times. The Tudors decided to finish with the old Gaelic order, and one of the first to accept this new dispensation was MacMorrough: 'on the 4th of November, 1550, Charles, or Cahir, macArt macmorough Kavanagh, of Polmonty, Chief of the Name, in the great council chamber of Dublin, and in the presence of the Lord Lieutenant, Sir Anthony St Leger, and other official and distinguished persons, submitted himself, and publicly renounced the title and dignity of Mac Morough, as borne by his ancestors.'

His son Brian became a Protestant and sent his children to be educated in England. One of them, Sir Morgan Kavanagh, was granted the forfeited estates of the O'Ryans in Idrone. The family were definitely Protestant by 1641. In the rebellion, which started in that year, their ancestry saved them from the confeder-ate Catholics, while Cromwell protected them because they were Protestant. Sir William Brereton visited Sir Morgan Kavanagh in his house at Clonmullen in County Carlow, 'a most solitary melancholy place', where he was given 'good beer, sack and claret.' He was told that there were wolves in the mountains. The castle, 'an old, high, narrow and inconvenient building', had a spiral staircase 'like a steeple stair' that led up to the dining room and bedchambers. At about this date, Sir Morgan's daughter, Eleanor Kavanagh, eloped with her lover,

Previous page
The entrance front of the house showing the three-bay porch and one of the towers with its octagonal lantern.

These pages
1   The entrance hall – although the room is square the arrangement of eight columns supporting a circular dish of plasterwork makes it appear round.
2   A fine view of Borris House, seen from across the parkland.

Borris House
Borris, County Carlow

[*33*]

Borris House
Borris, County Carlow

Cormac O'Daly. Such, at least, is the legend, which gave rise to the song *Eleanor* (or *Eileen*) *Aroon*, better known in Scotland as *Robin Adair*, after a later proponent of the tune. Its fame even reached France, where François Boïeldieu used it in the final act of his masterpiece, the opera *La Dame Blanche* in 1825.

A later head of the family, another Brian Kavanagh, built Borris House around the old keep at some time between 1720 and 1741. This house had three square towers that stood on the east and south fronts. They resembled those at Buncrana Castle in County Donegal and Castle Mary in County Cork. Brian's son, Thomas, married the extremely rich Lady Susan Butler, daughter of the 16th Earl of Ormond and in 1778, the Kavanaghs took charge of Susan's sister, Lady Eleanor Butler, after she had made a scandalous attempt to elope with Sarah Ponsonby. After three weeks of (not quite close enough) confinement, she managed to escape and tramped 12 miles southwest to Woodstock, the Ponsonby family home, where Sarah hid her in her room until Lady Eleanor's father, Lord Ormond, conceded defeat and the pair was allowed to go to Wales, via Waterford, in pursuit of the Gothic Pastoral Ideal.

They spent the next 50 years living together in what may, or may not, have been a lesbian relationship. Certainly, they never spent a night apart again and died within two years of each other. They became objects of curiosity, visited in their home, Plas Newydd, by the Duke of Wellington, Sir Walter Scott, William Wilberforce and William Wordsworth, who wrote a poem in their honour, and they were known as 'The Ladies of Llangollen' (after the local village). A contemporary account described what they did to their originally modest *cottage ornée* as 'fantastical, rather than tasteful, and shows more of the eccentricity than of sentiment.'

Borris was damaged in the rebellion of 1798 when there were a couple of attempts by the rebels to capture it, but on both occasions the attackers were met with murderous volleys of fire and retreated. On the first occasion General Asgill wrote that about 300 rebels had taken part in the attack, while two had been killed and 'three of the wounded have been taken, whom I have ordered to be hanged.' One defender was killed as he leant out of a window. At this period other members of the family who had left Ireland were making their mark abroad. Count Charles Kavanagh was General of Cavalry and Governor of Prague in 1766. Brian Kavanagh was created Baron Ginditz in the Austrian service and Maurice Kavanagh became Field Marshall and Chamberlain to the King of Poland.

Thomas Kavanagh, who succeeded his father in 1813, married his cousin, Lady Elizabeth Butler, the daughter of the 19th Earl of Ormond. A rich man – in 1818 the family had 28,000 acres in counties Carlow, Wexford and Kilkenny – he decided to rebuild Borris. To this end, he called in the most notable architectural partnership in Ireland at that date – Richard Morrison and his son, William Vitruvius. William's brother, John Morrison, wrote that the commission had come from Walter Kavanagh and J. N. Brewer supports this claim. However, as J.P. Neale, writing in 1819, states that the work was undertaken 'within the last seven years' and Walter Kavanagh died in 1813, the bulk of the work must have taken place after his brother, Thomas Kavanagh, inherited the estate.

The Morrisons' design included a three-bay entrance porch and tall, thin octagonal lanterns with conical roofs on the tops of the towers – all in the Tudor-Gothic style (the lanterns have since been demolished). The entrance hall is square, but eight columns with pointed arches support a circular dish of rich

plasterwork (probably by the Stapleton family of stuccodores). This plasterwork is like whipped cream, with swags, acanthus leaves and displayed eagles in the frieze and the ceiling. Because of the columns and the pilasters, the room now seems to be round – at Kilshannig in County Cork a room is made to appear oval by the same device. The drawing room has plaster trelliswork in the ceiling and the dining room has a screen of Ionic scagliola, or imitation marble, columns and pilasters. Behind the entrance hall is the staircase, with a ribbed ceiling, the banisters of which are similar to those designed by the Morrisons for Shelton Abbey (see p.197) and Killruddery (see p.135).

The staircase is overlooked by a gallery on the second floor. At the top of the stairs, and directly over the entrance hall, is the library, the ceiling of which features a design composed of alternate panels of barrel and rib vaulting. There was a servants' wing which ran from the northwest of the house and terminated in a chapel. The chapel remains, with a ceiling similar to that of the staircase hall; the service wing has been demolished. From the village, the demesne is entered by a fine turreted gate tower that serves as a lodge. This entrance is similar to a gate tower that the Morrisons built at Thomastown Castle in County Tipperary.

J.N. Brewer commented that 'the estate of Borris would appear to be formed by the hand of nature for the site of a baronial mansion. The extensive demesne abounds in inequalities of surface, and is richly wooded. The River Barrow flows along its borders, and a mountain-stream penetrates the interior, rolling over a bed of broken rocks. The Black-stairs mountains, which terminate the prospect towards the south-east, form a boundary, in that direction, of unusual grandeur … convenience, in this noble residence, is carefully blended with ornament; and, contrary to the perverse custom in many decorated dwellings, it may be safely affirmed that the genius of the builder is most forcibly displayed in the interior. The principal apartments are spacious, appropriate, and chastely, although sumptuously, adorned.' The Morrisons' patron, Thomas Kavanagh, died in 1837 and his second wife, Lady Harriet Trench, the daughter of the Earl of Clancarty, took over the running of the estate.

Lady Harriet had three sons. When her third, Arthur, was born in 1831, his mother is alleged to have remarked, 'Thank God he was born to me and not to anyone else', the reason being that he was horribly deformed, having only six-inch stumps where his legs and arms should have been. However, despite his physical condition, he grew up to be the most extraordinary member of his family, and a source of inspiration for handicapped people all over the world.

As a child, he was wheeled in a chair or carried on a servant's shoulders. When he rode, he did so tied on to a padded chair, with the reins tied around his arm stumps and his whip tucked into his side. He became a real all-rounder, excelling at billiards, boar hunting, shooting, yachting and fishing – he often landed eight salmon a day (including one of 36 pounds). Apart from his sporting achievements, he was an intellectual and particularly enjoyed Latin, Greek and mathematics. He wrote a thesis about a possible Pacific crossing a century before the Kon-Tiki expedition took place, and his other interests and expertise extended to astronomy, chess and even to Cossack dancing. One of his favourite sports was archery, in which he drew the bow with steel hooks that were attached to his stumps. His mother was a distinguished watercolourist and she taught him to paint holding his brushes in his teeth.

1 The dining room showing the Ionic columns and pilasters of imitation marble.
2 The chapel with a plasterwork ceiling, probably the work of the Stapleton family.
3 The library, which is over the entrance hall. The Charter Horn and the shrine of the Book of Saint Mo Ling are on the table in the foreground.

Borris House
Borris, County Carlow

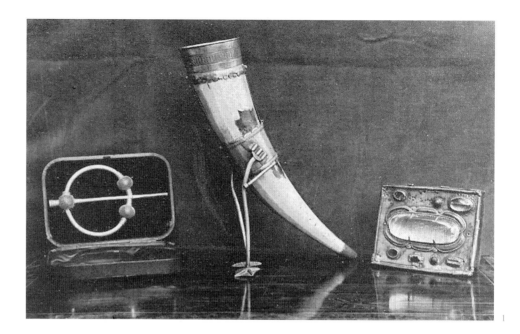

Borris House
Borris, County Carlow

As a boy he wrote in his diary,

Though dark my path and sad my lot,
Let me be still and murmur not.

and he admitted to his sister that 'I terribly want things which are impossible to have.' But, as a young man, other interests soon took over, and he was caught one night stealing out for a liaison with a local girl. His older brother, Tom, was suffering from tuberculosis and the family had determined to send him, under the care of his tutor, Mr Wood, to a healthier climate. They now decided that a sea voyage might do the romantically inclined Arthur a world of good as well.

And so it was that, in April 1849, Arthur set off with his brother and Mr Wood. The trip was fraught with incident. On the way to Moscow, the wheel of their coach caught fire when Arthur had eight pounds of gunpowder under his seat – 'a disagreeable experience', as he afterwards remembered. Later, the boys had to cross mountain paths, some only 14 inches wide. At one point, Arthur's horse fell over the edge of the cliff, with him strapped to it. A cactus bush broke the fall, and he had to be cut free from the unfortunate animal, which then fell to its death in the sea, 1000 feet below. In Kurdistan, they lost their way in the depths of winter and had to dig holes in the snow to sleep, with their clothes frozen to their bodies. Tom was by then in the final stages of consumption, and his tutor took him on to Australia by sea, leaving Arthur behind to fend for himself in India. Tom died on the journey and Mr Wood was killed in mysterious circumstances on his arrival in Australia.

Arthur got himself a job as a dispatch rider in India. His only complaint was that there was no word for 'thank you' in Urdu. He commented that, 'if the English had said "thank you" more often to the Irish, that country would not be in its present plight.' After two years of this way of life, he heard that his surviving brother, Charles, had died in a fire and that he was now the heir to Borris. He returned home to Ireland by the next boat.

Arthur was an enthusiastic landlord. When the weather was fine, he would sit beneath an oak tree in the courtyard, dressed in a black cloak and with his pet bear chained nearby, so that his tenants could come to him to discuss their problems. One of his hobbies was to 'stroll' around the estate with an axe and chop down trees – a dangerous pastime as he could not possibly have jumped clear had one descended on him. In an attempt to stimulate local industries, Arthur, who had seen the devastation brought to the country by the potato famine, brought the railway line to Borris at his own expense. In 1857, his mother visited Corfu and was impressed by the lace-making industry there. She brought lace making back to Borris and ran it as a cottage industry very successfully, encouraged by her son.

There is a story that, when he paid a visit to Lady de Vesci, daughter of the 11th Earl of Pembroke, at Abbeyleix in County Laois, he remarked 'It is quite extraordinary. I have not been here for over ten years, and yet the station-master still remembered me.' He married his cousin, Frances Leathley and together they raised seven children. He decided on a career in Parliament and, when he was 35, was elected as Conservative member for Wexford. Three years later he was returned as the Member for Carlow and remained so until 1880. More honours followed. He was made Lord Lieutenant of County Carlow and a Member of the Irish Privy Council. But the tide of history had turned against

Borris House
Borris, County Carlow

Conservatism and Unionism in Irish politics – Charles Stewart Parnell and the Home Rule Party now garnered the popular vote. Consequently, Arthur MacMurrough Kavanagh lost the 1880 election and was mortified to be jeered and burned in effigy by his tenants, whom he had thought of as his friends and supporters, and who had so often cheered him in the past. He died at Borris on Christmas Day, 1889, surrounded by his family – the best of all the Kavanaghs.

His grandson Major Arthur MacMurrough Kavanagh (Mac Murchadha Caomhánach) eventually succeeded. He had no son, but did have four daughters, one of whom married first Lord Kildare and then Lieutenant Colonel Macalpine Downie. Their son, Andrew, took his mother's surname, and still lives at Borris with his wife and daughters, having returned from a career as a professional jockey in England. In 1985, Andrew and his wife, Tina, decided to let the 12-bedroomed house for £1000 a month, but only during the summer months because, as he explained, 'we would like to live here ourselves for the rest of the year.' The demesne consists of a 650-acre farm and a nine-hole golf course.

Lady Rosemary Fitzgerald, the distinguished botanist and Andrew Kavanagh's half-sister, predicted in the magazine of the Irish Georgian Society that Borris would 'soon be empty and roofless' but that 'the Kavanaghs still have their Charter Horn of possession and will not abandon it.' Her predictions were wrong. Irish architecture and heritage would have been the poorer had she been proved correct.

An early 20th-century remodelling of the stables
of a late 17th-century house which had been
burnt down in 1811. Its parkland destroyed,
Castle Mac Garrett is now a home for the elderly.

Castle Mac Garrett *Claremorris, County Mayo*

The tragedy of Castle Mac Garrett lies not so much in what it has become but in what it might have been. Sitting in its park, denuded of most of the trees that were its glory, and serving as an old people's home, the grim, grey concrete façade (now cruelly exposed since its wall climbers have been cut down) underlines the fact that, had Dominick Browne, afterwards the 1st Baron Oranmore and Browne, spent a little more of his immense fortune on building the wonderful residence that Sir Richard Morrison had designed for him and a little less on reducing his putative electors in County Mayo to varying states of intoxication, the architectural heritage of the county would have been the better for it.

THE ANCESTRY of the Brownes of Galway is not to be confused with the much later arrivistes who acquired the Marquessate of Sligo, the Earldoms of Clanrickarde, Altamont and Kenmare, and the Barony of Kilmaine, as well as building mansions at Westport, Kenmare, The Neale and Breaghwy. These other Brownes are the descendants of those who came with the waves of Tudor and Cromwellian adventurers and land grabbers centuries after the Galway Brownes had arrived, and were the leading family of the 'Tribes of Galway' – merchant princes who had made that town the centre of their power.

Geoffrey Browne, the 3rd Lord Oranmore, wrote an account of his family's history in which he admitted that the earliest of his family from whom he could 'prove lineal descent' was a Stephen Browne who had lived during the latter part of the 15th century. He did, however, recount the family tradition that they were descended from a Norman knight, Sir David Browne (or le Brun) who had built the Castle of Carra Browne (on the Galway–Headford road) after the Battle of Athenry, which took place on 10 August, 1316.

This knight was alleged to be the descendant of Geoffrey le Brun who had come to England with the Conqueror. Hugh le Brun, a member of this family, married Isabel, the widow of King John, and William de Valence, the child born of this union was ennobled by Henry III as Earl of Pembroke. The Oranmore tradition relates that Hugh's cousin, David le Brun, came to Ireland with Prince John in 1185, and that Sir David Browne (who fought at Athenry in 1316) was the great-great-grandson of Prince John's companion. The family papers were largely destroyed in a fire at Castle Mac Garrett in 1811, and any evidence that might have existed to prove or disprove these claims has gone forever.

What makes this alleged pedigree at least probable (unlike similar claims to ancient noble ancestry)

Previous page
Castle Mac Garrett seen from the weir.

These pages

1 The old castle in the demesne. This is the original Castle Mac Garrett (also called Castle Mac Maryshe), which was declared unsafe in 1694.
2 The entrance porch of the house, over which is inscribed in stone, 'The house of O and OO and yours, my friend'.
3 The entrance front. The standard flying above the tower signifies that the owner is in residence.
4 Sir Geoffrey, 3rd Baron Oranmore and Browne and 1st Baron Mereworth (1861–1927).

Castle Mac Garrett
Claremorris, County Mayo

1 | 2

Castle Mac Garrett
Claremorris, County Mayo

was, and is, the existence of Carra Browne Castle (Ceathramhadh Bruna). The ruin of this edifice, which was built by Sir David Browne in 1316, was in the possession of Lord Oranmore until its sale in 1855; the feudal lordships of Carra Browne (in County Galway) and Castle Keele (in the Castle Mac Garrett demesne, not far from Ballindine, in County Mayo) are still the property of the present Lord Oranmore and, in addition, it was as Baron Oranmore of Carra Browne Castle that the 1st Lord Oranmore chose to be ennobled. The continuous ownership by the Browne family of these stones until 1855 is strong circumstantial evidence for the accuracy of the family tradition.

From Stephen Browne the line continued to his descendant Doiminic Mór (Dominick Browne), who was Mayor of Galway in 1575. His wife was Bé Bhinn Ní Flaithbheartaigh (O'Flaherty), the daughter of Sir Murchadh who was head of a rapacious crew whose deeds caused the people of Galway to pray 'from the ferocious O'Flaherties, Good Lord deliver us!' Her name translates, rather charmingly, as 'sweet-tongued girl.' Her husband is described in a letter to

3

Queen Elizabeth's first minister, William Cecil, Lord Burghley, as 'not a young merchant but of the gravest and wealthiest... of any one the wisest in all the town and so thought of. A dear friend of the Earl of Clanrickarde... and a friend indeed in all means judgements that never counselled him but to virtue.'

In 1592, the name of Dominick Browne was brought to the attention of Lord Burghley for a second time. On this occasion his informant was Sir Richard Bingham, who told him that after Lord Clanrickarde had devastated the town of Athenry, the Council had voted a sum of £1800 to compensate the freeholders. It

will be remembered that the Earl
was Dominick Browne's friend,
and so it may not come as too great
a surprise to discover that the same
Dominick Browne had bought the
poor freeholders of Athenry out of
their properties at a fraction of their
true cost. In consequence of this
piece of Tudor entrepreneurial
skill, the total amount that had been
voted to be paid in reparation was
given to none other than Mr Browne.
His gold signet ring, which bears
his Arms (a double-headed eagle)
and the date 1591, is still in the
possession of Lord Oranmore
and Browne.

On his death Dominick Browne,
described in the Calendar of State
Papers for 1588–92 as 'the richest
merchant in Ireland', was succeeded
by his eldest son, Geoffrey. He had
the good fortune to marry Mary, the
daughter and heiress of Edmund
Mac Muiris (or Prendergast), the
lord of Castle Mac Garrett in
County Mayo, and a descendant of
Maurice de Prendergast, who came
to Ireland with Strongbow, one of
the great Norman leaders, in 1169.
With Mary Prendergast came

thousands of acres in counties Mayo, Westmeath and Longford. The son of
Geoffrey and Mary was named Dominick after his grandfather. In fact, the
alternating of the names Dominick and Geoffrey for ten generations was to
become the rule in the family (and a source of constant confusion for its members and genealogists alike). A nephew of Geoffrey's, Martin Browne, built a
town house in Galway that is now demolished but whose doorway was re-
located to Eyre Square, at the expense of the 3rd Lord Oranmore and the
Galway Archaeological Society. It bears the date 1627 and is today one of the
best-known landmarks in the town.

The next in the pedigree, Dominick Browne, was one of the most colourful
and dangerous. In 1613, we find that he was imprisoned at the request of Walter
French for illegally grazing cattle on French's land, which had been given to
him when he married Dominick's aunt. In 1617, the same Walter French wrote
a pleading letter to the Lord Deputy in which he alleged that, in a case brought
between Dominick Browne and himself, he had expected the jury would be an
impartial one. But this one was, he claimed, nothing of the sort. Called by
Dominick Browne's brother-in-law, Nicholas Darcy, the High Sheriff, it had
been packed with Dominick's friends, servants and tenants. Moreover, several
of the jury had been provided with copious amounts of drink (at Dominick

Browne's expense) and, if that were not enough, he whined, some of the jurymen had left the jury room and had discussed the verdict in private with Dominick Browne. French begged the Lord Deputy to take the case into his own hands and see that a fair and impartial jury heard the case. Unfortunately, we do not know its outcome.

However, we do know that in 1620 Dominick Browne was found guilty at Athenry of the felony homicide of a builder, Henry Rany. The cause of the quarrel is unknown although, in 1602, Mr Browne had brought a William Rany to court over his failure to pay an annuity. For his part in the killing, Dominick was sentenced to be branded in the hand, to have his possessions confiscated and to be imprisoned. Having powerful friends (and being extremely rich) he appealed against the conviction. Strange to relate, a few months later, although the conviction was upheld, the sentence was drastically reduced to a fine of £5. Having literally got away with murder, it is not improbable that this event inspired the old Galway saying, 'He who bites a Browne dies!'

He may have been a murderer, but the townspeople elected him as their Member of Parliament in 1634, and he became Mayor of Galway in the same year. In 1635, Lord Wentworth, King Charles I's ill-fated Lord Deputy,

knighted him, but the victory of Oliver Cromwell, as well as Geoffrey Browne's services in the cause of the exiled Stuarts, saw his Galway estates confiscated in 1654. A man of strong opinions to the last, he left the following bequest to his wife, Anastitia Darcy, 'I will that my wife have what cannot be kept from her… and she be content with it.' He was a larger than life character and, by the time of his death in 1656, had more than justified his sobriquet of Doiminic Mór or 'Great' Dominick.

Dominick's brother, Father Stephen Browne, became a Jesuit in 1620. He is described in a contemporary report thus: 'He delights in too long a beard and wears wondrous strange clothes.' A chalice that he had made in 1634, which bears his name, was given by him to the parochial church in Galway and is one of the treasures of 17th-century Irish silver.

Geoffrey Browne, Dominick's eldest son, was the first of his family to move on to the European stage. A Member of Parliament in 1639 for his father's old seat of Athenry, he was elected a member of the Supreme Council of the Confederate Catholics when the General Assembly met at Kilkenny in 1642. At this period in Irish history, the people divided into three camps: those who supported Cromwell and the Parliament (such as Lord Inchiquin); those who wanted to get heretics out of Ireland and to have complete independence (such as Eoghan Ruadh Ó Néill); and those who wished to ease the laws against the Catholic majority but who were loyal to the Crown (such as the Protestant Marquess of Ormond and the Catholic Earl of Clanrickarde). Both Sir Dominick Mór and his son Geoffrey belonged to this third group.

The Papal nuncio, Cardinal Rinnuncini, arrived in Kilkenny and, horrified at the peace treaty that had been agreed between Eoghan Ruadh and Ormond, ordered the imprisonment of all the members of the Supreme Council. Geoffrey Browne was in Galway at the time and so a warrant was sent to the Mayor and Corporation ordering his immediate arrest. A second one followed that directed his transfer to a Castle in County Cavan. Faced with this dilemma, the citizens decided on a Judgement of Solomon. They detained Mr Browne but refused to move him from the town 'for he being a Gentleman allied to the prime men of

1 The dining room which was decorated in eggshell blue and had a stucco ceiling copied from one at Leinster House in Dublin.
2 The head of the staircase with portraits (left to right) of the 4th Lord Oranmore and Browne (b. 1901) as a child, Major the Honourable Myles Ponsonby (1881–1915) and Olwen, Lady Oranmore and Browne (1876–1927).
3 Lord Oranmore's bedroom, located beneath the tower and over the gunroom.

Castle Mac Garrett
Claremorris, County Mayo

the town and generally dear to all the inhabitants by reason of the merit of his fair carriage and abilities they were no way inclined to put his life into the power of his enemies.' When the Papal nuncio returned to Kilkenny, after his disastrously unsuccessful attempt to capture Dublin, all the prisoners were released.

In 1644, Geoffrey Browne was at the court of Charles I in the company of Mac Carthaigh Mhúscraighe, Lord of Muskerry, and Sir Nicholas Plunkett; 1647 saw him in France as an envoy to Queen Henrietta Maria and the Prince of Wales. While there, he was told that Her Majesty distrusted him. He asked Lord Taafe to intercede for him and got a reply back from Lord Ormond, who stated that the rumour had been put about in order to cause trouble for the Queen who had only the best opinion of Mr Browne and, in consequence, he could 'rest secure in her favour'. Ormond added 'I shall never forget your loyalty to the King and your friendship to me and how I may remember them to your credit and advantage.'

In 1651, the Bishop of Ferns, on behalf of the clergy and people of Ireland, took it upon himself to approach Charles, Duke of Lorraine, with a view to his becoming Protector of 'the Nation and Religion'. Geoffrey Browne, Lord Taafe (sent by the Duke of York) and Sir Nicholas Plunkett, were sent to open the negotiations with the duke. They arrived in Brussels, via Amsterdam, but nothing emerged from their discussions. Geoffrey Browne did take with him a map of Galway, which in 1855 his descendant, the 1st Lord Oranmore presented to University College, Galway. Geoffrey married Mary, the daughter of Sir Henry Lynch, and was the Member for Tuam in the Restoration Parliament of 1661, when those lands in Galway that had been confiscated were returned to him. His will, which was made on the day that he died, is the first document to mention Castle Mac Garrett, where the oldest trees that survive were planted by him in about 1664.

Castle Mac Garrett
Claremorris, County Mayo

Colonel Dominick Browne, Geoffrey's son and heir, was born in about 1635 and was Mayor of Galway in 1688 and again in 1689. When William of Orange invaded Ireland, Dominick took up the cause of James II and commanded a troop of dragoons at the Battle of Aughrim. When Galway surrendered to General Ginkel (afterwards the 1st Earl of Athlone), Colonel Browne was one of the hostages taken as surety for the town's good behaviour. On the lighter side, he was given to composing anagrams and epithets in English and Latin. The best (and the worst) that could be said of him was that he survived through those perilous times with his inheritance intact.

The next to hold Castle Mac Garrett was Colonel Dominick Browne's son, Geoffrey. In 1694, when the old Prendergast Castle became unsafe, he moved to a site nearby and built a new house, the stables of which survive, imbedded in the core of the present Castle Mac Garrett. Following his father's example, Geoffrey planted extensively around his new residence. In 1732, Mr Carte, an antiquarian, wished to examine some papers which belonged to Geoffrey Browne concerning his ancestor's embassies on behalf of the Stuarts. Lord Athenry asked if the gentleman could stop by to see the documents only to be told by Mr Browne that he had too much business of his own, his children and his grand-children to lay out time in rummaging through old papers. This prompted an outburst by the Reverend Thomas Sheridan, the grandfather of the dramatist, 'Mr Browne confesses that he has letters and memoirs for Carte's purpose but he is such a lazy Irish brute that he refuses to give himself the trouble of search.' On the other hand, Geoffrey Browne, who (considering the activities of research-ers) may have got his priorities right, is described in a death notice as 'charitable to those in distress, benevolent to Mankind which makes his loss greatly lamented'. Born in 1664, he died in 1755 in his 91st year. He was probably the last Roman Catholic member of his family.

Geoffrey Browne's heir was his son, Dominick, who waited until his father was a few months from his end, and too ill (or too senile) to realize what was going on, and then conformed to the Established Church. This was almost certainly done in order to prevent the loss or diminution of the family estates under the Penal Laws. They may have 'turned' but, after all, the family had remained

Castle Mac Garrett
Claremorris, County Mayo

Catholic for most of the period that the Penal Laws were in force, which is an achievement that could not be claimed by most of the landed families in Ireland. Dominick's first wife was Elizabeth Martyn from Tulira. Her collateral descendant was Edward Martyn, the author and moving light in the Gaelic Revival Movement at the end of the 19th century (and, incidentally, the President of Sinn Féin). The Bow Gate at Castle Mac Garrett was erected to celebrate their union. After his first wife died, Dominick married Henrietta, the daughter of Sir Henry Lynch.

Their son, Geoffrey, who was born at Ashford House in County Galway, was known to his family as 'The Vain'. He made the Grand Tour with his father and attended the Coronation of Louis XVI at Rheims in 1774. On his return to Ireland he chose as his bride, Mary, the granddaughter of the 1st Earl of Altamont from Westport House. In 1793, he was Colonel of the South Mayo Volunteers and then raised the Castle Mount Garrett Volunteers to serve in his local district. The latter company had a uniform of scarlet faced with pomone green. His estates were considerable and, in 1799, he was the 22nd largest landowner in Ireland. We can get some idea of the family in a letter written in 1807 by the 13th Viscount Dillon. Mrs. Browne is mentioned as 'uncommonly clever – very witty sarcastic… and she devotes her time to the education of her children, she is about 38 and was a great beauty.' Lord Dillon described her husband's family as 'one of the best in Ireland having the same property seven hundred years from King John, Mr Browne has 23,000 green acres in Connaught so that his son has £20,000 a year. He is a most high-minded honourable gentleman highly esteemed and could have represented the county often but would not give himself the trouble.' The family were, Dillon claimed, 'all stout Protestants, 'tho not violent against the Catholics.' Disaster struck the family in 1811, when their seat was destroyed by fire. It was reported in *The Gentleman's Magazine* – 'This night the mansion at Castle Mount Garrett, Co. Galway the seat of D.G. Browne Esq. was totally consumed by fire. It originated in the kitchen and the Cook perished.' Most of the family papers were lost in the blaze.

After this event, it seemed that things could only get better, but in the next generation they went from bad to worse. The heir, Dominick Browne, married Catherine, the daughter and co-heiress of Henry Monck. This gentleman was the heir-general of George Monck, 1st Duke of Albemarle, and the soldier who had facilitated the restoration of Charles II in 1660. Mr Browne became a Member of Parliament for County Mayo in 1814 and held his seat until 1836 (with a break during the years 1826 to 1830). He planned to rebuild Castle Mac Garrett in a palatial style. Sir Richard Morrison was engaged and, although the design was laid out on the grass, it never rose from the plans. A later scheme, in the 1840s, also came to nothing and so the stables that had survived from the 1811 fire were pressed into service and were soon incorporated in an enlarged structure. This is the oldest part of the present Castle Mac Garrett.

Dominick Browne supported the Whig, or Radical, cause in Parliament. In 1830 he came up with a scheme to give vested property rights to Catholic Churches and Glebes in Ireland. Daniel O'Connell wrote to him, 'I do assure you that it gave me most sincere pleasure to have any opportunity, however trivial… of showing you how anxious I am to evince to you my strong sense of the manly independence of your Parliamentary conduct. The country never wanted men of your constitutional principles so much as it does at present.' Dominick Browne spent a fortune in winning the seven elections that took him

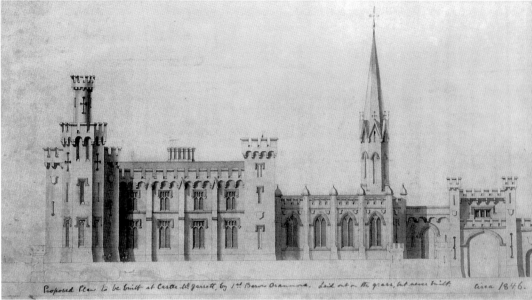

Proposed Plan to be built at Castle McGarrett, by 1st Baron Oranmore. Laid out on the grass, but never built.   circa 1846.

to Westminster. On the last occasion, he laid out some £40,000 for the privilege – £600 of it going on lemons for whiskey punch. A lemon cost one penny and twelve were used in order to make a quarter of a gallon of punch. Simple arithmetic will show that Mr Browne had provided some 3000 gallons of alcoholic beverage to the constituents of Mayo during his last appearance at the hustings. He was returned with a large majority.

His reward came in 1836 when he was raised to the Irish peerage, with the title and style of Baron Oranmore of Carrabrowne Castle, in the County of the Town of Galway, and Baron Browne of Castlemagarret, in the County of Mayo, by King William IV who instructed him, in the patent of creation, to enjoy his title 'magnificently'. This, however, did not satisfy him. An Irish title did not give him an automatic right to sit in the House of Lords, whereas a peerage of the United Kingdom of Great Britain and Ireland would. And so he began to lobby the Government in order to get one. He wrote to the Prime Minister, Lord Melbourne 'as to my accepting an Irish Peerage, I can call Lord Mulgrave that I took it only as a step to an English one.' In a moment of blind optimism he decided that he would like not one but two English titles and had even chosen their names. He wanted to be Lord de Valence and Lord Monck of Potheridge.

Unfortunately for Lord Oranmore, man proposes but government disposes. No fewer than three Prime Ministers, Lords Melbourne and Palmerston, and Lord John Russell refused his request. The reason was that they had heard he was on the verge of bankruptcy. He denied it and claimed that he had an annual income of £25,000 a year from his rents (whereas it was nearer to £13,000) while his debts amounted to the staggering sum of £199,320. He had borrowed money from, among others, Sir Moses Montefiore, Mr Gurney and the Marquess of Salisbury. The Great Famine of the 1840s had ruined Lord Oranmore, as well as an entire nation, and his creditors came yapping at his heels. In a series of sales between 1852 and 1855 most of the Browne estates were sold. A large portion of the town of Galway, as well as Salthill and Roundstone, went under the hammer at the Encumbered Estates Court. The trustees of Sir Benjamin Lee Guinness bought Ashford. Castle Mac Garrett was saved only through the intervention of Lord Oranmore's son and heir, the Honourable Geoffrey Browne. The first Baron died five years later, leaving his heirs a decimated inheritance – and two Irish peerages.

Geoffrey Browne, the 2nd Lord Oranmore, married Christina Guthrie, the daughter and (fortunately for the depleted family coffers) the heiress of Alexander Guthrie of The Mount in Ayrshire, and served at Westminster, as a Representative Peer for Ireland, from 1869 until his death in 1900. His son, Geoffrey Browne, the 3rd Baron Oranmore and Browne, married Lady Olwen Ponsonby, the daughter of the 8th Earl of Bessborough KP and, in 1902, he followed his father to the House of Lords as a Representative of his Order. In 1902, he engaged Richard Caulfield Orpen, the elder brother of the painter Sir William Orpen, to remodel Castle Mac Garrett. From new entrance gates, which were made in Stresa near Lake Maggiore, the drive led up to a particularly ungainly building in architectural terms. The friendly atmosphere that reigned inside the house tempered the choice of grey cement and the uninspired design of Mr Orpen in his extension, which was, mostly, to the left of the entrance.

1 | 2

1 The coat of arms of the 3rd Baron Oranmore and Browne. They show the double-headed eagle of the Brownes with his wife's arms – those of the Ponsonbys – a chevron between three combs. It also displays his crest and supporters.

2 Lady Olwen Ponsonby, Baroness Oranmore and Browne and Baroness Mereworth (1876–1927), painted by Ellis Roberts, 1907.

3 The gates to the house. They were made in Stresa near Lake Maggiore.

Castle Mac Garrett
Claremorris, County Mayo

The front hall was decorated in white and contained a spacious staircase, whose plaster swags were late-17th century in style and enclosed the family arms quartered with those of the heiresses that they had married; on the walls was a superb collection of 'Mrs. Mee' miniatures. The drawing room and dining room were given stucco ceilings that were copies of those at Leinster House in Dublin. The dining room had walls of eggshell blue, the morning room was decorated in primrose and the drawing room had a colour scheme of two contrasting shades of grey. The Meissen porcelain in the drawing room had been part of the famous collection that was assembled by Lady Charlotte Schreiber, who was the present Lord Oranmore's great-grandmother. The library was a typical Edwardian room. No expense was spared in the decoration. Chimneypieces came from Hicks in Dublin, panelling from Crowthers in London, while the lighting fixtures were provided by the firm of Osler, who had provided glass furniture to the royal courts of India in the 19th century. The cost for all of this splendour came to £21,422.7s.6d.

In the last year of World War I Geoffrey Browne was made a Knight of the Most Illustrious Order of Saint Patrick – one of the last to be created. During the troubles that culminated in the partition of Ireland, Lord Oranmore was an Irishman of moderate Unionist opinions. In 1921 he was made a member of the King's Privy Council in Ireland and elected as a Senator for the new Free State. The Union peerage, so long sought by his grandfather, came his way in 1926; however, the title and style chosen was not 'de Valence' (as his grandfather had requested for himself and his descendants) but Baron Mereworth of Mereworth Castle in Kent. This mansion was his home during the early 1920s. Designed by Colen Campbell in the early 18th century, Mereworth Castle is one of the most beautiful and important Palladian houses in Britain. Tragically, Lord and Lady Oranmore were killed in a car accident in 1927 and were buried in Mereworth Churchyard.

The titles and the remaining estates came to Geoffrey's eldest son, Dominick, who was only 26 years old at the time of the tragedy. He decided to sell up in England and return to Ireland. He married Mildred Egerton and had two sons, Dominick and Martin, and three daughters, Patricia, Judith and Brigit. His second wife was Oonagh Guinness, the great-granddaughter of the gentleman who had bought Ashford from the 1st Lord Oranmore in 1852. They had two sons, Garech, the hero of Irish traditional music, who founded Claddagh Records and The Chieftains. The second son was Tara, whose tragic death in a car crash prompted the song *A day in the life* by the Beatles.

Lord Oranmore worked hard to make Castle Mac Garrett pay for itself. His kitchen gardens produced and sold vegetables and fruit, including more than 80 varieties of cooking and eating apples; eels were caught and shipped to the London markets; land was reclaimed, reseeded and stocked with a herd of Aberdeen Angus cross-breeds; and Suffolk and Galway sheep were cross-bred in order to provide a better strain. Some 1200 pheasants were raised for the shoots, which took place every November and January. In addition, there was an extensive snipe and woodcock shoot at Cong, near Ashford, and grouse stalking at Luggala.

The shooting that took place at Castle Mac Garrett was not limited to birds. As a boy, the present peer was in the habit of taking pot shots at the dairymaid as she went about her business. The reason given is that she had an extremely ample figure and the temptation proved to be too much for a small boy. He was eventually summoned before his father for a scolding, but whether the rebuke was for shooting his airgun at the lady or for missing her is not known. Another to experience Lord Oranmore's love of firearms (and his sense of humour) was the Marchese Malaspina, the Italian Minister to Ireland in the 1940s. Tired of hearing him boast about what a good shot he was, Lord Oranmore adjusted the sights on his gun, with the result that the gentleman missed everything at which he took aim. At length, on being told that he could not even shoot his own hat, he accepted the challenge. Lord Oranmore surreptitiously readjusted the sights on the gun and, with the rest of the house guests, watched with quiet amusement

Castle Mac Garrett
Claremorris, County Mayo

as the diplomat proceeded to blast his own headgear into small pieces. Perhaps
it is not without a sense of irony that the present owners of the Castle have
turned the former gunroom into a morgue.

Despite his best endeavours to keep the place going, which included engaging
his friend, the distinguished Irish architect Michael Scott, to build new stables
for his stud at Castle Mac Garrett, the end was in sight. Heart-broken, Lord
Oranmore and Browne (whose third wife was Constance Stevens – the actress
Sally Gray) sold the contents of the house and moved to London in 1961. In 1964,
financial considerations forced him to sell the house and demesne to the Land
Commission who, as might have been expected, destroyed the estate. Lord
Oranmore and Browne now lives in Eaton Place in London and has just reached
his hundredth birthday. This achievement is surpassed by the fact that since he
took his seat in the House of Lords on his father's death in 1927 (as the 2nd Baron
Mereworth), and was still there when the hereditary element of that body was
abolished in 1999, he was a Member of the British Parliament for longer than
anybody else in history – a record that, in present circumstances, is unlikely to
be surpassed.

An era has come to an end and there are some who would argue that the
neighbourhood is the poorer for it. Recently, a former footman from Castle
Mac Garrett approached Garech Browne in a Dublin pub, where he was in the
company of a distinguished member of Dáil Éireann. The man described the
long hours he had to work and, by today's standards, the low wages that he
had received. The elected representative, thinking to score a point against
Mr Browne, asked him, 'And would you like to be working back there again?'
'In the morning, like a shot' came the unexpected reply. Unfortunately, the
parliamentary gentleman's reaction has not been recorded.

A late 19th-century house designed by Frederick Pepys Cockerell for Charles O'Conor, Ó Conchobhair Donn (O'Conor Don). Clonalis contains one of the greatest collections of Irish manuscripts still in private hands.

Clonalis *Castlereagh, County Roscommon*

Beyond Castlereagh, among level fields and woods contained between branches of the River Suck, lies Clonalis. This, the first Irish country house to be built of concrete, is perhaps the most curious building in this collection. Behind its formidable mixture of Queen Anne and High Italian architecture is a residence which, until quite recently, was the home of the last family to hold the High Kingship of Ireland. When Father Charles O'Conor, Ó Conchobhair Donn (O'Conor Don) died in 1973, he left the estate to his sister's family and the connection between the place and the head of the family was broken. The title went to a cousin, Denis, who was living in a small but elegant villa in Dun Laoghaire in County Dublin.

2

THE PRESENT HOUSE AT CLONALIS was commissioned by Charles, Ó Conor Don, O'Conor Don, in 1872 and built to the design of Frederick Pepys Cockerell, who had already built Bithan in Buckinghamshire for his client's cousins, the Perrys. Among other considerations, he thought the original residence too near to the River Suck to be healthy. Work started in 1878 and the house was left two-thirds finished in 1880. It is a country house in the style of the innumerable villas that had sprung up after the building of Osborne, Queen Victoria's house on the Isle of Wight.

The avenue stretches for a third of a mile through the parkland, over a bridge with wrought-iron balustrades, and then up to the western side of the mansion, where a large porch below a tower-like structure greets the visitor. The Royal Coronation Stone of Connacht, removed from Rathcroghan, stands beside the front door. The front hall is the most ornate room in the house. The staircase is separated from this space by arches, as at Gurteen le Poer in Tipperary. It has an oak handrail and pitch pine balusters, and is fronted by columns of pink Mallow marble. The north side of this hall leads to a small lobby off which is the billiard room. There is a mahogany screen in the hall which contains small paintings of those properties, civil and ecclesiastical, that are connected with the O'Conor family. Immediately above the screen hangs the Standard of Ireland, which was last carried by O'Conor Don, as Standard Bearer of Ireland, at the Coronation of King George V in 1911. Cockerell transferred the Georgian chimneypieces from the old abandoned house to his new building. The chimney-piece in the hall contains niches for turf and logs on either side of the main section, while beside it is Carolan's Harp – the harp of bard and harper/composer Turlough O'Carolan (1670–1738).

The three main reception rooms are on the garden front. The drawing room faces the staircase and takes up the southwest angle of the house, while the dining room occupies that of the southeast part. The house contains the finest collection of Irish manuscripts in private hands.

The O'Conors of Connacht have a long and complex history. The family produced no fewer than 11 high kings of Ireland and 24 kings of Connacht until

Previous page
The entrance front of Clonalis seen from the avenue.

These pages
1 The ornate entrance hall and staircase. The harp of Turlough O'Carolan can be seen in a case to the left of the chimneypiece.
2 Clonalis seen from the southwest.

Clonalis
Castlereagh,
County Roscommon

the Norman invaders finally put an end to the old Gaelic way of things. In 1106, Toirdhealbhach Ó Conchobhair was inaugurated as King of Connacht at the ford of Termon, on the River Shannon. The internal dissension among the Irish kings and lords was one of the factors that facilitated the Plantagenets in their conquest of the country. In 1118, Muircheartach Ó Briain, the son of Toirdhealbhach Mór (the 'Great'), died, and as the King of Aileach, Domhnall Mac Lochlainn, was too weak to defend any claim that he might have had to the High Kingship. Toirdhealbhach Ó Conchobhair of Connacht (accompanied by the Kings of Ossory, Leinster and Tara) invaded Munster and 'hurled Kincora (O'Brien's palace)... stone and wood, into the Shannon.' In 1151, he presided over the Synod of Kells where the Sees of Dublin, Cashel, Armagh and Tuam were raised to Archbishoprics. The Cross of Cong, a processional cross which was commissioned by Toirdhealbhach Ó Conchobhair in about 1123 and is now in the National Museum of Ireland, bears this inscription, 'A prayer for Turlough O'Conor, King of Erin, for whom this shrine was made'. He ruled as King of Ireland until his death in 1157.

When Diarmuid mac Murchadha landed with his Norman allies on the coast of Wexford, the High King of Ireland, Ruaidhrí Ó Conchobhair (Rory or Roderick O'Conor) did not realize what was about to happen. He failed to move on Dublin in 1171, failed to accept an offer from Strongbow (the great Norman leader) to become his vassal as King of Leinster, and had been compelled to do homage in the same year to Henry II in Dublin. In 1175 he agreed to the following: 'Henry grants to Roderick, his liege King of Connacht, as long as he faithfully serves him, that he shall be King under him... and as his man'. This agreement is known to history as the Treaty of Windsor, which St Laurence O'Toole had negotiated on behalf of the Irish High King. It was, effectively, the end of Irish independence for almost 750 years, and Ireland received a foreign overlord, backed by the Pope.

Roderick observed the Treaty faithfully, but it was a covenant that the Normans had no intention of honouring. A comment made by a Native American chief in the 19th century is particularly apposite regarding the treatment of the native

Irish by their Norman conquerors, 'They made us many treaties and they kept but one. They promised to take our land and they took it.' The prospect of owning vast tracts of land was too much of a temptation for the Normans – de Lacy, de Burgo, de Coghlan – they all came. They even persuaded Roderick's own sons to plot against him and so, in 1187, he abdicated and spent the remainder of his life as a religious in the Abbey of Cong in the west of Ireland, where he was buried in 1199. Roderick's brother, Cathal Crobhdhearg, succeeded him and is the direct ancestor of the present head of the family, Desmond O'Conor (Ó Conchobhair Donn). Henry II confirmed his status as King of Connacht in a second treaty. He died as a grey friar in the Abbey of Knockboy.

In 1260, at the Battle of Drumderg, the Irish were defeated because they were not equipped to fight a Norman army. Ten years later revenge was possible thanks, in large measure, to hired galloglasses (mercenaries) from the Hebrides. At the Battle of Athenkip, Aodh Ó Conchobhair defeated Robert d'Ufford, the Justiciar of Ireland, and Walter de Burgo at the head of 'all the foreigners of Ireland', and *The Annals of Ulster* recorded that 'no greater defeat had been given to the English in Ireland up to that time.'

Less than a year after Robert I, King of the Scots, had defeated the English at the Battle of Bannockburn, his brother Edward landed at Larne in 1315 with 15,000 men in search of an Irish Crown. His arrival offered a rallying symbol to the embattled Irish. It did not seem to matter that Bruce was just as much a Norman as Edward II of England. In a curious twist of fate, it seems to have been a case of 'better the devil that you don't know than the one that you do'; besides which, the Bruces had gone native and could hardly be regarded as Normans in any real sense. The Kings of Thomond, Breffni, Uí Maine (Ó Briain, Ó Ruairc and Ó Ceallaigh) joined Feidhlim Ó Conchobhair of Connacht. They met the English army at Athenry in 1316, when the Irish turned tail and fled. The English archers made a slaughter among the Irish ranks and, at the end of the day, Feidhlim lay dead. With him the sovereign power of the family ended, and de Burgo set up a tame member of the dynasty as a puppet king.

In 1385 there were two claimants to the Kingdom of Connacht. They agreed to divide the territory between them and, from that time, there were no longer kings of Connacht but only kings of half of Connacht. The two claimants were Toirdhealbhach Ruadh, the grandson of Feidhlim, and Toirdhealbhach Óg

Ó Conchobhair Donn, the grandson of Feidhlim's older brother. From Toirdhealbhach Ruadh descended the family of O'Conor Roe, the last of whom was Roger O'Conor (Ó Conchobhair Ruadh), the Governor of Civita Vecchia in 1734. From Toirdhealbhach Óg comes the line of O'Conor Don.

The Annals of Lough Cé in 1585 stated that 'O'Conor Don, a man who subdued and humbled his enemies, the best that came of the race of Turlough Óg for a long time, died and was interred at Ballintubber under the protection of God and Brigid.' His son, Hugh O'Conor, had been no more than a boy when he had rescued his father from

1 The staircase with the 'Standard of Ireland' on the left. This was last carried at the Coronation of King George V in 1911.
2 A giltwood mirror in the entrance hall.
3 Roger O'Conor, Governor of Civita Vecchia in 1734

Clonalis
Castlereagh,
County Roscommon

Athlone Castle where Sir Edward Fytton, the Governor of Connacht, had imprisoned him. Ten years later, Hugh O'Conor was accused of inciting his father-in-law, Brian na Múrtha Ó Ruairc of Breffni, to rebellion against the Crown. O'Conor Don submitted to the English in 1583.

This was 40 years after the Ó Briain had submitted to Henry VIII, but unlike the Munster king, there was no peerage offered, nor was the amount of land that O'Conor Don was allowed to keep anything like the vast tract that had been returned to Lord Thomond. However, Ballintubber Castle and the lands around it were returned to him. His father-in-law, Brian Ó Ruairc, fled to Scotland but was arrested and sent south to face a trial, followed by execution.

The lord of Breffni was drawn along the ground to the gallows on a hurdle and hanged until near death; he was then cut down and revived only to be castrated and have his entrails and heart torn out. The beheading that followed was a mere formality. His head was stuck on a pike on London Bridge, while pieces of his quartered body were nailed on the gates of English towns as a warning to anybody else who might try to oppose the Crown. To the squeamish, it should be pointed out that compared with the sentences meted out to those convicted of treason in Europe, this execution was comparatively humane.

Hugh O'Conor Don returned so far to the English fold that he commanded
a troop of horse at the Battle of the Curlews against Aodh Ruadh Ó Domhnaill.
The battle was won by the men of Breffni, led by the son of Brian Ó Ruairc.
The English ranks broke and those who survived fled the field. Hugh O'Conor
Don took refuge in Ballintubber Castle, but his own family, disgusted by his
alliance with the foreigners, turned a great gun on the fortalice (a small fort)
forcing him to surrender. His life was spared at the request of his brother-in-
law, Brian Óg Ó Ruairc.

He was knighted in 1598 by Robert Devereux, Earl of Essex, becoming the
one and only member of his House to accept an honour from the English. Such
at least is his descendants' proud boast. However, it should be borne in mind
that this was the only title that the Tudors (ever the realists) were prepared to
offer the representative of a now diminished power. To the heads of other – and
stronger – families, such as the MacCarthys and the O'Donels, they gave the
earldoms of Clancar and Tyrconnell.

Sir John Perrott, Elizabeth's representative, was inclined to allow the native
Irish to settle down as good subjects of the Queen. However John O'Donovan
wrote that, 'Like many of those who preceded him, and came after him, he
was thwarted by the English garrison in Ireland, who wished for no settlement
with the Irish but rather their destruction and the division of their lands among
themselves.' On Hugh's death, O'Conor Don was succeeded by his first three
sons. The family supported Charles I, notwithstanding a rumour that Charles,
O'Conor Don had proclaimed himself King of Connacht. The result of their
support for the Stuart cause was that two of them died outlawed and in poverty,
while all the others fled to France and Spain.

Although Charles II officially returned O'Conor Don's confiscated lands
at the Restoration, they were unable to gain possession of the vast majority of
their estates, and what they did get was mostly bog land, with a few hundred
good acres beside the River Suck. Despite this betrayal, they fought for James II
at the Battle of the Boyne. Major Owen O'Conor of Ballinagare raised three
troops of horse for his Sovereign and, as Governor, surrendered the castle and

1   The drawing room
2   The dining room, the walls of which
    are hung with O'Conor portraits.

Clonalis
Castlereagh,
County Roscommon

Clonalis

Castlereagh,
County Roscommon

The Antient Coat Armour of O'CONOR Don.

town of Athlone to the victorious Williamite army. The Major was imprisoned in Chester Castle where he died in 1692.

Arthur Young wrote of Charles O'Conor, who died in 1790, 'At Clonalis, near Castlerea, lives O'Connor, the direct descendant of Roderick O'Connor who was King of Connacht six or seven hundred years ago... I was told as a certainty that the family were here long before the coming of the Milesians. Their possessions, formerly so great, are reduced to three or four hundred pounds a year, the family having fared in the revolutions of so many ages much worse than the O'Neills and O'Briens. The common people pay him the greatest respect, and send him presents of cattle, etc., upon various occasions. They regard him as the prince of a people involved in one common ruin.'

Charles's sons were members of the United Irish movement but took no part in the rebellion of 1798. The next generations produced several Members of Parliament who were elected on behalf of the Irish National Party, which was led by Isaac Butt. The O'Conor Don at the close of the 19th century was Solicitor-General of Ireland. On his death, in 1904, Douglas Hyde paid him this tribute: 'It was owing to his foresighted statesmanship that the Irish language was originally placed by Parliament upon the curriculum of the Board of Intermediate Education and from that day until his death he never ceased... to champion its cause. Few men in Ireland know how much they owe to the watchful care of the O Conor Don in this matter.' It was he who in the 1870s built the Victorian house to replace the 17th-century house, down by the river.

The family are a curious mixture. They have remained steadfastly Roman Catholic but, at the same time, are the only family to have accepted a grant of supporters to their arms, as Irish lords, from the British monarch (Lord Inchiquin has his as a peer of Ireland). The present Ó Conchobhair Donn (O'Conor Don) is Desmond, the grandson of Father Charles O'Conor, O'Conor Don. Clonalis is now the home to Father Charles's nephew, Piers O'Conor Nash, his wife and children. They have fought hard to keep the house, which is open to the public in the summer months, and its demesne in the family and have, thus far, succeeded.

Dromoland Castle was until 1962 the seat of The Baron Inchiquin, The Ó Briain, senior direct descendant of Brian Bóruma, High King of Ireland, who died on 23 April 1014 at the Battle of Clontarf, near Dublin. Dromoland is today run as a comfortable and luxurious hotel.

Dromoland Castle   *Newmarket-on-Fergus, County Clare*

Three miles south of Quin, and just across the Limerick from Ennis railway line, is Dromoland Castle, which until 1962 was the seat of Lord Inchiquin, head of the former royal dynasty of Thomond. This name derives in history from the genitive case of the Irish word 'Tuadhmhumhal', meaning north Munster, and the rulers of this territory claimed descent from Cormac Cas, a son of the semi-legendary Oilioll Olum, a king of Munster who supposedly lived in the 3rd century of the Christian era. His descendants and their followers are known as the Dál gCais (or Dalcassians) on account of their alleged descent from this Cormac. It was said that 'they were always the first into the fight, but the last out of it.'

In 1002 THE LEADER OF THE O'BRIEN FAMILY became the most famous monarch in Irish history. He was Brian mac Cennétig, but he is better known as Brian Bóruma or Ború. *The Book of Rights of the King of Cashel* (*Leabhar na gCeart*) was written to celebrate his achievements, although until then Cashel had been a MacCarthy and not an O'Brien stronghold. In the last, and greatest, victory of the Gaels over foreign invaders, King Brian's army completely defeated that of the Norsemen and their Irish allies at Clontarf, near Dublin, in 1014. The old king did not take part in the battle, but he was killed by Brodir of Man, who found him on his knees at prayer and brained him with a battleaxe. So Brian died at the moment of his greatest triumph. The Irish caught Brodir, cut into his stomach, and nailed the end of his intestines to a tree. They then pulled him around the trunk until he became disembowelled.

Brian was succeeded by his son, Donnchad. There is a story that, as the survivors of Clontarf were on their way back to the late king's capital at Cenn Coradh (Kincora), they were attacked by the men of Osraighe under their leader Mac Giolla Phádraig (Fitzpatrick), who decided to cast off their allegiance to the Dál gCais. Half of Donnchad's men were wounded and so their companions tied the injured to wooden stakes and each healthy warrior then lashed himself to a wounded comrade and let it be known that they would not leave their fellows while one strong man remained alive. On hearing this, the men of Osraighe crept away in terror. The event is still commemorated in the name of the townland of Gortnalea, or the Field of the Stakes, in County Laois. Donnchad reigned for 50 years. Ruthless as well as powerful, he murdered his ambitious brother Tadhg, and, having presented the royal regalia of Munster to the Pope, he died at Rome in 1064,

Toirdhealbhach Ó Briain, followed Donnchad in 1064. The Archbishop of Canterbury, Lanfranc, described him as 'the magnificent Torlagh, King of Ireland.' He died in 1086 and was succeeded by his son, Muirchertach Mór Ó Briain, who moved his capital from Kincora to the former Norse town of Luimneach (Limerick). These were bitter and bloody times. The century that had started in war and destruction finished it in much the same way. In 1087,

Previous page
The north front of the castle seen from across the lake.

These pages
1 The entrance hall with a portrait of Queen Anne and the great hall beyond.
2 The chimneypiece in the great hall with an equestrian portrait of Sir Edward O'Brien, 2nd Baronet, by James Seymour.
3 The castle seen from the southeast. A new banqueting and conference centre has been added to the left of this.

Dromoland Castle
Newmarket-on-Fergus,
County Clare

Mac Lochlainn, King of Aileach, sacked the palace of Kincora. It was not a
sensible action to take: Muirchertach retaliated by levelling Mac Lochlainn's
seat. All that now remains of that residence is the much-reconstructed fort
known as the Grianán of Aileach. Muirchertach died at Kincora in 1119 and
was the last O'Briain High King of Ireland.

Less than a century later, in 1171, Domhnall Ó Briain, King of Thomond,
was one of those who greeted Henry II of England on his arrival at Waterford.
This rapprochement did not last very long. In 1174, he defeated the mighty
Richard de Clare at Thurles, and then followed this up by beating Strongbow's
lieutenant, John de Courcy, in 1178. King Donal died in 1194. The O'Brien
kings founded many religious houses. Among the beautiful abbeys that owe
their existence to the kings of Thomond are the Abbeys of Corcomroe and Holy
Cross, as well as St Mary's Cathedral in Limerick.

Conchobhar Ó Briain (Conor O'Brien), became, in 1526, the last properly
inaugurated King of Thomond. On his death in 1540 he was succeeded by his
younger brother, Murchadh the Tanaiste (or heir), despite the fact that, under
English law, the next king should have been Conor's son, Donnchadh. Not that
any of this sophistry really mattered for, a brief three years later in 1543, both

Murchadh and Donnchadh, with the Lord of the Bourkes, were summoned by Henry VIII, who was newly proclaimed as King of Ireland by an obsequious parliament in Dublin, to submit themselves, their lands and their people to English authority.

And so it was that on 1 July 1543, they came to the court of Henry VIII at Greenwich. There in the Queen's Closet, after High Mass, they were invested as Irish peers under the English Crown. Murchadh came as an independent lord and left as the Irish Earl of Thomond, which dignity was to be his only for his lifetime. Thereafter it was to pass to his nephew Donnchadh – his elder brother's son. Murchadh was given the compensation prize of the hereditary barony of Inchiquin for himself and his heirs, and it is this title that survives today. The other titles conferred on that day – the earldoms of Thomond and Clanrickarde – have become extinct. This event recalls the occasion, nearly 400 years later, when His Serene Highness Prince Louis of Battenberg was made to exchange his German titles for a British marquessate. As he left Buckingham Palace, he wrote in the visitor's book 'Arrived Prince Jeckyll, departed Lord Hyde.' It is questionable whether Henry's Irish visitors took their demotions so flippantly.

The Chiefship of the O'Briens passed on the death in 1551 of the 1st Earl of Thomond to his nephew Donough, who became the 2nd Earl. The barony of Inchiquin passed to the elder son of the 1st Earl, while the younger son, Donough, was left the estate of Dromoland (which name means, according to various sources anything from 'The Hill of Litigation' to 'The Hill of the Lake' or even 'Beautiful Summit'). This gentleman was deprived of his property (and his life) when the English hanged him in Limerick in 1582; another account states that he was hanged in the old tower house at Leamaneh. The Sheriff of Limerick, George Cusack, then took possession of Dromoland, which was subsequently claimed by Lord Thomond. After many legal wrangles he received the freehold, and in 1613 he compensated Donough's grandson with the princely sum of £132.13s.6d. A William Starkey leased the estate from Lord Thomond in 1614 and his family were still there in 1641 in the person of Robert Starkey, who fled when rebellion broke out in that year. At this point, Colonel Conor

2

O'Brien of Lemanagh arrived to claim the estate. He brought with him his heavily pregnant wife, Máire Ruadh. Their son, Donough – or Donat – was probably born at Dromoland in 1642.

Máire Ruadh was a forceful lady. She is supposed to have hung her men servants by their necks, and the female servants by their hair, from the corbels of her stronghold. She is also credited with keeping a blind stallion in her stables, so fierce that when it was released the grooms had to conceal themselves in specially built niches in the yard. What is certain is that, in 1664, she received a Royal Pardon for all the murders she had committed.

It was her son Donough who finally

1   The drawing room, which is called the 'Keightley' room after the collection of portraits that hangs there. The paintings were brought to Dromoland by Catherine Keightley, wife of the 2nd Baronet.

2   Máire Ruadh, the wife of Conor O'Brien of Lemanagh and the mother of Sir Donough O'Brien, the 1st Baronet.

Dromoland Castle
Newmarket-on-Fergus, County Clare

Dromoland Castle
Newmarket-on-Fergus,
County Clare

obtained the freehold of Dromoland from the Thomonds in 1684 and was said to have built a wing on to the old Castle. He married Lucy Hamilton, whose mother was the sister of the 1st Duke of Ormonde (and whose first cousin was the unfortunate wife of the 4th Earl of Fingall). Donough O'Brien managed to stay apart from the vicissitudes of the 'Glorious Revolution', having been created a baronet by James II in 1686.

Lucius, the son and heir of the 1st Baronet, was constantly at odds with his father. He moved to London where, in 1713, he was tried for, and acquitted of, the capital murder of his friend Colonel Hickman. He died in 1717 in Paris and, because he was a Protestant, he was refused decent burial in a churchyard by the French authorities, still triumphant after the Revocation of the Edict of Nantes, some 32 years earlier. He was, in consequence, taken 'in a Dung Cart into a garden wherein the Swedish envoy has priveledge to have his people interr'd.' His son, Donough, became the 2nd Baronet and married Catherine Keightley, who was first cousin to both Queen Mary II and Queen Anne. The best portraits in Dromoland came to the family as a result of this union. Lady O'Brien sought advice from Thomas Burgh, the Surveyor-General for Ireland, about alterations to Dromoland but very little, if anything, was done about it.

Encouraged by the fortune that his grandfather had left him, Sir Donough consulted both Thomas Roberts and John Aheron about building a new mansion at Dromoland and decided that he preferred the designs of the latter, who was the author of Ireland's first book on architecture. Accordingly, there arose a splendid new mansion, of nine bays, with a three-bay pedimented breakfront, over a raised basement. The windows in the breakfront were interspersed with Corinthian pilasters, and there was a broad flight of steps up to the front door.

The rear of the house appears in a watercolour from the 1820s by Grace O'Brien, the daughter of Sir Edward O'Brien, the 4th Baronet. The painting shows that this elevation was ten bays wide and two storeys high over a raised basement, and with a four-bay, pedimented, breakfront. There was an *oeil de boeuf* window in the pediment, which was flanked by a pair of dormer windows. In the demesne of this 'handsome Grecian building', Mr Aheron also designed a temple, a gazebo, a turret and an obelisk (which no longer survives). In 1786, Daniel Beaufort described it as 'a large old house – not regular and only part of a vast design, intended to connect with the castle, since pulled down.' He went on to describe it as 'cheerful as well as magnificent'.

The 2nd Baronet was a great gambler and always in debt. He managed easily

1 The 'Armada' table, which is now on
   loan to Bunratty Castle, County Clare.
2 The long gallery with portraits of Ann
   Hyde, Lady Frances Keightley (by
   John Reilly), the 2nd Earl of
   Clarendon (by Sir Geoffrey Kneller),
   and Sir Edward O'Brien, the 2nd
   Baronet (by Eckhardt).

Dromoland Castle
*Newmarket-on-Fergus,
County Clare*

1

to squander the fortune that his grandfather had left to him. He loved racing and commissioned a set of equine portraits that used to hang in the house. In general, affairs went on in a high old style at Dromoland. In 1723, the household accounts show that the family drank 16 quarts of plain brandy, 7 gallons of white Lisbon, three hogsheads of Galway wine and unspecified quantities of sherry and white wine.

It was left to Sir Lucius O'Brien, the 3rd Baronet, to restore the family's finances after the extravagance of his predecessor, and it was his son, Sir Edward O'Brien, the 4th Baronet, who took the decision to rebuild the house and to transform it into the castellated building that we see today. In 1812, Sir Edward asked Thomas Hopper to provide plans for the reconstruction of Dromoland. Hopper had already been consulted by Lord Conyngham with regard to alterations at Slane Castle in County Meath and would, in 1819, design Gosford Castle in County Armagh, the first Norman-revival building in Ireland. But Sir Edward did not take to Hopper's design or to the idea that he should only make a few additions to the existing structure. He wrote: 'I think it would be almost as well to build a new House entirely & to content ourselves with the one we have till we can do it to suit our Purse & wishes in every respect as we are in no hurry about the matter.' In 1814, Richard Morrison supplied a design, of which a plan and two sketch elevations survive.

The decision was finally taken in 1829 and the architect chosen was James Pain, who eventually settled in Limerick. He had arrived in Ireland with his brother, George Richard, to oversee the construction of Lough Cutra Castle, which had been designed by John Nash. They saw the lucrative possibilities of working in Ireland and established a thriving practice there. They designed Strancally Castle, County Waterford; Castle Bernard in County Offaly; Blackrock Castle in County Cork; and Adare Manor in County Limerick, among many others; but their best-known house is Dromoland Castle, for which they produced classical as well as gothic plans. The large ashlar castle with four linked irregular towers was completed to Pain's design in 1835. The northwest façade fronts on to Dromoland Lake. To the rear are 18th-century walled gardens approached by the 17th-century gateway that once stood at Lemanagh Castle, near Corofin, while the 1736 stable block is part of the current building. Lady Chatterton, who saw the castle during its construction, remarked 'that phenomenon in Ireland, or indeed in any country, a magnificent place erected without ruining its possessor.'

The Pains were told to design a residence that would excel any of a similar description. This is not dissimilar to the instruction they had received from Lord Kingston with regard to his new castle at Mitchelstown. James Pain was 'assisted' in his designs by Sir Edward who wrote to him that the 'End window of the Gallery looking on to the yard have a Handsome Gothic Head & it gives an appearance to all of the windows of Cloisters which I have seen in some Houses... so that it would have the appearance of a Chapel'. It is regrettable that, despite this seeking after the gothic, Sir Edward omitted to tell Mr Pain to give the gallery and the state rooms of the castle vaulted ceilings, as he had done at Mitchelstown Castle. As it is, they are all as flat as pancakes with nice,

although simple, gothic cornices. There are oak doors and wainscotting throughout the main part of the residence.

The hall contained a table constructed from the timbers of one of the ships of the Spanish Armada, which was presented to the family by Boethius Clancy, the Sheriff of County Clare. It was, consequently, always called the 'Armada Table'. It is now on loan to Bunratty Castle, County Clare. A flight of stone steps leads to the long gallery with the great staircase at the far end. The principal rooms are to be found to one side of this gallery. In 1837, Samuel Lewis described Dromoland as a 'superb edifice in the castellated style', and in 1855 Sir Bernard Burke claimed that the Pains had started their work in 1822 and it had cost 'not much less than £50,000. It is built entirely of dark blue limestone'. He finished by stating that 'Dromoland [was] one of the most beautiful and desirable residences in Ireland.'

Sir Edward was a most liberal and, in the best sense of the word, Christian gentleman. He wrote, 'I never feel so devote as when I hear a ripening cornfield murmur in the wind; it makes me say to myself "God is preparing bread for his people."' However, his wife, Charlotte Smith, armed with Protestant missionary zeal, was determined to reclaim for salvation as many of the poor ignorant people about her as she could. The parish priest was the victim of one of her tirades, after which her husband remarked, 'This reverend gentleman, as I informed you before, did not come here for a controversy with you, but to buy my little yellow pony; and he has been worried and molested in my house; and now I will not sell him the pony, for I will make him a present of it.' There are two ash trees at Dromoland that are known as the 'Famine trees' because it was there that soup was supposedly doled out to the hungry during the Great Famine of the 1840s. The want was not as great at Dromoland as elsewhere, but the family still tried to do what they could to help.

Edward's younger son was William O'Brien, who added his mother's maiden name of Smith to his own in order to receive an inheritance. He was the Member of Parliament for County Limerick and initially opposed Daniel O'Connell. He later changed his opinion, but was never really forgiven by some of the 'Liberator's' followers for the trouble he had caused the great man. Smith O'Brien's mother (the Protestant zealot) was devastated when he decided to support O'Connell's Repeal movement; she wrote that he was 'A Rebel & a supporter of Rebels'. 1848 saw all of Europe torn apart by Revolution.

Ireland's contribution to the general spirit of unrest and upheaval took place on 26 July 1848, at 'The Battle of the Widow McCormack's Cabbage Garden' in Ballingarry, County Tipperary. It occurred when William Smith O'Brien and a few friends attempted to take over the local police station with the intention of somehow driving the British out of Ireland, but they were soon arrested by the local constabulary. This pathetic little incident was later to attain heroic and mythological stature, completely out of proportion to what it had any chance of achieving, since it was referred to by Patrick Pearse in his 1916 Declaration of Independence as one of the six attempts 'in the last three hundred years' in which the people of Ireland had asserted their right to Independence in arms.

No sooner was the little band of conspirators in custody than the authorities, predictably, over-reacted. Smith O'Brien and his companions were charged not only with treason (which Smith O'Brien did not, at first, believe he was guilty of) but also with conspiring to kill Queen Victoria which, as Her Majesty was at Windsor on the day and consequently nowhere near the Ballingarry Royal Irish Constabulary Station, might be thought to be stretching the charges somewhat. The inevitable trial and predictable sentence of death was commuted to transportation to what is now Tasmania. Smith O'Brien and his friends spent a few years there, but in 1854 he was allowed, with those of his friends who had not already escaped, to return to England. Permission to go back home came two years later and he returned to a hero's welcome. He died in 1864. The only penalty that remained with him at the end was the Government's refusal to allow him to use the prefix 'Honourable' before his name, as his siblings had been permitted to do when their brother Sir Lucius had officially inherited the barony of Inchiquin (as the 13th Lord) in 1861, on the death of his remote cousin, the last Marquess of Thomond. A headstrong but essentially noble gentleman, William Smith O'Brien was the most notable O'Brien of recent generations. His statue stands in O'Connell Street, in Dublin.

William's nephew, the 14th Baron Inchiquin petitioned continually to be granted the Earldom of Thomond but successive governments refused. He was given the Order of Saint Patrick, perhaps as a consolation prize. The family continued the political involvement that William Smith O'Brien had started and the 13th, 14th and 15th Barons were all Representative Peers of Ireland.

Dromoland Castle
Newmarket-on-Fergus,
County Clare

In the latter part of the 19th century the Inchiquins continued to live well, despite the political disturbances in the country and the fall in rents generally. For example, in 1873 there were 18 indoor servants at the castle and the family retained the privilege given to them by Henry VIII of putting their servants into a royal livery of scarlet. And on their coat of arms, which is carved over the entrance porch of the castle, are the same three Lions found today in the coat of arms of the British monarch. The only difference is in the blazon of the colour: at Dromoland, the forequarters of the O'Brien felines are gold and their hindquarters silver, while the British beasts are all in gold.

Electricity was introduced into the house after World War I. One of Lord Inchiquin's employees had the job of running the engine that made the whole system function. Unfortunately, he did not quite understand its complicated workings and turned on the machine without first turning on the water. When, after about ten minutes of strange sounds emanating from the machine, he realized his mistake and let the water loose, it merely had the effect of cracking the cylinders. Until replacements arrived the whole castle was plunged into utter darkness.

The 14th Baron's daughter, Beatrice, married Guglielmo Marconi, the inventor of radio, who was afterwards created a marquis by the King of Italy. Despite this connection, his mother-in-law, Ellen, Lady Inchiquin, would never permit a radio inside the front door at Dromoland. In 1902, Lord Inchiquin moved the gateway from Lemanagh Castle to Dromoland, where it still forms a feature of the walled garden.

The 16th Baron became a furrier in London. His mother, the Dowager Lady Inchiquin, continued to live at Dromoland until her death in 1940. There was a rumour that Eamon de Valera offered the position of President of Ireland to the 16th Baron, who, far from thinking about high affairs of state, had turned the castle into accommodation for paying guests in order to keep a roof on the place. His butler was Patrick O'Dowd, and, in a curious cross-fertilization, the footman was Nicholas Meyers, who started out his working life at Dromoland, and ended up as the butler at Luggala in County Wicklow, working for the

The castle seen from the 'Limerick' avenue. Dromoland Castle is approached from the Limerick to Ennis road. Coming from Limerick, this was the avenue that brought one to the castle – hence the name 'Limerick' avenue.

Dromoland Castle
*Newmarket-on-Fergus,
County Clare*

Honourable Garech Browne, the son of Lord Oranmore, a cousin of the Inchiquin family.

In 1962, the 17th Baron sold the castle, together with 350 acres, to Bernard P. McDonough, from West Virginia. He retained 1000 acres for himself and built a new residence, Thomond House, to the designs of Donal O'Neill Flanagan. His widow and daughter lived there until Lady Inchiquin's death, when the house became the home of Conor O'Brien (the present, and 18th, Baron), his wife Helen and their daughters Slaney and Lucia. The castle is now a luxury hotel and has been well served by its subsequent owners.

It should not be forgotten that Lord Inchiquin (Ó Briain) is the heir to one and a half millennia of Irish history. The year 2002 will be the 1000th anniversary of the Coronation of Brian Bóruma as High King of Ireland, while 2014 is a millennium on from the Battle of Clontarf. Conor O'Brien is the Chairman of the Standing Council of Irish Chiefs and is actively involved with the welfare of the O'Briens throughout the world.

A 17th-century house, transformed into a Palladian mansion by Richard Castle in about 1729, French Park was the seat of the French family, the head of which became Baron de Freyne in 1839. Today the family has gone, the desmesne is destroyed and the house has been demolished.

French Park *County Roscommon*

One day, early in the last century, a priest knelt down on a deserted country road in County Roscommon. After a while, he looked up and found to his astonishment a troop of local inhabitants down on their knees in the mud beside him. Encountering a religious, seemingly at his devotions and in such an out of the way spot, they had concluded that he must have seen a miraculous apparition and so had joined him in what they imagined to be his prayers. Unfortunately for their hopes, as well as for the prospects of religious tourism in County Roscommon, there had been no celestial vision. The good cleric turned out to be the distinguished photographer, Father Frank Browne SJ, who had merely been adjusting his camera in order to record the gates of French Park, which were among the finest in Ireland.

AT FIRST GLANCE, FRENCH PARK, originally known as Dungar, appeared to be the *beau ideal* of an 18th-century Palladian residence. Appearances, however, can be deceptive for beneath the outer skin lay a much older building. The construction of the house commenced in about 1650 and was completed by 1667, according to the date on the pediment. It was built of red bricks brought over from Holland and was probably the first brick house in Connacht. The gates that had so attracted Father Frank Browne were constructed in 1704 (and restored in 1915). Around 1729 the house was altered and two wings were added to the building. These were connected to the main house by curved sweeps that were the same height as the wings. This feature is to be found at Strokestown Park in County Roscommon and at Summerhill in County Meath, both of which have been attributed, in whole or in part, to the architect Richard Castle. This and other similarities have led to the suggestion that the altered and extended French Park may well be Castle's work.

Born at Hesse in Germany in about 1690 or 1695, Castle arrived in Ireland in 1728 at the invitation of Sir Gustavus Hume, the Irish politician, and in 1733 he married June Truffet, an Irish girl of Huguenot origin. After the death of Sir Edward Lovett Pearce, whose assistant he had been, Castle became the most successful architect in the country. Three of the finest houses in Ireland, Powerscourt, Russborough and Carton (where he died in 1751), were built to his designs.

In its final state, French Park was a three-storey, seven-bay house, with a three-bay pediment breakfront. The wings were five bays wide, four bays deep and two storeys high. A pillared portico was added in the late Georgian period. This led into a two-storey entrance hall, panelled and grained to resemble walnut, which contained a staircase with finely turned balusters above a carved Adamesque frieze. To the left of the hall was an octagonal boudoir panelled in pale wood. The entrance hall led directly into the dining room, which originally had walls lined in 'Queen Anne' leather. When this was found to be beyond repair, it was taken down and those fragments that were still usable were inserted into a screen. Over the dining room was the drawing room, reached by the

French Park
County Roscommon

French Park
County Roscommon

staircase, which contained two late 18th-century chimneypieces, one of them by Pietro Bossi, a renowned Italian craftsman. The ceiling appeared to date from the mid-18th century, but was in fact commissioned by the 4th Lord de Freyne as part of the renovations that he carried out on the house during the 1870s. These included, among other things, the insertion of a stained glass window into the entrance hall.

Isaac Weld, the author of *A Statistical Survey of Roscommon*, wrote of French Park, which he visited in 1832, 'everything at this fine old place is upon a grand and extended scale and the mansion has been for a long time distinguished for its hospitality'. In his case, the famed hospitality fell somewhat short of the mark, since the family was away from home when he called and he had to make do with a view of the pack of 25 black and white hounds that served the French Park Hunt.

The Irish gentry took great pride in what they imagined to be their ancient lineages and the Frenches of French Park were no exception. Their pedigree, recorded in *Burke's Peerage* and copied, more or less accurately, in the *Weekly Irish Times* and the *Irish Tatler and Sketch*, provided a list of ancestors that went back nearly a thousand years. John D'Alton concluded his *Memoir of the Family of French* with the words, 'In 1839 Arthur French (the Fourth) was raised to the peerage of the United Kingdom by the title of Baron de Freyne of Artagh, Co. Roscommon, and is living: the seventeenth in lineal succession from Fulco de Freyne, the descendant of Rollo, first Duke of Normandy.'

In 1837 when Sir William Betham, Ulster King of Arms, registered their family pedigree in his Office, he wrote (with rather more enthusiasm than accuracy) that 'the family names of the Freyne's (of Kilkenny, Tipperary, Cork and Waterford) were Oliver, Patrick, Robert, John and Geffery, equally those of the French's of Galway, they were undoubtedly the same family'. In reality, they were undoubtedly nothing of the sort for the excellent reason that the earlier part of their family tree was pure invention.

According to the family mythology, Patrick French, who had been Sheriff of Kilkenny in 1425, was dispatched in 1444 to Galway 'to try the Blakes for the murder of the Athys'. Love followed in the footsteps of justice for Patrick French's son, Oliver, married Mary d'Athi, sometime after the conflagration in Galway of 1473, and thus another surname was added to 'The Tribes of Galway' – or so the story goes.

In fact, the earliest known ancestor of the family was a certain Walter French, who was living in about 1425 and who, it is claimed, was the Chief Magistrate of County Galway in 1444–45. There is, however, no record of anyone of that name holding such a position during those years. His descendants came to hold the baronies of de Freyne and ffrench, as well as the earldom of Ypres. Walter's descendant, Nicholas French, was the Mayor of Galway in 1583–84.

During Nicholas's term as Mayor of Galway, Sir John Perrott, Queen Elizabeth's Lord Deputy, visited the place and was obviously disturbed by the 'disorderly practises' that he saw, for he ordered the Mayor and Corporation to put matters instantly to rights. A draconian list of byelaws followed in 1585, including one that forbade women to wear 'gorgiouse aparell'; in headgear their choice of colours was to be limited to black and they were particularly prohibited from wearing hatbands or cap bands of gold thread – mayoresses only excepted!

According to the de Freyne version of history, Nicholas's older brother, Francis, married Úna O'Conor, the daughter of Sir Donough O'Conor, Ó Conchobhair Shligigh, who settled extensive lands upon her son, Stephen, in

The dining room with a portrait of the
Right Honourable Fitzstephen French
MP over the chimneypiece and, beside
it, a portrait of Colonel Arthur French
MP who died in 1799. The third
portrait from the right is of Colonel
John French MP (An Tiarna Mór).

French Park
County Roscommon

1609 while Sir Charles O'Conor gave him more lands in 1622. In reality, it was Stephen's son, Patrick, who by various methods acquired confiscated lands in counties Sligo and Roscommon, and it was he who built the house at French Park, then known as Dungar. These were troubled times for the French family. The Earl of Strafford, King Charles I's Lord Deputy, confiscated Patrick's lands in 1635–36 during the English Civil War. Restored to him by an Act of the English Parliament, the lands were confiscated again in 1654 by Oliver Cromwell, whose commissioners then proceeded to return to him some 6000 of his Roscommon acres in the years 1656 and 1657. This holding was increased by a Royal grant of 1667 that gave him back a very considerable portion of his original estates.

Patrick French died in 1669, leaving his estates to his second son Dominick. John French, Dominick's son, acquired the sobriquet of 'An Tiarna Mór' ('the great landowner' – rather than the literal meaning of the words: 'the great lord'). He conformed to the Established Church, fought for King William during the so-called 'Glorious Revolution' and commanded a troop of Enniskillen Dragoons at the Battle of Aughrim. With an eye to the main chance, in 1703 he acquired from the trustees of the Forfeited Estates the greater part of the lands of Major

The dining room with a portrait of the Right Honourable Fitzstephen French MP over the chimneypiece and, beside it, a portrait of Colonel Arthur French MP who died in 1799. The third portrait from the right is of Colonel John French MP (An Tiarna Mór).

Owen O'Conor of Ballinagar and started the family connection with Parliament when he was elected the Member for Carrick-on-Shannon in 1695. His heirs would continue this involvement in politics for almost 150 years, culminating in the granting of a peerage to his great-great-grandson. John's father-in-law was Sir Arthur Gore, the ancestor of the earls of Arran, whose Christian name would be passed on to many of his daughter Ann's descendants. John French left a bequest of £1000, an enormous sum of money for those days, in order to provide for a 'wake' that would be long remembered in the vicinity. For three whole days and nights his tenants, together with all the other locals, drank themselves into oblivion in the best Irish tradition beside his corpse, which had been propped up in its coffin for the occasion.

John's eldest son, Arthur French, succeeded to the family estates and died in 1769. He left four sons, three of whom would follow him to the grave within six years. The first to go was his youngest son, George French of Innfield (or Enfield). He had taken deep offence at certain remarks that had been made concerning the alleged fraudulent activities of a member of his family who had been Treasurer of the County. A neighbour, Sir Edward Crofton, the 2nd Baronet of Mote, and a Member of Parliament for the same borough, made these accusations during the election campaign of 1770. Despite the attempts of both families, nothing could shake George French in his determination to fight a duel in order to redeem the family honour. The outcome was that, in the early hours of the morning, just behind the ruins of Roscommon Castle, he fell at the first exchange of shots. He did not die immediately but lingered on for some days in considerable pain after his leg, which had been struck by the bullet, was amputated from 'the thick part of the thigh'.

In 1775, the late George French's two older brothers – Robert, who was a Major in the Army, and John – were drowned while returning to Ireland from London where John, who was known as Seán Dubh, or 'Black John', had been a Member of Parliament since 1743. As a reward for his political services it had been decided to confer a peerage on him and he had chosen the title of Baron Dungar, which suggests that the name of the house was not changed from Dungar to French Park until after his death. A family legend tells that, as the household was waiting for the return of the two brothers, the spectral sound was heard of an invisible carriage drawing up to the front door, quickly followed by the unearthly shriek of the family 'bean sí' (banshee). In this way were the wives of the two unfortunate gentlemen given notice that they had just become widows. In the best convention of such ghostly and gothic tales, a particularly fierce thunderstorm was raging outside the mansion at the time.

The heir was the surviving brother, Arthur, who was a prosperous wine merchant in Dominick Street, Dublin. Family tradition has it that he refused to accept the Barony of Dungar that had been intended for Seán Dubh. But this disinclination to accept a proffered 'inheritance' did not deter him from taking over both the family estates and his brother's seat in Parliament.

What is even more curious is that the same family tradition claims that his son, yet another Arthur, supposedly rejected both an earldom, which was proffered as a bribe to vote for the Act of Union, as well as a barony that was offered without any strings at all. Writing about such 'family traditions' as these, Sir Robert Peel made the comment, 'I never yet met with a man in Ireland who had not himself either refused honours from the Crown, or was not the son of a man, or had not married the daughter of a man who had been hard-hearted enough

French Park
County Roscommon

to refuse the solicitations of the Government. In general it is a peerage that has been refused.'

But, whether or not Arthur French turned down two peerages, his views on the Act of Union with Great Britain are a matter of public record, for he issued an address, together with Lord Kingsborough (his kinsman and fellow member of Parliament for Roscommon) that included the sentiment 'The independence of Ireland must always be for us a most favourite object and to transfer for ever, without consent, the trust you reposed in us for a limited period only, would in our opinion be an unjustifiable usurpation.'

If two generations of the French family had problems with the prospect of ennoblement, the next one, in the person of yet another Arthur French, had no such qualms. Inheriting French Park in 1820, he sat as a Member of Parliament at Westminster until 1839. In that year he was created Baron de Freyne of Artagh in County Roscommon. Having no male heirs, he was in 1851 additionally created Baron de Freyne of Coolavin, County Sligo, in the peerage of the United Kingdom, with remainder to his brothers and their male heirs. Upon his death in 1856, the first barony became extinct while the second one devolved upon his brother. The newly created Lord de Freyne chose an ancient Irish warrior as one of the supporters to his coat of arms. Just why this should have been selected

baffles the imagination since, not even in their wildest claims for noble lineage, did this family ever suggest that they were descended from the pre-Norman inhabitants of Ireland. In passing, it might be mentioned that, in addition to acquiring his peerages (and giving enough money to purchase 51 tons of food for the locals during the Great Famine of 1845–49) Arthur French had the distinction of being hung in effigy by his tenantry. Which just goes to show that no good deed goes unpunished.

Although the 1st Lord de Freyne had taken good care to ensure the continuation of his title, by including his brothers as potential heirs in the patent of creation, it must be said that his siblings did not do very much to assist him with his schemes.

Neither the 1st nor the 2nd Barons left any sons and so the title and estates came to their next brother, Charles, in 1863. He had married in a Roman Catholic chapel at a time when such unions were illegal for members of the Established Church, and the upshot was that his first three sons, Charles, John and William, were all deemed to be illegitimate and consequently ineligible to succeed to the title. Charles French eventually rectified matters, as far as the law was concerned, by re-marrying his lady in a Church of Ireland ceremony. As a result, he was followed as the 4th Lord de Freyne by his fourth son, Arthur, who, being the first son born after the Protestant marriage, was his senior legitimate male offspring. As might  have been expected, the first-born son disputed the inheritance, but the House of Lords ruled against him. If it were not for that decision, the present peer would be Seán de Freyne French, who was born in 1936, and the heir to the peerage would be his son Lance, who was born in 1963, as they both descend from the second, but deemed illegitimate, son of Charles French, 3rd Lord de Freyne.

A question remains; why did Arthur French choose the title of 'de Freyne'? It might have been that he thought de Freyne was an older form of his surname or perhaps he believed that he really was descended from the Fulco de Freyne mentioned by d'Alton. In either instance he was wrong, but in fairness he was not alone in such delusions. The quest for ancient lineage, which had started with the 'new men' of the Tudor court, had reached fever proportions by the 19th century. In England, the Howard dukes of Norfolk got it into their heads that they were somehow descended from Hereward the Wake, the Saxon hero who had opposed the Conqueror, rather than from respectable Norfolk knights who had lived centuries later. Their Graces of Somerset and Manchester, each with a similar type of ancestry, decided that they were really descended from ancient noble dynasties that had originated, respectively, in St Maur in France (for Seymour) and Monte Acuto in Italy (for Montague).

In Ireland, too, perfectly respectable families such as the Veseys opted to become 'Norman' de Vesci's; while another branch of the Frenches, descended from the same Walter French who was living in Galway in 1425, pretended that their surname had been written as ffrench since the 15th century, and this spelling was used for the peerage that one of these cadets received in 1798. The fiction that they had used this orthography for more than five centuries is perpetuated by their entry in the millennium edition of *Burke's Peerage*.

As the author of *The Complete Peerage* wrote in a footnote to the ffrench barony, 'The ludicrous mode of spelling the name with a double 'f' has been stereotyped by its adoption in the patent of 1798. It probably arose from ignorance that the form of the capital 'F' in manuscript was that of the small 'f' duplicated (a duplication presumably arising from a prolongation of the tick at the extremity of the upper horizontal line of the capital 'F'), so that not only every 'Fool' but also every 'Felon' (if spelt with a capital 'F') would be as much entitled to the double 'f' as these scions of the house of French. The ffoolish ffancy, which is aggravated if the 'f' be written 'Ff', has happily not been repeated by any other member of the peerage and, considering the spread of education, is not likely now to occur

French Park
County Roscommon

again.' The same author, bewildered as to why Arthur French should have chosen de Freyne for the name of his peerage, commented, 'but at any rate he secured a title with an archaic sound, which is always something'.

For the record, the name Frene or Freign was that of an old English family, a member of which was summoned to Parliament in 1336. A certain Sir Humphrey de Freyne allegedly came into Ireland with Strongbow in 1172, his grandfather having arrived in England with the Conqueror in 1066. The first mention of the name de Freyne occurs in the Irish State Papers for 1286, when Fulco de Freyne was appointed Seneschal of Kilkenny. This family, whose surname was de la Freign and, afterwards, Freyne, remained on their Kilkenny estates until they were deprived of them in 1650.

By 1883, the family estates consisted of French Park, together with some 38,788 acres. In 1915 the 5th Baron and his half-brother, George, had died in the muddy trenches of the Western Front during 'The war to end all wars'. Dr Douglas Hyde, the founder of the Gaelic League and, in 1937, the first President of Ireland, was their friend and neighbour in County Roscommon (his father had been the rector of Tibohine, Frenchpark). On hearing the news, he wrote 'Poor Lord de Freyne and his brother were shot the same day and buried in one grave... noblesse oblige'. In fact, of the six sons of the 4th Baron, four were to die before the conflict ended in 1918.

Francis French, the 7th Baron De Freyne now lives in London, having sold French Park in 1953. Soon afterwards the roof was removed in order to avoid the payment of rates on the building, which was subsequently razed to the ground. All that now remains is a dilapidated brew house, a souterrain and a lake. Everything else has gone.

A cadet branch of this family made a mark in history in the person of Field Marshal Sir John French, who became the Supreme Commander of the British Expeditionary Force in France in 1915. Descended from John, the third son of An Tiarna Mór, he was created a Viscount in 1916, as Lord French of Ypres, and advanced to the Earldom of Ypres in 1922. Between 1918 and 1921 he served as the penultimate British Viceroy of Ireland and, during his three years of misrule, he presided over a concerted campaign of arrests, burnings and bloody reprisals that were carried out by a crack force, who were officially called the Auxiliaries, but who are better known to history and to infamy, as 'The Black and Tans'. Their nickname came from the colours of their improvised uniform – one half police black and one half army khaki. It is on record that, never one to let the murder and mayhem of a war distract him from doing things correctly, Lord French insisted that only the finest champagne was served for his Vice-regal receptions and levées.

The lustre given to this branch of the Frenches tarnished rather quickly. A mere 50 years after Lord French had ceased to be the Viceroy of Ireland, his grandson, the 3rd Earl, was declared a bankrupt in a London Court. The previous year he had sold off the Field Marshal's treasures, decorations and other heirlooms. These had been bought back by his uncle, who was then forced to obtain a court order in order to prevent his nephew from publishing the French diaries. The 3rd Earl's obituary in *The Times* reported that, after his bankruptcy ' a life of petty vexations followed, in which stints as taxi driver and hotel porter were interspersed with court appearances'. In 1988 his title died with him.

A large, handsome house belonging
to the Smyth family and dating from
the late 18th century, Gaybrook has
now been levelled to the ground.

Gaybrook   *County Westmeath*

Built in 1790, Gaybrook was a handsome three-storey building over a basement. There was a bow in the centre of the garden front, which was flanked by a Wyatt window, and a semicircular Doric portico was added in the early 19th century. The house was five bays deep and a one-storey west wing was built in 1830 which contained a smoking room, a billiard room and, strangely, the bathrooms. This wing was afterwards converted into kitchens and the basement was closed off. The house was meant to have been twice its size – flanked by two wings each as large as the main block – but a lack of funds prevented further building. It might have been a better, if over-large, composition had the other wings been built.

THE MAIN ROOMS OF GAYBROOK, the library, sitting room, drawing room, dining room and staircase hall (the largest room in the house), as well as the front door and the servant's wing, were all accessed from the entrance hall. The sitting room was in the east corner of the house. It had three long windows and a Wyatt window facing south. In the 1950s, at the time of these photographs, this room was decorated in pale green and earth brown. The dining room had yellow walls with white curtains and the drawing room pale blue walls and gilt-wood pelmets, with ruby accents. The writing room, or study, was a fine example of the late Georgian style. There was a good neoclassical stucco ceiling, and the marble chimneypiece had a central tablet that depicted *Diana and the Hound* by Arthur Darley, a monumental sculptor.

Now demolished, Gaybrook once belonged to the senior branch of the Smith family, two of whose other houses, Ballynegall and Glananea, are also described in this book. The progenitor of this tribe was a William Smith who came to Ireland from Yorkshire in 1630. His heir, Captain Ralph Smith, left a son, the Right Reverend William Smith, who was successively Bishop of Killala (1680), Kilmore (1682) and Raphoe (1693). He married Mary, the daughter of Sir John Povey, who may have been happy to see the Restoration of 1660 and to marry his daughter to an Anglican cleric but who had, in 1653, sworn an oath of loyalty to the Puritan Commonwealth. The Bishop's son was the Venerable James Smith, the Archdeacon of Meath, who was a friend of Jonathan Swift (author of *Gulliver's Travels*). Continuing the clerical connection, the archdeacon's wife was the daughter of the Archbishop of Tuam. His son, Ralph Smith, who married the granddaughter of James Butler, 1st Viscount Lanesborough, purchased the estates of the Gay family in County Westmeath.

John Gay, the author of *The Beggar's Opera*, was reputedly a member of this family. Gay lost his original fortune in the South Sea Bubble – a financial disaster that occurred in 1720 with the collapse of the South Sea Company – but made a second one with his theatrical successes. *The Beggar's Opera* (1728) was a 'ballad' opera – a play interspersed with popular melodies to which new words had been added. This, and the fact that it was in English, put the genre

Previous page
The garden front of the house.

These pages
1   The entrance gates of Gaybrook.
    The last Smyths to live at Gaybrook
    bred horses.
2   The house seen from the southeast.
    The single-storey extension to the left
    was built in 1830.

Gaybrook
County Westmeath

into direct and successful competition with the Italian *opere serie* of Handel. It was said of the author of the words (Mr Gay) and the impresario (Mr Rich) that 'It made Rich very Gay, and probably will make Gay very Rich.' John Gay was buried in Poet's Corner at Westminster Abbey – he even wrote his own epitaph:

> *Life is a jest, and all things show it*
> *I thought so once, and now I know it.*

The success of the piece also made a duchess of its leading lady, Lavinia Fenton, who went on to marry the Duke of Bolton. The forgotten character in all of this is Dr John Pepusch, the founder of The Academy of Ancient Music, who chose and arranged the music for the work.

Two more Ralph Smiths followed, the first of whom changed the spelling of his surname to Smyth (in conjunction with his cousins), demolished the 17th-century house of the Gay family and in 1790 built the residence known as Gaybrook. The High Sheriff of County Westmeath, Ralph (d.1751) married Anne Maria, the daughter of Sir Robert Staples, 5th Baronet of Dunmurry. Their son Ralph married Georgiana, the granddaughter of the 4th Earl of Essex but they had no children and so his brother Robert eventually inherited Gaybrook. Robert revived the family's penchant for marrying the daughters of clerical gentlemen when he wed Henrietta, the daughter of the Right Reverend Nathaniel Alexander, the Bishop of Meath. This Bishop had, as an impecunious cleric, fallen in love with a Miss Jackson, the daughter of the Speaker of the House of Commons. Although the Alexanders were a great family (including among its members the Earl of Caledon and Earl Alexander of Tunis), the Reverend gentleman was too poor to be considered a suitable husband for the daughter of Speaker Jackson. The couple consequently eloped.

Their plans were discovered and Mr Jackson followed in hot pursuit. As he had better horses than those hired with the coach by the unfortunate pair, he was soon in sight and it was plain that he would overtake them in a few minutes. With great presence of mind, the Reverend Mr Alexander stopped his coach, got out with his intended and, pulling out his prayer book, proceeded to read

1 The sitting room.
2 The dining room, with a portrait of Ralph Smyth over the door.
3 The drawing room.
4 Another view of the drawing room, showing what the family called 'the Angelica Kauffman table'. It was named after the painter because it may have belonged to her.
5 The dining room.

Gaybrook
County Westmeath

Gaybrook
County Westmeath

the marriage service over Miss Jackson and himself so that, when the irate father arrived, he was presented with a *fait accompli* and a new son-in-law.

To return to the Smyths, Robert and his wife Henrietta had a difficult time to start with since they occupied the top floor of Gaybrook, the rest being the preserve of his parents and his unmarried sisters. In 1831, there were 20 indoor servants. Four men slept in a dormitory in the basement, while two footmen had to make do in so-called 'press beds', that is, beds that folded up into cupboards when not in use. Robert was prey to fits of melancholia which were not improved by a series of letters that he received from his aunt, who had moved to Bath: 'I wish it was in my power to make you happier than you seem to be, you live so much alone that your spirits sink and everything appears gloomy. I trust you will not have the affliction to lose either of your sweet girls, who can say such cruel things to you as that Bess's complaint is a forerunner of consumption, how many have I known that have worm fever and were very healthy after – asses milk and riding would be of great use...'. Robert Smyth's son, another Ralph, married the daughter of Admiral the 17th Baron Somerville but, as proved to be the case for the males of this family who married into the peerage, they had no children.

Gaybrook next passed to Ralph's brother, Colonel James Smith, whose grandson James Robert Smyth was the last Smyth to own Gaybrook. He sold up in 1960 and moved to England. Gaybrook was left for years to rot and was, eventually, levelled to the ground.

It is the way with most Irish houses that there is a story that connects even the most innocuous estate with great deeds in the past, and Gaybrook is no exception. The story here is that the demesne had belonged to the Tyrells (which it did) and that it was here that Walter Tyrell fled after he had killed William II of England (the tale relates that Walter's father, Simon Tyrell, lived here in his castle). Unfortunately for the legend, the murder of William 'Rufus' in the New Forest took place about three-quarters of a century before the Normans arrived in Ireland and started building fortifications. This myth was, almost certainly, prompted by the fact that a family called Tyrell did build a castle on this land at a later date, the ruins of which may still be seen.

Glananea
Collinstown, County Westmeath

A classic late 18th-century house
'of the medium size' which belonged
to a branch of the Smyth family
of County Westmeath. Although
the house still stands, the Smyths
have long gone from it

Of the many houses that the Smith family used to own in County Westmeath, Glananea is the only one of those featured in this book that survives. Built by Ralph Smith, the third son of William Smith and his wife, Mary King, a ward of the Archbishop of Dublin, it was called Ralphsdale until at least the 1880s. Glananea has two storeys over a basement and is six bays wide with a two-bay breakfront (as at another Smith house, Ballynegall). Here, however, instead of a portico, there is an elegant pedimented doorway, which is approached by a small flight of steps. The garden front is of seven bays with a three-bay breakfront. The house is decorated with plaster in the manner of the English architect James Wyatt and the entrance hall has a frieze of swags and shallow arcading. The ceiling in the staircase hall has a radial pattern and the balusters are of brass (again, as at Ballynegall). In a moment of *folie de grandeur*, Ralph Smith's son, William, engaged Samuel Wooley to build an impressive entrance to the demesne in the form of a triumphal arch with Corinthian columns. The arch was surmounted by a unicorn couchant, flanked by urns and covered in Coade stone decorations; it was one of the most elaborate entrances to an estate in Ireland.

WILLIAM SMYTH (as he had now become) soon acquired the sobriquet 'Mr Smyth of the Gates' in order to distinguish him from his numerous relations with country houses in County Westmeath. After a while, this sort of celebrity began to irk him, so he sold the offending gates to a neighbour who lived at Rosmead, near Delvin, and who rejoiced in the equally commonplace surname of Wood (which, mercifully, did not become de Wood, as it might have done in those days). Unfortunately, Mr Smyth's travails were only beginning for, no sooner was the offending entrance removed, than he was dubbed 'Mr Smyth without the Gates' – a nickname he carried with him to the grave. As a footnote, it should be noted that, in the Irish way of things, the gates survive, albeit in a distressed state, whereas Rosmead has gone the way of so many Irish houses and has been demolished.

Ironically, the other good story about Irish gates concerns those designed and built by another Mr Smith, who was gardener to the Kiely family at Ballysaggatmore, near Lismore in County Waterford. His employer Mrs Arthur Kiely had persuaded her husband to erect a house that would eclipse Strancally Castle, the home of her brother-in-law, John Kiely, farther down the River Blackwater. The entrance naturally came first and, as no expense was to be spared, a large turreted gateway, complete with twin lodges, and a huge bridge rose up in the demesne. The impressive castle that was intended never materialized for the reason that, since Mr Smith's designs had proved so expensive to construct, there was no money left to build the main residence.

Arthur Young, an 18th-century writer and traveller, described this type of landowner as 'little country gentlemen… who drink their claret by means of profit rents… bucks, your fellows with round hats edged with gold, who hunt in the day, get drunk in the evening and fight the next morning.' Another portrayal of the type describes them as 'the very best of commonalty and just next to the quality'.

The next couple of Smyths at Glananea were High Sheriffs of their county. William, the grandson of 'the Gates' married his cousin, Margaret Smyth of Barbavilla. It is at this point that Irish history interjects itself into the quiet

Previous page
The east, or entrance, front.

These pages
1   The gates designed for the house by Samuel Wooley. They are now in a derelict condition at Rosmead in County Westmeath.
2   The front door with a breakfront pedimented doorcase.
3   The garden front, very similar in style to the garden front of Ardbracken in County Meath, which was designed in 1734 by Richard Castle.

Glananea
Collinstown, County Westmeath

world of the Smyths of Westmeath, for Margaret's mother had been murdered in an outrage that shook Ascendancy Ireland to its core, as much for the way it was received by the ordinary rural Irishman as for the deed itself.

The landed gentry and the peerage owned most of land in the country. For example, in Westmeath, the Smyths owned, in a single parish – that of St Mary's, Collinstown – nearly 8000 acres (Drumcree had 4431 acres, Barbavilla 2108 acres and Glananea 1256 acres). The owners of these estates were all descended from Bishop William Smith, who had purchased confiscated land in Westmeath in 1670. The Barbavilla estate sustained the village of Collinstown, while the other two estates supported the village of Drumcree.

During the land war in 1882, William Barlow Smyth of Barbavilla had found himself in trouble with the Land League, whose policy was to encourage those tenants who had genuine grievances; promote discontent among those who were satisfied; and intimidate those who did not go along with its ideology or schemes. The League was founded by Michael Davitt in 1879, as a response to evictions that had been carried out by some landlords (more than 2000 in that year alone), following a disastrous harvest. Their aims were to achieve the three 'F's': fair rent, free sale and fixity of tenure. The League, following a speech by Charles Stewart Parnell in Ennis in 1880, adopted a new form of protest. They shunned or 'boycotted' offending landlords and their agents (the word boycott derives from the most famous victim, Captain Charles Cunningham Boycott, the Earl of Erne's agent, who lived at Lough Mask House in County Mayo). As affairs got steadily worse, Lord Clanrickarde wrote to his agent, 'tell the people they cannot hope to intimidate *me* by shooting *you*!' Violence and killings began, however, including the murder of the villainous 3rd Earl of Leitrim in 1878, as well as two innocents, his coachman, Charles Buchanan, and a youth named John Makin. Their murderers were never caught.

The trouble for the Smyth family started with a tenant called Richard Riggs, whose family had been tenants on the Barbavilla estate for three generations. When Riggs was eventually evicted for non-payment of his rent it was recorded that he '…had been getting worse and worse for sixteen or eighteen years, an utter beggar from his own conduct, with a moderate rent, no stock, always in arrears, only paying for the past by bills of men to whom he was allowed to sublet for the future…'.

Glananea
Collinstown,
County Westmeath

Glananea
Collinstown,
County Westmeath

Local testimony suggests that Riggs, who was fond of the drink, had been constantly in arrears for 17 years. In March 1880, Smyth made him an offer of £152 in forgiveness and £70 to go away, but Riggs refused. He was reinstated in the house as a caretaker and given a final opportunity to pay his rent and arrears within six months. He failed to do so and was eventually evicted. William Smyth had never evicted a tenant before for non-payment of rent and, even after the eviction, he told Riggs that he would pay him £10 a year on the understanding that no injury was done as a result of the eviction and that his life would be insured for £100 for his family.

The Land League decided to stir things up and one Sunday, as the Smyth family was returning from church, shots were fired at their carriage. Inside were the landlord, William Barlow Smyth, his sister-in-law Lady Harriet Monck and another sister-in-law Mrs Henry Smythe, who was the daughter of Captain Robert Carr Coote and mother of the Margaret of Barbavilla mentioned previously. The first shot entered the carriage through the front glass panels. According to *The Westmeath Chronicle*, 'the ball struck Mrs. Henry Smyth on the right side of the back of the head, shattering the skull… Mr Smyth's coat was splashed with blood and Lady Harriet Monck's dress was shockingly stained and smeared'. A number of local men were arrested and, although they were not charged with the actual murder because they were not present at the scene, they were given prison sentences ranging from one to ten years for complicity. Among the defence team for the men accused was Edward Carson, later to be the champion of Ulster Unionism.

What distressed the Smyth family was that the local population, whom they looked on as their friends, supported by the Catholic clergy, came out on the side of the men and helped to raise money for them and their families. The actual murderer was never caught. The Smyths sold Barbavilla in 1955.

The murdered woman's daughter, Margaret, who married William Smyth of Glananea, had three children. Her second son, Abel Smyth, pursued a military career with commissions in the Inniskilling Dragoons and the Royal Berkshire Regiment. He was the last of the family to own Glananea, which he sold in 1960 with 165 acres. It was described in the sales brochure as having four reception rooms, six family bedrooms and two gate lodges, together with stables and farm buildings.

Gormanston Castle   *Gormanston, County Meath*

A large, half-finished, Gothic Revival castle, Gormanston was built for the 12th Lord Gormanston, the Premier Viscount of Ireland. The building, and some of the family demesne, now belongs to the Franciscan Order who use it as a private boarding school for boys.

There are many legends about harbingers of death among Irish families. Of all of these, the most uncanny and creepy (and the best documented) is the phenomenon of the appearance of the foxes at Gormanston when the head of the Preston family dies. This weird occurrence was reported by the Honourable Lucretia Farrell who wrote, 'on the day before my grandfather, Jenico [Preston], the 12th Viscount Gormanston, died [in 1860] the foxes came in pairs, an unusual thing, into the demesne from all the country round. They sat under his bedroom window, which was on the ground floor, and howled and barked all night. They were constantly driven away, only to return.'

LUCRETIA CONTINUED, 'We found them the next morning crouched in the grass in front and around the house. In those days there were many hares in front of the house and the foxes merely wandered through them and the same among the poultry and, even when driven away, they only crouched down before one. On the day of the funeral the keeper saw them all leaving and going across the fields towards the woods where the burial took place, but they did not turn up there but all disappeared.' When her father died in 1876 Lucretia was ill in bed, but the family told her that the foxes had returned, although not in such numbers.

The Honourable Richard Preston remembers that in 1907, while watching over his father's coffin through the night in the private chapel, he heard sounds coming from outside the door at about 10 in the evening. When he opened it he saw many foxes gathered outside which then entered the chapel and walked around the bier. One came close enough to brush against his foot. He tiptoed out, and the whining carried on until about five in the morning when it suddenly stopped and not a trace of a fox remained in the chapel, or in the park. Two servants later confirmed this account. The story goes that Lord Fingall rode out to a meet that morning but was stopped by a local who told him that he might as well go home as 'every fox in Meath will be at Gormanston today.'

The editor of *The Complete Peerage* remarked that 'It is a pity that this strange behaviour does not take place in the case of a family where there is a doubt as to the limitations of the patent, for the fact that the foxes continued to visit the farmyards on the death of the heir male, but were found in floods of tears outside the castle or chapel on the death of the heir general, would be conclusive. Doubtless, too, in cases of questionable legitimacy evidence as to the conduct of the foxes would be held by the Committee for Privileges as rebutting the legal doctrine, *Pater est, quem nuptiae demonstrant*' – a rough translation of this is 'If they are married – then he's the father' or more formally 'He is the father, where a marriage can be shown'.

The Prestons arrived in Ireland from the town of that name in Lancashire in the early 14th century. They were a family of tradesmen and as early as 1318–19

Previous page
The side of the castle showing the now demolished family chapel in the northwest corner.

These pages
1 The entrance front of Gormanston.
2 The centre of the oak armorial chimneypiece in the entrance hall. The coats of arms were carved by Georgina, the wife of Jenico Preston, the 14th Viscount Gormanston. This robust lady also carved the oak chairs in the hall.

Gormanston Castle
Gormanston, County Meath

William and Richard de Preston were buying up shops in Drogheda. The family that was to become one of the most venerable in the Irish peerage had not arrived in Ireland as lords or landed gentry. As *The Complete Peerage* remarked 'It is a common error in popular genealogy to assume that 'de' implies lordship of the place name that follows it'. Not only were they not lords of Preston, but 'they were not lords even of one of the townships within the parish of Preston. Nor are they so described in any of their family charters as calendered.'

All of this was to change. In 1326, Robert de Preston was appointed a second justice of the Justiciar's Court and, in 1361 his son, Roger de Preston, Lord Chancellor of Ireland, was knighted by the Duke of Clarence on the field of battle, after an engagement with the O'Tooles of Wicklow. Sir Roger followed up this honour by buying the lands and lordship of Gormanston (Baile Rinn Uí Ghormain) from Lord St Armand two years later. He had been summoned as a Peer of Parliament before 1390, but it should be remembered that such 'baronies' in Ireland were feudal baronies by tenure, and did not constitute hereditary peerages as we know them today. In fact, the first hereditary title that was bestowed on the family was the viscountcy in 1478.

The 2nd Lord fell from grace and, accused of treason, was imprisoned in Trim Castle. The 4th claimed, by virtue of his possession of the Barony of Kells-in-Ossory, to be superior in rank to David Fleming, Lord Slane, and complained that he had only yielded precedence to that nobleman 'through fear and compulsion'. The Yorkist monarch Edward IV created the 4th Lord a viscount, making Gormanston the Premier Viscount of Ireland. After the Battle of Bosworth Field in 1485, there were some who refused to accept that their side had lost. Among these was the 1st Viscount Gormanston. He was involved with the rebellion that saw Lambert Simnel crowned king in Christ Church Cathedral in Dublin. When Simnel – a 15-year-old boy who, persuaded by Richard Simon, an Oxford priest, claimed to be the imprisoned Edward Plantagenet, Earl of Warwick – was defeated at the Battle of Stoke, Henry VII brought the Irish rebels before him and, pardoning them, merely remarked, 'My Masters of Ireland, you will crown apes at length!'

By the time of the 3rd Viscount, who was married to Catherine Fitzgerald, the sister of 'Silken Thomas', the family had understood that one did not oppose the Crown if one wished to survive. Consequently, in 1541, Lord Gormanston was a member of the Irish Parliament that eagerly voted to allow Henry VIII the title of King of Ireland – all other kings of England, since the reign of Henry II, had called themselves Lord of Ireland, or Dominus Hiberniae. The Irish Council was told that this viscount had 'fair possessions, but is of mean wit, and less activity, and keeps no defense.' The 4th Viscount vacillated between near rebellion (he refused to condemn the Earl of Desmond's treason) and offering to inform on the rebels. The name of Lord Slane appears again in this story because Lord Gormanston was fined £100 for beating him up (they were brothers-in-law). On the viscount's death, Sir Geoffrey Fenton, in 1599 or 1600, wrote to Sir Robert Cecil that 'The Viscount Gormanston is dead, by whose death Her Majesty is rid of a froward nobleman, contentious, and backward in all duties.'

Gormanston Castle
Gormanston, County Meath

In 1611, the next Lord received a grant of land in various counties that had been confiscated as a consequence of the flight of the earls of Tyrone and Tyrconnell. The Prestons fought on the King's side in the Civil War and in 1641 the 6th Viscount acted as Commander-in-Chief of the Catholic forces. He was outlawed after his death in 1643, and his estates declared confiscated. His uncle, the Honourable Thomas Preston, was created Viscount Tara in 1650 and was, with Owen Roe O'Neill, one of the Confederate generals in Ireland during the Civil War. The title died out 24 years later, when his grandson, the 3rd Viscount, was murdered by the Blundel brothers (who were acquitted at their trial).

The 7th Viscount Gormanston went into exile in Europe, only returning at the Restoration in 1660, when his estates were restored to him. If the Irish aristocracy had learned any lessons as a result of their support for the Stuart cause in the 1640s, the Gormanstons were not among their number for in 1690 we find the 7th Viscount assisting in the defence of Limerick for James II, only to be indicted for high treason for his trouble by William of Orange. The Marquis d'Albyville wrote to Charles II, '... my Lord Gormanston deserves highly of your Majesty.' The viscount died during the siege, and his reward was to be declared an outlaw a month after his death.

For the next 109 years the title was believed to be under attainder. The estates were restored to the 9th Viscount, Anthony Preston, under the terms of the Treaty of Limerick, but it was not until Easter 1800 that the Court of the King's Bench declared that the peerage attainders of 1643 and 1691 were void. Accordingly, the 12th Viscount received a Writ to attend the Irish House of Lords. But, with superb timing, the House had just been abolished and so he never took his seat. It was this viscount who demolished the family's old manor house and, perhaps prompted by the official restoration of his title and the craze for the Gothic, employed Francis Johnston as architect and started to rebuild the house, using the old stones of the demolished building. His father having died when he

was eight, the 12th Viscount had accumulated years of rent rolls and on a Grand Tour had developed an interest in architecture. But when his wife died before the house was completed, all further construction stopped. 'This day the light of my life has gone out', he confided to his diary on the day of his wife's death.

There is a contemporary account of his creation which states 'Gormanston Castle is… about eighteen miles distant from Dublin, and about a mile and a half from the Sea, of which there is a pleasing view from the windows of the principal rooms. The upper grounds in the park command a fine view of the house in the foreground, with a more distant and extensive one of the Bay of Dundalk, bounded by the lofty mountains of Mourne and Carlingford.' It goes on, 'The Castle is of very great antiquity, and originally belonged to the Knights Templars. The present Viscount Gormanston has made some well-judged alterations, and changed the Front of the Edifice from the East to the South, by which the grandeur of its external appearance is considerably increased, and its interior more commodiously arranged. The great Entrance Hall… with a fine groined ceiling, springing from ten large handsome carved corbels.' The author concludes by mentioning that the house contains a drawing room, a dining room and a library, as well as 'other excellent apartments'.

This account also mentions the Yew Walk, a feature of the grounds which still partly remains. 'There is still in preservation a curious Yew garden, of great antiquity, the original appearance and form of which was intended to represent the cloisters of a Monastery. The outer walls, and open arches towards the centre being of clipt yew, and the space, so surrounded, answering to the quadrangle laid out as a flower garden.'

1 The drawing room. The portraits are, from the left, the 12th Lord Gormanston, the 3rd Viscount Tara (who was murdered in 1674), the 10th Viscount Gormanston (1707–57) and General Thomas Preston, 1st Viscount Tara. The portrait resting against the door at the far end of the room shows Anthony, 2nd Viscount Tara, on his deathbed.
2 The interior of the private chapel, now demolished.
3 The dining room chimneypiece by Italian craftsman Pietro Bossi.

Gormanston Castle
Gormanston, County Meath

Apparently a daughter of the Gormanston family wished to become a nun. Although the family had remained staunchly Catholic and had not 'turned' during the period that the Penal Laws were in force, her father, Lord Gormanston, was unwilling to allow her to enter a nunnery. He planted the Yew Walk and constructed a small cell-like building, also in Yew, to act as a cloister and a dwelling to compensate her for her loss of convent life.

If the circumstances of history had denied the 12th Viscount a seat in the Irish Parliament, this was rectified in the next generation when his son, the 13th Viscount, was created a peer of the United Kingdom, Baron Gormanston of Whitewood in County Meath, in 1868. The 14th Viscount, was successively Governor of the Leeward Islands (where his portrait still hangs in the President's Palace in Antigua, the capital); of British Guiana, and of Tasmania (the last from 1893 until 1900). The mining settlement of Gormanston in Tasmania is named after him and for all of this good work he received the GCMG. He died in 1907.

In 1883, the family owned 9657 acres in County Meath, around Gormanston Castle, and another 1300 acres in County Dublin (which is today some of the most valuable building land in Ireland). In 1883, the Gormanston's revenues amounted to £9364 a year.

The 15th Viscount married the daughter of Elizabeth, Lady Butler, the Victorian painter of the *Roll Call*, bought by Queen Victoria, and other military subjects. In 1940, his son, the 16th Viscount went missing in action and was presumed killed. His widow, Pamela, Lady Gormanston, subsequently married Lieutenant Maurice O'Connor and, because of financial pressures, she decided to sell the castle. (When Lady Gormanston asked Sir William Joynston-Hicks what she should do with the castle, his answer was short and to the point: 'I'd give it away with a pound of tea.')

Nevertheless, Gormanston Castle attracted the attention of the novelist Evelyn Waugh, who had been persuaded by Nancy Mitford to buy a residence in Ireland to avoid socialism in England. On the morning of his 43rd birthday, Waugh received the *Country Life* sales details of Gormanston Castle: '1806 Gothic, fifteen bedrooms, chapel, seductive "unfinished ballroom", 124 acre park.' Waugh arrived in Ireland and rolled up to the castle, which he described as 'a fine, solid, grim, square, half-finished block with tower and turrets. Mrs. O'Connor, Lord Gormanston's widow, opened the door, young, small, attractive, common'. (This is the moment to reflect on the fact that Mrs. O'Connor was the granddaughter of the Earl of Denbigh and Desmond, whereas Evelyn Waugh was the descendant of plain working folk – indeed, as a youth, he used to travel from his modest family home in Golders Green to neighbouring Hampstead in order that his correspondence would have a more impressive postmark.)

Waugh ungraciously continued: 'She had lit peat fires for our benefit in the main rooms but normally inhabited a small dressing room upstairs. The ground floor rooms were large and had traces of fine Regency decoration. Pictures by Lady Butler everywhere. There were countless bedrooms, many uninhabitable, squalid plumbing, vast attics…the chapel unlicensed and Mrs. O'Connor evasive about the chances of getting it put to use again…', but he did admit that 'she gave us a substantial luncheon.' On the whole he liked the house, but thought 'the grounds dreary with no features except some fine box alleys'.

The asking price was £13,000 (with another £5000 tacked on for repairs).

1   The Yew Walk, known as 'The Cloisters', in the grounds of Gormanston.

2   The chapel at Gormanston was built by Jenico, 7th Viscount Gormanston during the reign of James II and the revival of Catholic hopes in Ireland. Over the doorway is a carved stone 'Jansenist' crucifix, showing Christ's arms uplifted, under an armorial panel inscribed with the date 1687.

Gormanston Castle
Gormanston, County Meath

Gormanston Castle
Gormanston, County Meath

If Waugh had any doubts about the wisdom of making such a purchase, the information that Butlin's were planning to open a holiday camp nearby put a halt to any idea that Gormanston would make a suitable home for such a distinguished personage as himself. He saw the headline in the *Evening Herald* as he boarded the mail boat at Dun Laoghaire and instructed his companion and old friend, 'Cracky' Wicklow, to cancel his offer. He wrote to Nancy Mitford about his experiences 'among the countless blessings I thank God for, my failure to find a house in Ireland comes first. The peasants are malevolent. All their smiles are false as Hell. Their priests are very suitable for them but not for foreigners. No coal at all. Awful incompetence everywhere. No native capable of doing the simplest job properly. No schools for children.' The writer J.B. Priestly thought that Waugh had gone mad in trying to ape the manners of a country gentleman.

The estate was eventually sold in 1947 to the Franciscan Order, which opened a private boys' boarding school there. It is a great irony that the family chapel at Gormanston, which had remained Catholic throughout all the centuries of oppression, was no sooner in the hands of the Franciscans than they demolished it to make room for a squash court. The stone bearing the family coat of arms and the date 1687 is now placed in the chimneypiece of the entrance hall, where it resembles nothing so much as a fireback. The Order decided that they needed some new accommodation and proceeded to erect a large range of ghastly new buildings beside the existing castle (to the design of Mr John Thomson).

And so it was that the family came to leave the house that they had occupied for 584 years. The present and 17th Viscount lives in London and lost his first wife in tragic circumstances. There are two sons of the marriage, Jenico and William. The present Lady Gormanston is Lucy Fox, the daughter of Edward Fox, the distinguished actor.

Headfort
near Kells,
County Meath

A very large, grim,
18th-century pile,
Headfort was enlivened
by interiors designed
by Robert Adam.
It was sold by the family
in 1982 and is now
a preparatory school

The Great Cromwellian Irish land grab took place in 1649 after the Civil War. Those who had been so misguided as to oppose the future Lord Protector's grand plan were shipped off to the far side of the River Shannon – 'to Hell or to Connaught'. Their tenants remained, as tenants, and the land was doled out to the dour Puritans and other unscrupulous adventurers who supported the winning side. This legalized theft was presided over by Dr William Petty, Professor of Anatomy at Oxford University, who abandoned his chosen vocation in order to slice up what little remained of Catholic landholdings in Ireland. His assistant was Thomas Taylor, a school friend of Petty, who was born at Ringmer, Sussex, in 1631. Their achievement in cartography is known as the 'Down Survey'.

2

THE TAYLOR FAMILY liked to claim that that Thomas Taylor had paid for the land he acquired in Ireland. It is true that he sold what property he had in Sussex in order to finance his purchases. However, when one considers that by 1660 he had acquired some 21,772 acres in Ireland, it demonstrates that the English government were almost giving away the confiscated Irish lands. The Stuarts returned in 1660 and Mr Taylor, seeing the new order, changed his coat; abhorring all things to do with the Commonwealth, he became sub-commissioner of the Court of Claims. He died in 1682, as the Treasurer of War.

Part of the property which Mr Taylor acquired was the forfeited walled town of Kells, in County Meath. It was listed by the Commonwealth Commissioners in Dublin and was given to a Parliamentary soldier, Colonel Richard Stephens, who was confirmed in his estate at the Restoration. No sooner was this done than he promptly sold the property to Thomas Taylor, with whom he had been involved on the Down Survey. Kells, or Ceanannus Mór, was an ancient monastic settlement. The ubiquitous Hugh de Lacy had been granted Meath, where he built one of his many castles and erected a high wall around the town which is sometimes called Kenlis.

The next Mr Taylor was another Thomas and the Member of Parliament for Kells in 1692. He, like his father, supported the winning side and was created a baronet in 1704 and a Privy Councillor for Ireland in 1728. The earliest plans for Headfort are those that the architect Richard Castle produced in 1750 for Sir Thomas Taylor, the 2nd Baronet, whose family had lived at Headfort Place until then. These magnificent designs show a two-storey, seven-bay house over a raised basement, with a pediment supported by columns over the central three bays. High single-storey wings over a basement connect with a pair of 'campanile-like' three-storey, single-bay towers, reminiscent of those at Summerhill (also by Castle) in the same county. These return, for seven bays, at right angles on either side to form a forecourt which is flanked by wings, four bays wide by four bays deep, on either side. When Richard Castle died in 1751, John Ensor was asked to produce a set of plans for the house but, by the time the 2nd baronet died in 1757, nothing had been built.

Previous page
The staircase hall with its old mahogany staircase.

These pages
1   The eating parlour, the finest room in the house. Over the white Carrara marble chimneypieces are painted panels by Antonio Zucchi, which feature classical scenes.
2   The garden front of the house, described in 1789 by the Duke of Rutland as 'a long range of tasteless buildings'.

Headfort
near Kells, County Meath

1 An alcove in the entrance hall.
2 The Chinese drawing room. The
   wallpaper has been removed and sold.
3 The drawing room. The large portrait
   is of Lady Madeline Crichton.

Headfort
near Kells, County Meath

The 3rd Baronet, also Sir Thomas, commissioned George Semple to build the unlovely house that we see today. It is 11 bays wide and three storeys high over a raised basement, and resembles an institution rather than a home – the presence of what Desmond Guinness calls 'the lifeless stare of plate glass' in its windows does nothing to improve its appearance. In 1789, the Duke of Rutland called it 'a long range of tasteless buildings'. Sir Thomas had taken one look at Semple's proffered design 'more like a college or an infirmary' and changed his mind. He then went from one extreme to the other – from the penny plain of Semple to the tuppence-coloured of Sir William Chambers. Chambers (who incidentally held a Swedish and not a British knighthood) produced wonderful designs that were – like his Casino for Lord Charlemont at Marino in Dublin – also extremely expensive. And so the baronet returned to the more economical plans of Mr Semple.

Sir Thomas had begun to buy materials for his new house as soon as he came into the estate – oak beams, 14,000 slates and more than half a million bricks – and the stonemason Joseph Briggs started work in February 1761. The house rose up slowly and eventually reached a length of over 500 feet. Built of silver-grey Ardbracken stone, it would be a full decade until the house was ready to be decorated. In 1760, Sir Thomas was created a peer of Ireland as Baron Headfort; in 1762 he was advanced to a viscountcy and, in 1766, made Earl of Bective, of Bective Castle in County Meath. His new lordship's father-in-law was Hercules Langford Rowley, who had engaged Robert Adam in 1765 to decorate his town house in Dublin, Langford House. Lord Headfort was obviously impressed by what he saw there, for in 1771 he engaged Adam to design the interiors for his new residence. This house would be one of only three in Ireland for which Adam undertook to provide designs.

As financial precautions had prevented Lord Headfort and his father erecting the designs of Castle and Chambers, the same carefulness stopped them from fully implementing the spectacular designs that Adam produced for their seat. The entrance hall, although splendid, lacks the plasterwork that should have adorned the walls. Lord Headfort's economies prevented the staircase hall achieving the magnificence that Adam's imagination had planned. Quite simply, his lordship did not see why the perfectly good mahogany staircase had to be removed and replaced by a stone one. The old stairs remained in place and this prevented the stuccodore, John McCullagh, from putting in the elaborate wall panels that Adam had designed. (Italian stuccodore Roberto Zuchelia is also known to have worked at Headfort.) The ceiling of the staircase hall is the only part of Adam's plan to be fully implemented. The walls were covered with family portraits and a set of Gobelins tapestries that were woven for the family, although not perhaps for the staircase hall.

The finest room in the house is the eating parlour. It is four bays long and constructed out of two rooms on the south front of the house and the two rooms above them, whose windows are blocked out. Antonio Zucchi, the husband of the artist Angelica Kauffmann, decorated the coved ceiling with rich plasterwork and painted panels. The pair of white Carrara marble chimneypieces are surmounted by painted panels by Zucchi depicting classical scenes and dated 1776. Unfortunately, the planned large canvasses of classical scenes in the style of Panini or Vanvitelli were never executed, with the consequence that the pictures that now hang in the plaster frames are much too small for them and detract from the room's design. The colour scheme of blue and white there now is not what

Adam intended: his plan was for a room with pale cream and light olive-green walls. The floor is of Irish oak and contains more than 3500 pieces laid in a herringbone pattern. The enormous pier mirrors that hung here came from a factory in Vauxhall, London, which produced glass of a faint blue tinge with a wide, shallow bevel known as 'Vauxhall bevel'.

The saloon, with roundels by Zucchi depicting 'Peace' and 'Plenty', became the dining room during the 19th century when the eating parlour was judged too large for everyday use. The Chinese drawing room next door has a ceiling which is an exact copy of the now demolished drawing room at Langford House in Dublin. The Chinese wallpaper that hung on the walls of this room may have been the inspiration of Sir William Chambers, whose design for the house was rejected and who had published a book on Oriental gardening. As the Adam brothers never came to Ireland, either Thomas Cooley or Richard Charles is believed to have supervised the work. The rooms that Adam designed for Headfort are the only examples of his art that have survived in Ireland.

In 1776 Arthur Young wrote, 'reached Lord Bective's in the evening, through a very fine country, particularly that part of it from which the very fine prospect of his extensive woods was got. The improvement at Headfort must be astonishing to those who knew the place seventeen years ago, for then there were neither building, walling nor foundations. At present almost everything is created necessary to form a considerable residence. The grounds fall agreeably in front of the house to a winding narrow vale, which is filled with wood: where also is a river, which Lord Bective intends to enlarge. On the other side the lawn spreads over a large extent, and is everywhere bounded by fine plantations. Besides these plantations, he has also walled in twenty-six acres for garden and nursery. He has also built a farmyard two hundred and eighty feet square totally surrounded by offices of various kinds. All Lord Bective's gates are of iron, which cost him £5.5s., and as wooden ones come to £3.3s., he finds them the greatest improvement, saving the expense very soon.'

What Young described as 'the state of the lower classes' prompted this last remark. He wrote 'they steal everything they can lay hands on: all sorts of iron,

Headfort
near Kells, County Meath

hinges, chains, locks, keys etc. – gates will be cut in pieces & conveyed away in many places as fast as built; trees as big as a man's body, & that require ten men to move, gone in a night… turneps are stolen by car loads; & two acres of wheat pluckt off in a night. In short, their pilfering and stealing is a perfect nuisance!' He also mentioned that Lord Bective 'transplants oaks 20 feet high without danger, and they appear to thrive perfectly well; but he takes a large ball of earth up with the roots… besides these numerous plantations a considerable mansion and an incredible quantity of walling.'

When the Most Illustrious Order of Saint Patrick was instituted by George III in 1783, Lord Bective was one of the founder Knights. The 1st Earl, who opposed the concept of political union with Great Britain, died in 1795, but his son was created Marquess of Headfort in recognition of his support for the Act of Union. Two years after the coronet came to rest on the new marquess's head, he was in the courts on a charge of criminal conversation. It transpired that his Lordship had seduced and eloped with the wife of a Limerick clergyman, the Reverend Charles Massey. The offended cleric had sought damages in the sum of £40,000. John Philpot Curran who distinguished himself with 'perhaps the greatest of his non-political speeches' represented the plaintiff – in consequence of which the Marquess was forced to pay out £10,000 and costs. It would be a century before the Headforts put love before propriety again. Incidentally, it was at this time that Lord Headfort decided that being a Taylor was far too plebeian a surname for him to bear and so, like the Smiths and Frenches who are featured in this volume, he added a letter to his name and become Taylour, which spelling has remained to the present day.

In 1802, the architect Francis Johnston was asked to produce plans to gothicize the house. This extravagance was possibly prompted by the building of Charleville Forest, near Tullamore in County Offaly, which had been commenced in 1800 to designs by Johnston. Certainly his designs for Headfort include a central lantern that is very similar to the one at Charleville. However, the rather uninspired alterations that he designed, which included towers, battlements and gothic fenestrations were never executed.

In the Coronation honours of William IV, the 2nd Marquess (yet another Thomas) was created a Peer of the United Kingdom as Baron Kenlis of Kells in 1831. (This adoption by Irish peers of titles that differed from those by which they were known prompted the remark that it was, perhaps, done by their possessors 'as if on purpose to puzzle the uninitiated and so escape from their own identity'.) Described by Creevy as 'a chattering, capering, spindleshanked gaby', Thomas was nonetheless made a Knight of Saint Patrick in 1839. Thirty years after this event, the Gothic finally arrived at Headfort when he erected a mausoleum to the design of James Franklin Fuller, the architect of Ashford and Kylemore castles. This is down in the woods by the River Blackwater and looks like a miniature version of the Temple Church in London – octagonal, with a tall pointed roof over a raised rotunda. Lord Headfort was buried there a year later.

His son, the 3rd Marquess, who was made a Knight of Saint Patrick in 1885, retained Fuller's services and he designed the farm buildings for the estate in 1874. In 1883 the family estates comprised some 21,000 acres in England, together with 14,251 acres of County Cavan and 7,544 acres in County Meath. The rent roll produced an income in the region of £39,606 a year. The 3rd Marquess's principal residences were at Headfort House, near Kells in County Meath, and Virginia Park Lodge in County Cavan.

The 4th Marquess, Geoffrey (the first head of the family not to be called Thomas in over 300 years) married the delectable Miss Rosie Boote – a Gaiety Girl and the protégée of producer and impresario Mr George Edwardes. She had risen from working-class obscurity in County Tipperary to fame with a song *Maisie was a darling, Maisie was a dear* that took London by storm. Mercifully, it is now forgotten.

The happy couple arrived in Headfort in May 1901, and 'so popular was the event that crowds travelled from as far as Virginia, Drogheda and Dundalk to see the Marquess's Gaiety girl. The whole town was decorated with flags and bunting with banners of good wishes strung across the streets.' Lord Headfort was forced to resign from the Brigade of Guards when he married Rosie, but Ascendancy circles in Ireland accepted her. She was a Roman Catholic and the 4th Marquess converted to her faith shortly after their marriage.

Their son was born in 1902 and the event was celebrated by a grand display of fireworks. A few years later, Rosie persuaded Lord Headfort to shut up the house and live in a rented house in Hampshire. By 1907 they had returned home again, and Lady Headfort's prudent economy enabled her husband to maintain a small staff of a butler, footman, cook and two maids. Eventually, Rosie's

The 300-year-old Yew Hedge in the
garden, part of the arboretum started
by Lord Headfort, the 4th Marquess.

Headfort
near Kells, County Meath

husband was made a Senator in the first Free State Dáil (parliament) in
December 1922

Lord Headfort also started to plant an immense arboretum at Headfort.
Christopher Hussey, author, gardener and owner of Scotney Castle, wrote in
Country Life in 1936 that 'Headfort is a place where a complete garden education
can be received or, equally well, an interesting and enjoyable day spent. The
gardens combine in a rare degree all that can be desired by artist or botanist, little
as they are apt to see alike. Catholic in his tastes there is scarcely a family of trees
or shrubs which he does not favour and all are represented.'

The 5th Marquess inherited in 1943 and in 1949 turned the house into a boys'
preparatory school. An apartment was created for the family in the east wing.
The first headmaster, Romney Coles, was followed in 1950 by David Wild, who
remained until 1975 and oversaw the introduction of girls to the school. Sir
Lingard Goulding was the next headmaster and, during his period in charge,
Lord Headfort decided to sell the estate. In 1982, B.J. Kruger, a Canadian paper
manufacturer bought it. The demesne was sold again after Kruger's death in
1994 and a consortium purchased it. The school now owns the house (excluding
the east wing) together with 66 acres of land. It is the only all-boarding preparatory school left in Ireland.

The land south of the house has been sold and is now yet another golf course.
The farmyard has been developed in a way that has destroyed the integrity and
beauty of the original. It is now a 'luxury' development of mews-type houses
and apartments.

The present marquess has had a somewhat unconventional life. On one
occasion, he was wrestled to the ground by security officers in a cinema in the
Scilly Isles. The reason for this was that he was armed with a starting pistol
and was believed to be about to assassinate the prime minister, Harold Wilson,
who was in the building at the time with his wife Mary. Lord Headfort, who
is an honorary Hong Kong police officer, has remarried and now lives with his
wife in the Philippines.

An imposing fortalice of the Earls of Kildare, afterwards
the Dukes of Leinster. The house was sold by the family in
1960 and is now a successful and comfortable hotel.

Kilkea Castle   *Castledermot, County Kildare*

At the foot of the hill called Mullachreelan, on the banks of the River Greese, near Castledermot, lies Kilkea Castle, the oldest continuously inhabited castle in Ireland. The place used to be called 'Omurethi', which is the old Irish name for the district. The castle lies halfway between a pagan and a Christian burial ground, each being only 100 yards from the house. The barony of Kilkea (Cill Chathighe) derives its name from the Christian church, which was dedicated to Saint Caoidhe, a disciple of Saint Patrick. In the 12th century, the land belonged to the family of Saint Laurence O'Toole, who, in 1162, became the first Irishman to be Archbishop of Dublin.

WHEN RICHARD DE CLARE, Earl of Pembroke, presented the demesne of Kilkea to his follower, Walter de Riddlesford, Baron of Bray, in 1180, Hugh de Lacy had already built one of his many castles there. Walter de Riddlesford died in 1244 leaving two daughters, Emelina and Ela. The elder daughter had a daughter of the same name who married Maurice Fitzgerald, 1st Baron of Offaly.

Maurice Fitzgerald is described by Giraldus Cambrensis, the distinguished Welsh chronicler, as 'a honourable and modest man; with a face sunburnt and well-looking, of middle height, a man well modelled in mind and body, a man of innate goodness, desiring rather to be than to seem good; a man of few words… having more in the heart than of the mouth, more of reason than of volubility … and when it is required, earnest of purpose. In military affairs valiant… neither impetuous nor rash… constant, trusty and faithful… a man not altogether without fault, yet not spotted with any great or notorious crime.' The 2nd Baron, his grandson, was famed for his piety. He brought the Franciscans to Ireland in 1216, followed by the Dominicans in 1231.

In 1316, Edward II created John Fitzgerald, Maurice's great-grandson, Earl of Kildare, and he was given the castle and town of Kildare. Kilkea Castle appears in the State Papers several times over the following centuries. In 1314, the Wogan family seems to have taken possession of Kilkea Castle in the person of a John Wogan, and in 1417 Anastacia, the widow of Sir David Wogan, is recorded as receiving the manor house of 'Kylka' as her portion under his will. In 1356, Edward III ordered Maurice, the 4th Earl of Kildare, to strengthen and maintain his castles at Kilkea, Rathmore and Ballymore, under pain of forfeiting the same. The castle was restored in 1426 or 1427 by John, 6th Earl of Kildare, having probably been sacked by the native Irish.

The castle is essentially an 18th-and 19th-century rebuilding of a 15th-century L-plan tower-house, with round and square turrets. About 100 yards from the front of the castle on the right-hand side is the original motte of the castle that was mentioned by Giraldus Cambrensis in 1181. The motte is 40 feet high and is now covered with trees. High in the wall that overlooks the entrance is a carving known as the 'Evil Eye' Stone. It is designed to attract the evil eye of anyone entering the building, thus preserving the inhabitants of the castle from evil – for anybody might possess it without knowing. Originally the entrance had a portcullis, and the grooves remain to show where it hung. The stone table

in the garden came from Maynooth and was the Council Table of the Earls of Kildare. It is inscribed in Latin with the name of Gerald Fitzgerald, 9th Earl of Kildare, the date 1533 and the family motto 'Crom-a-Boo'. A chimneypiece in the dining hall bears a sculptured crest and the inscription *Si Dieu Pled, Croaabo*

Previous page
The entrance front of the castle seen from the avenue.

These pages
1 The castle seen from the 19th-century formal gardens
2 The impressive massing of the entrance front.
3 The Treaty table on which the Confederation of Kilkenny was signed. It was brought to Kilkea Castle from Carton, near Maynooth in County Kildare.

Kilkea Castle
Castledermot,
County Kildare

1573. A second carving has the Earl's arms and a third shows an eagle, the arms of his wife. Also in the castle was a manuscript dated 1503 called 'The Earl of Kildare's Red Book'. It contained detailed lists of all of the lands then in the Earl's possession.

The castle boasts a ghost, that of Gerald, 11th Earl of Kildare and half-brother of the 10th Earl, 'Silken' Thomas Fitzgerald (who was executed in 1537 for treason and his earldom attainted). Aged only 10, Gerald had been taken abroad two years before the execution to be educated, and for a time he served under Cosimo de Medici in Florence. In 1568, Elizabeth I permitted the attainder against the family to be reversed, but, although the titles and estates were restored to them, the Fitzgeralds never again achieved the power they had exercised in the past.

The 11th Earl, Gerald, returned to Kilkea in 1573. An amateur alchemist, he was known as Gearóid Iarla, or the 'Wizard Earl', and legend has it that one day he was at his ease in a room on the ground floor of the castle, when his wife came in and asked him to demonstrate his powers as a great magician. He refused at first but then agreed to her request on the sole condition that she should not cry out in fear. If she did so, he warned her, he would vanish and she would never

see him again. He gave her three tests. For the first he caused water to flood the room until it reached all the way up to her mouth. Despite this, she held her tongue. He then caused a friend, recently deceased, to enter and shake her by the hand. Again she kept silent. Finally he conjured up a giant snake to coil itself around her and lick her face. Even now, she did not utter a sound but, with the three tests finished, the earl decided on a fourth. He transformed himself into a small bird, which perched on her shoulder. A large black cat crept up behind her and pounced and at this the countess shrieked and fainted. When she came to, her husband had vanished and was never seen alive again.

This famous old tale has to be one of the most improbable and silliest stories ever told about an Irish house. The 11th Earl is supposed to return to the scene once every seven years when, mounted on a white horse shod with silver shoes, he rides across the county from the Rath of Mullaghmast to Kilkea Castle. He then rides up the stairs to the haunted room and is not seen again until another seven years have passed.

During the rebellion of the 1640s, the Countess of Kildare leased the castle to the Jesuits. A manuscript at Clongowes Wood College in County Kildare tells what happened next: 'In the reign of Charles I, 1634, the good and ever to be honoured Countess of Kildare gave the Castle and all of its furniture to Father Robert Nugent, the Superior of the Jesuits of Kilkea. Father Nugent was a near relative of the Earl of Inchiquin of the noble House of Thomond. In the year 1646 Father Nugent entertained, for twenty days, the celebrated Rinnuccini, the Pope's nuncio, and several companies of soldiers on their way to besiege Dublin. The nuncio wanting pecuniary means Father Nugent leant him four thousand pieces of gold which the nuncio never repaid; and, consequently, the Jesuit mission was much neglected as they had not sufficient means to support them.'

The Jesuits remained at Kilkea until 1646. As for Lady Kildare, she was implicated in the rebellion of 1641 and outlawed in 1642. After the destruction of Maynooth Castle in 1641, George, 14th Earl of Kildare, resided at Kilkea Castle from 1647 until 1660, and it continued as the family's principal seat until Robert, the 19th Earl, made Carton House his home in 1738, after his marriage

1   The drawing room. The portrait over the chimneypiece is of William, Duke of Leinster.
2   The oriel window in the sitting room.
3   The small dining room. The furniture and pictures in this and other rooms were brought from Carton, County Kildare.

Kilkea Castle
Castledermot,
County Kildare

to Lady Anne O'Brien, the daughter of the 3rd Earl of Inchiquin. The 20th Earl of Kildare was made the 1st Duke of Leinster in 1766.

In 1787 Kilkea was redecorated and then leased to Thomas Reynolds, through the influence of his relation, Lord Edward Fitzgerald. Reynolds is supposed to have had some of the tall lancet windows put in at Kilkea. One of the most notorious informers in Irish history, Reynolds was born in Dublin in 1771, the son of a prosperous poplin manufacturer, and became the brother-in-law of Theobald Wolfe Tone, one of the founders of the Society of United Irishmen. The Society was founded on 14 October 1791 in Belfast to lobby for parliament-ary reform, Catholic emancipation and, as Wolfe Tone said, 'the unity of all of the people – Catholic, Protestant and Dissenter – under the common name of Irishmen'.

In 1797, Reynolds joined the Society (he was to betray their plans for inde-pendence to the authorities in Dublin Castle for a large sum of money as early as March of that year); at about the same time he also obtained a lease on Kilkea Castle. Reynolds's son said that his father paid £1000 as a fine to his landlord the 2nd Duke of Leinster and to pay Mr Shannon, the duke's builder, for new flooring, roofing and ceiling at the castle and 'making such other improvements as would put the castle into substantial repair'.

Reynolds was in residence at Kilkea until 1798. Having been informed that Lord Edward Fitzgerald, who had escaped arrest after Reynolds's betrayal of the Society, was hiding at Kilkea, Colonel Campbell, who commanded the military in the district, arrived there and ordered his men to find the fugitive patriot. The 9th Dragoons and a company of the Cork Militia proceeded to tear the place apart; they ripped up the floorboards, slashed the wainscotting from the walls and forced open the doors, but all to no avail, since Lord Edward was hiding in Dublin. Reynolds was arrested and held in custody until May. On his release he surrendered the lease of the castle to the duke who then re-let it to a Mr Daniel Caulfield in 1799. This family was to stay at Kilkea for half a century. The last Mr Caulfield to rent the place stated that 'some tasteless person' (probably Reynolds) had covered a wonderful carved oak medieval ceiling, in the room that had once been the private chapel, with a modern one.

In 1849, following a fire, Augustus, the 3rd Duke, recovered possession of the castle and undertook a programme of restoration and refurbishment. The great solar on the top floor was divided in two to provide an extra room. The existing windows were enlarged and brought down, or up, so that the façade presented a more balanced and regular appearance, with rows of trefoil-headed windows. The ground floor was made habitable and the outhouses were rebuilt in stone and designed to form a forecourt.

Jeremy Williams has suggested that the architect of this remodelling may have been Frederick Darley, who had been engaged by the duke to build the Church of Ireland and the model schools in nearby Athy. In the course of the reconstruction, the great hall was divided to provide a new dining room below, with extra bedrooms above. The table that was in the dining room is the same one on which the Confederation of Kilkenny was signed and had been brought to Kilkea from Carton. The Irish battlements were extended from the former great hall to cover the whole edifice and, in the gardens, French-style parterres were introduced.

In the 19th century the castle was used as a dower house or as a residence for the Marquess of Kildare, the duke's son and heir. The most famous inhabitant of the place during this time was Hermione, the beautiful wife of the future 5th Duke of Leinster. Her unhappiness and boredom led her to compose the following couplet on her situation:

> *Kilkea Castle and Lord Kildare*
> *Are more than any woman can bear.*

Tragedy hit the family early in the 20th century. The 6th Duke was mentally ill and was detained until his death in a lunatic asylum in Scotland. His next brother, Lord Maurice Fitzgerald, died without a male heir and the youngest brother, Lord Gerald, eventually became the 7th Duke. The real problem with this scenario was that Lord Gerald had previously sold his birthright. He had contracted an unsuitable marriage to a Gaiety Girl, just as Lord Headfort had done (see p.113); however Gertie Miller was no Rosie Boote. The couple ran up

1 The formal gardens seen from the dining room.
2 Hermione, 5th Duchess of Leinster, was the daughter of William Duncombe, 3rd Baron Feversham of Duncombe Park. She married the Marquess of Kildare who later became the 5th Duke of Leinster. She died at Menton in the South of France in 1895 and was buried at Carton, County Kildare.

Kilkea Castle
Castledermot,
County Kildare

debts and, in order to pay them, Lord Gerald sold his inheritance, should he ever become Duke, to Sir Malaby Deeley, the '50-shilling tailor'. Lord Gerald was to receive £1300 a year for life, while Sir Malaby would inherit Lord Gerald's prospects, should he ever come into them. On the death of the 6th Duke in 1921, he did. Carton was seized by Deeley and subsequently sold to Lord Brockett. It is currently being destroyed as a country house hotel, with hideous and inappropriate new buildings; in the demesne are the usual golf course and chalets aplenty.

The new duke was apportioned Kilkea Castle in the subsequent settlement, but he never accommodated to his reduced state of aVairs. He was bankrupted and later stated that the annuity of £1300 was his sole annual income. Gerald Fitzgerald, Premier Duke, Marquess and Earl of Ireland, committed suicide in 1973. His son, the Marquess of Kildare married, as his first wife, Joane Kavanagh, the daughter of the MacMurrough Kavanagh from Borris House in County Carlow. She was the chatelaine of the castle when these photographs were taken. In 1960, the castle with 100 acres was sold for £8000. It was reopened as a health farm, which must have proved financially unhealthy since it had to be closed quite soon afterwards. The castle was sold on and is now a successful luxury hotel.

The flag tower at the rear of the castle.

Kilkea Castle
Castledermot,
County Kildare

Killeen Castle *Tara, County Meath*

Killeen Castle possessed some of the finest Gothic
Revival interiors in Ireland. The seat of the senior
branch of the Plunkett family, the Earls of Fingall,
it was sold by the last earl and passed to a succession
of horse owners only to be burnt out. It is now being
restored as a hotel with a golf course.

The demesnes of Irish country houses have been acquired in many ways, among them purchase, confiscation, marriage, inheritance and theft. But the demesne of Killeen is, with its sister estate of Dunsany, perhaps unique in that their boundaries were allegedly settled by means of a foot race in about 1438. The contestants were the wives of the two sons of Sir Christopher Plunkett, 1st Baron of Killeen. The story is that each of the ladies had to run from her husband's castle and wherever they met would form the boundary between the two properties. The wife of the elder son from Killeen, which is placed on higher ground, had a distinct advantage in the contest, the predictable outcome of which was thereafter given as the reason why the lands of Killeen were so much greater in extent than those of Dunsany.

SIR CHRISTOPHER PLUNKETT had married the daughter of Sir Lucas Cusack in 1403 so bringing the demesnes of Killeen – built in 1181 by Hugh de Lacy – and Dunsany into Plunkett hands. The Cusacks had arrived with the first wave of Normans, and Geoffrey de Cusack, the Lord of the Manor of Meath (Hugh de Lacy's companion), was in Ireland by 1175. His descendant, Sir Lucas Cusack died in 1388.

Deputy Lord Lieutenant of Ireland in 1432, Sir Christopher Plunkett was created Baron of Killeen. His ancestors were not Normans – a Mr Campion, who visited Ireland in 1566, wrote that the Plunkett family possessed 'special monuments proving that their ancestors came with the Danes'. After they arrived in Ireland they lived first at Beaulieu, near Drogheda.

Together with Lady Killeen, Sir Christopher endowed a confraternity known as 'The Guild of the Blessed Virgin' and built a chantry chapel at Killeen. This foundation was recognized as a religious corporation by Henry VI and Henry VII for 'diffusing the blessings of piety and charity among the people'. It survived the Tudor confiscations of religious property but was closed down by James I, who re-granted its lands to the 1st Earl of Fingall, rather than taking them for himself. The 1st Lord Killeen died in 1445 and is buried in the chantry at Killeen.

Lucas Plunkett, the 10th Baron, was known as 'An Tiarna Mór' ('Great Lord') and was elevated to the Earldom of Fingall in 1628. Charles I wrote to Lord Falkland that the new peer was 'one of the ancient nobility of that our Kingdom of Ireland and the chief of a very honourable and well-deserving English family planted there since the first conquest'. 'Fionn Ghaill' (Fingall) translates as 'Fair Foreigners', the Irish name for the Danes. It is today, as Fingal, the name of the local county council. Lord Plunkett's first wife was Lady Elizabeth O'Donel, daughter of Rory O'Donel, the 1st Earl of Tyrconnell and King of Tír Chonaill, and his second was the Honourable Susan Brabazon, the daughter of Lord Brabazon of Ardee.

The 2nd Earl, Christopher Plunkett, was a leading player in the Confederate gatherings at Tara and Duleek and commanded the cavalry at the siege of Drogheda. He was seven times outlawed, which was either overkill or else suggests that he submitted and asked for pardon on at least six occasions. Wounded and captured after the Battle of Rathmines (in which his leader, Lord Ormond, was defeated by the Cromwellian leader, Jones), he died two weeks later in Dublin Castle. Three years after the 2nd Earl's death, Oliver Cromwell deprived him of his estates in his so-called 'Act of Grace'. His younger brother, the Honourable Edward Plunkett, was sent abroad by his family during this time of civil unrest and was captured by the Turks. He was kept as a slave for five years, but eventually escaped and returned to Ireland, where his father had settled a small estate on him.

Peter, the 3rd Earl, married a daughter of Mac Carthaigh Múscraighe, Lord Clancarty, whose brother-in-law was the Great Duke of Ormonde, Charles II's Lord Deputy in Ireland. Lord Fingall, the 3rd Earl, detested his MacCarthy wife. Her uncle, Ormonde, wrote 'to let Her Majesty know what kind of man my Lord Fingall is, and how unreasonable his calumnies against his wife are. From the first three years of her marriage her father and friends were for a separation but she always refused their advice'. His Lordship died in 1684 but, even then, his troubles were not at an end since he was outlawed in 1691, under the name of 'Luke', as an adherent of James II. This sentence was later reversed on the

Previous page
The imposing entrance front of Killeen Castle as remodelled by James Sheil.

Facing page
A view of Killeen Castle from the southeast

Killeen Castle
Tara, County Meath

Killeen Castle
Tara, County Meath

perfectly reasonable grounds that since he had been dead for some four years
before James was overthrown in 1688, he could not be guilty (*post mortem* as it
were) of treason.

Robert, the 6th Earl, a captain in Berwick's Regiment, lived in France where
his son, the 7th Earl, was brought up. The 7th Earl petitioned for a restoration
of his title in 1762. The family left the castle in the 1720s and, when in Ireland,
lived in their Dublin residence – Killeen House, 5 Great Denmark Street. As for
Killeen Castle, in 1763 a report stated that 'everything about it has been a ruin
for a great number of years and what remains of the old castle is but very small
and not even capable of being made a habitation for a family'. Despite this
pessimistic view, it was let in 1778 and in 1780 the 7th Earl attempted to make
the place habitable. To this end, he engaged a mason named Ian Quinn to make
repairs. After this, the demesne was landscaped and a lake added.

The 8th Earl, on succeeding to the title, took steps legally to assure himself
of it and of his other possessions. On 9 May 1795, he wrote to the Bishop of
Meath (Dr Patrick Plunkett) '... on Thursday last my claim to the title of Fingall
etc., was established by a unanimous resolution of the House of Lords. We shall,
I hope, soon become inhabitants of this old Castle…' He decided to remodel his
ancestral home and consulted Thomas Wogan Browne, a prosperous merchant
and amateur architect, who had built Castle Wogan (now Clongowes Wood
College) in County Kildare. Professional help came in the person of Francis
Johnston, the architect of the General Post Office in Dublin, and Charleville
Forrest in County Offaly, which is the most important Gothic Revival castle
in Ireland.

The 8th Earl led the Catholic Peers in their attempt to obtain relief from their
political disabilities; the Lords Gormanston, Southwell and Ffrench supported
him in his actions. He was a member of the Catholic Committee and advocated
a limited measure of relief for his co-religionists. However, on discovering that
Daniel O'Connell was demanding 'unqualified emancipation' he withdrew his
support for the cause. Lord Byron called him 'The Irish Avatar'. In 1831, he
was created a peer of the United Kingdom as Baron Fingall of Woolhampton

1 The staircase hall – the staircase leads up to the bedrooms. The portrait over the door is of Franz Joseph I (1830–1916), Emperor of Austria and Apostolic King of Hungary.

2 The dining room – an elegant chamber decorated with elaborate plasterwork.

3 The lobby at the head of the entrance stairs, which lead to the oak hall. The Fingall coat of arms can be seen on the walls.

4 The oak hall. The splendid ceiling is by the architect Francis Johnston.

Killeen Castle
Tara, County Meath

Lodge in Berkshire. When George IV visited Ireland in 1821 (the first British monarch to come to Ireland since William III and James II had fought over it – and much more – in 1690), Lord Fingall became the first Roman Catholic to be appointed a Knight of the Most Illustrious Order of Saint Patrick, an award that was also given to his son, the 9th Earl, in 1846.

The award of this Order to the 8th Earl brought forth this stinging rebuke from Byron

> *Will thy yard of blue ribbon, poor Fingall, recall*
> *The fetters from millions of catholic limbs?*
> *Or has it not bound thee the fastest of all*
> *The slaves who now hail their betrayer with hymns?*

When the 8th Earl received the Ribbon, Lady O'Brien from Dromoland, a very strong member of the Established Church snorted, 'I have very little doubt that this is preparatory to His Majesty granting emancipation to the Catholics.' (In fairness, the O'Brien family more than made up for this incipient bigotry in the next generation when, to Lady O'Brien's horror, her son William Smith O'Brien was sentenced to death for high treason, see p.72.)

The 9th Earl was born in Geneva and was a Liberal MP until he succeeded to the title. He obviously thought that the castle that Francis Johnston had designed for his father was not large or grand enough for in 1841 he engaged the architect James Sheil to enlarge it. The entrance to the castle, when Sheil had finished his work, was by way of a front door flanked by tall battlemented towers. From there a flight of oak stairs led up to the reception rooms. The decorative motif in the entrance hall, and elsewhere in the castle, was the quatrefoil. Quatrefoils were on the ceilings and under the balusters of the staircase, and they ran as a frieze half way up the room. At the top, the stairs were divided from the landing by a series of lancet arches. The landing gave on the left to a large vaulted room known as the oak hall, which contained the family coat of arms in full relief and colours. More full achievements of arms were on the walls of this room as well as in the porch that led from the staircase to the oak hall, off which were the library and the dining room.

The plasterwork in all of the main rooms was of supreme richness. The dining room, which was painted a soft stone colour, had been the drawing room until the wife of the 11th Earl got round to redecorating the castle with the assistance of Sir Hugh Lane. Sir Hugh was a confirmed bachelor, about whom the plain,

1 The library with bookcases designed by Sir Hugh Lane.
2 The plaster ceiling of the library, designed by Francis Johnston.
3 The vestment worn by Saint Oliver Plunkett, who was martyred in 1681 and canonized in 1975.
4 The west side of the picture gallery.

Killeen Castle
Tara, County Meath

fox-hunting 11th Earl once remarked: 'He is a good fellow… it is a pity that he is like that!'

As a result of the new arrangements, the library became, *faute de mieux*, the drawing room of the house. It had a very elaborate plaster ceiling and a series of bookcases designed by Sir Hugh and made at a cost of £1000 by the firm of Hicks of Dublin. In a glazed cabinet between the windows on the southern side of the library were preserved the vestments worn by Saint Oliver Plunkett, the Archbishop of Armagh and Primate of All Ireland, who was martyred in 1681 and proclaimed a saint by the Catholic Church in 1975. Across the oak hall was the great staircase. This was built in 1841 and was allegedly the largest room in the house. It was certainly the tallest, being some 60 feet in height. The carving on the staircase was very fine, even the underside of the stairs was carved. Off this staircase, and over the oak hall, was the picture gallery. The ceilings of the library, the oak hall and the adjoining porch are all by Francis Johnston, while the entrance hall and the great staircase are by James Sheil. As Jeremy Williams has noticed, the castle was adorned with heraldic devices 'including a self-consciously modest Adam, surprised beneath a tree…' He suggests that the figure was 'probably an ancestor'.

Born in Rome, the 11th Earl, Arthur Plunkett, had been raised in France with the result that he spoke with a soft French accent. On his 21st birthday, the butler got uproariously drunk and set fire to the dining room at Killeen, thereby destroying the most valuable pictures in the house, including a pair of Van Dycks of Charles I and his Queen, Henrietta Maria. A quiet man, Arthur was much given to falling asleep at State Balls in Dublin Castle, where he was the State Steward. Once, at dinner, he was obviously asleep and his wife asked the gentleman who was sitting beside her to kick him. Her neighbour did as he was bid but missed his mark and kicked the Vicerene, Lady Spencer, instead.

Arthur married the beauty Miss Elizabeth, or 'Daisy', Burke, whose memoirs *Seventy Years Young* are the most telling account of the final years of the old order in Ireland. Lord Wolseley, the soldier who had arrived too late to save General 'Chinese' Gordon at Khartoum, wrote to his wife in 1891, 'Lady F. is a Catholic, a nice pretty little woman, very fond of hunting, and her maiden name was Murphy [*sic*].' She wrote about her engagement: 'Of course it was a disappointment to them all that Fingall had not married some great and rich lady to bring money to the castle and estate which so badly needed it.' In the end, all that mattered was that her husband loved her to distraction.

In Daisy's time there were 12 indoor servants at Killeen and a much larger number of outside 'employees with unspecified duties, self-appointed perhaps, who dragged brooms or spades about the place happily.' One of Lady Fingall's servants described a 'great house' as one where 'as much was thrown out as used.' The 11th Earl would have liked to pay higher wages to his servants but, since this would have caused discontent among those of his neighbours, he made up the difference by giving milk, meat, fuel and similar items to those who worked for him. He refused to keep powdered footmen, although there was one at the castle, a ghost. Lady Fingall wrote: 'Fortunately for me the Clammy Hand never moved over my face as I slept. Nor were the bedclothes pulled off me as happened to somebody sleeping in one of the rooms.'

Killeen was dark – it took 'a hundred lamps to light the house, and even then there were many dim corners' – and freezing. Arthur and Daisy once let it to an

Killeen Castle
Tara, County Meath

American who said that he used a ton of coal a day to heat it – according to Daisy 'our fortunes… went blazing up the chimney'. This transatlantic tenant must have been the Mr Thomas Nevins whom *The Complete Peerage* records as having purchased the castle in 1894 for £60,000.

The Earl was Master of the Meath Foxhounds and held that that 'if you didn't hunt in Meath you might as well be dead'. Apart from killing foxes, he loved cats and built a special 'cattery' in a tower of the Castle. There were 60 of them at any one time, and the window was left open in case any other feline wanted to join their company. Lady Fingall wrote that her husband 'brought them food at regular intervals. No one else dared approach them as they were perfectly savage.' The tombs in the church were damaged in the early 1900s when servants of an English gentleman, who had taken the castle for the hunting season, got hold of some ladders, placed them against the walls of the church and, climbing up, proceeded to throw stones down into it.

The 11th Earl was chairman of the great Unionist Convention that was held in Dublin to oppose the introduction of the First Home Rule Bill in 1892; he once stated that 'You should not give the Irish anything that they do not ask for.' The tragedy of Unionist and, consequently, British policy towards the Sister Island was that they did not even give the Irish what they did ask for, with the result that those who live on this island are still suffering the consequences of their misguided policies.

One evening in 1923 a message was received at Killeen from the pro-treaty politician John Dillon warning Lord Fingall that the IRA were in the process of burning his home at that very moment and would be at Killeen shortly. The old couple gathered up their jewels and a few other possessions, Daisy put on a fur coat against the cold, and waited in the study for what they believed would be the inevitable knock on the door from the terrorists. Daisy wrote, 'we waited all night. But they never came. They burned a small place on the way and then, perhaps, had had enough of it,' and Killeen certainly 'would take a bit of doing.' And perhaps they were weary. When dawn broke, the Fingalls pulled back the shutters, 'the study was grey and chilly in the morning light. They won't come now.' And so we climbed stiffly and wearily up the great staircase to bed...'

Prophetically, however, Daisy also wrote about what would happen to Killeen if the house-burners got their way. 'How Killeen would burn. Badly – that old Norman Castle of stone that had been built as a pale fortress. Then I remembered the big oak staircase; that would send up a glorious flame. Then I remembered, too, how I had often thought that Killeen would make a lovely ruin. And I saw it in my mind, with the light falling through its empty window spaces and its battlemented walls lifted gauntly against the sky.' It is, perhaps, a mercy that she did not live to see the evil day in 1981 when the old place was torched. All that remained, apart from the stout old walls, was the plasterwork in the entrance hall and the dining room (the former drawing room) which, somehow, survived; everything else was destroyed.

The remainder of the story of this residence is brief and perhaps all too predictable. The 12th Earl, who served with the 17/21st Lancers in World War I, was destined to be the last. In 1952, Lord Fingall sold the castle to Sir Victor Sassoon, who never lived in it but ran the estate as a stud with Lord Fingall as his manager. Town and Country Estates sold the contents over five days. Among the treasures that were snapped up and dispersed were paintings by Hobbema,

van der Capelle, Gainsborough, Guido Reni, Hondecoeter, Lancret, Ruysdael and Van Dyck. Sassoon sold it on in 1963 to Daniel Wildenstein, an art dealer and racehorse owner.

The Fingall motto was '*Festina lente*', but no matter how slowly the family hastened, the inevitable day dawned in 1974 when the 12th and last Earl of Fingall died. Less than a century before, the Earls of Fingall had owned 9589 acres around Killeen Castle. Now it was all gone. The only thing that did survive was the old Barony of Killeen, which passed to his kinsman Lord Dunsany, who decided not to use it.

Basil Brindley, a Dublin advertising executive, bought the house from Daniel Wildenstein, but it lay empty until the day in May 1981 when a hooligan decided to pour petrol all over the main rooms and set fire to them. The ruin of Killeen Castle was sold to Chris Slattery in 1989 and its present owners have plans to turn it into a country house hotel. There will be the inevitable golf course in the demesne and probably ancillary chalets as well. At least, one ought to be grateful that the place is being restored and not levelled, as happened with the great Vanbrugh-like palace of Summerhill, in the same county.

The stables. In the 1950s the estate was run as a stud which was managed by the 12th Earl for the then owner, Sir Victor Sassoon.

Killeen Castle
Tara, County Meath

This Regency house was designed by
Sir Richard Morrison in Elizabethan
Revival style for the 10th Earl of Meath.
The 14th Earl demolished two-thirds
of the mansion in the 1950s.

Killruddery   *Bray, County Wicklow*

After the restoration in the 19th century of Killruddery, the home of the Brabazon family, J.N. Brewer wrote, 'The mansion of Killruddery was, until lately, a low and rather old building, quite destitute of architectural interest; but a new and very estimable structure is now in progress… the style adopted is that which prevailed in the reign of Henry VIII; a mode assuredly combining the advantages of picturesque effect and convenience of internal arrangement. The plan of the house is an irregular quadrangle, enclosing a court-yard. The entrance is through an ante-hall, which communicates by a broad flight of fourteen steps with the great hall, an extensive apartment that rises to the height of thirty feet… the roof is supported by carved beams. The grounds are laid out in a manner peculiarly adapted to the character of the present building, and present nearly an unique instance in this country of the old Dutch style of gardening'.

THE GARDENS AT KILLRUDDERY are among the finest in Ireland. They were principally laid out between 1682 and 1750, and may be seen in a marvellous painting belonging to the house that depicts the Killruddery Hunt. Also in the grounds is a pair of canals measuring 550 feet long and known as the 'Long Ponds'. It has been suggested that these may have been used to keep fish and indeed a similar pair of ponds at Stonyhurst College, near Blackburn in Lancashire, are still known as the 'Fish Ponds'. Beyond the canals is a hidden circular pool 60 feet across, where four cherubs accompanied by turtles surround a central fountain head. Around the pool is a hedge, known as 'the Beech Circle', which was described in 1827 as having reached 20 feet in height. On a plan of 1740–50 there was also a lime avenue, which began halfway across the park and led to the crown of a hill.

Another feature of the garden is the arrangement of hedges – of yew, hornbeam and lime – known as 'The Angles'. These hedges stand 10 feet tall and form triangles within a rectangular frame, a shape known as a *patte d'oie* or 'goose foot'. There is an example of this design at Howth Castle in County Dublin, and something similar with Irish yews at Charleville Castle in County Offaly. There was once a real maze on this site as well as a bowling green.

An ornamental dairy, designed by Sir George Hodson, was built in the mid-Victorian period. Sir George lived nearby at Hollybrooke House and had been the chairman of the Royal Horticultural Society of Ireland for 20 years. A pool in the shape of the ace of clubs has long since vanished, but there is still a 'Sylvan Theatre', which the 10th Earl told Sir Walter Scott (who visited Killruddery in the 1820s) had been the scene of amateur theatricals in both his and his father's time.

The Brabazon family's connection with Killruddery dates back to 1618. John Brabazon, from Eastwell Manor in Leicestershire, had been slain fighting at Bosworth Field in 1485. His son, another John, married a Miss Chaworth (her Christian name is unknown), and their son William arrived in Ireland to found his family's fortune in this benighted island. Sir William (as he became) was appointed Vice-Treasurer and Receiver-General of Ireland in 1534, and remained in office until his death in 1552. Sir William's son was created Baron Brabazon of Ardee (or Baron of Ardee) and in 1627 his son, another Sir William, was raised to the Peerage as Earl of Meath.

In 1618, James I had given William a grant of the lands of Killruddery in County Wicklow as a reward for his services. A report states that 'The Castle, Town and Lands of Kilrothery, in the Counties of Wicklow and Dublin, were granted by the Crown to Sir William Brabazon, eldest son of Lord Brabazon of Ardee, in 1619, as assignee to the Lord Cromwell. In 1634, he had a grant for ever of free warren throughout his lands in the County of Wicklow, with licence to enclose three thousand perches [about 18 acres] for a park, and to store the same with deer'. The property came with a small castle and its outbuildings. Lord Meath later stated that he had spent some £10,000, (a huge amount in those days) on improving his Wicklow estate.

Killruddery (or Cill Ruadhrach) means 'Church of the Knight', although the name of the particular gentleman after whom the church is named has not come down to posterity. Eugene O'Curry records that in 1820 bones were found near 'the north side of the house where the Clock is now', and later on an ancient graveyard and a small stone cross were discovered when an avenue was being laid out. In the 13th century, a Nicholas de la Felde had leased the lands of

Killruddery
Bray, County Wicklow

Kidretheri to the Abbey of Saint Thomas à Becket in Dublin. These lands had been granted to de la Felde by the ancient proprietor, Dermait Mac Giola-Maholmock (Mac Colman). This Abbey has long since disappeared although its name is preserved in Thomas Street, Dublin. The monks of St Thomas's Abbey in Dublin had a 'garden' and a 'grove' at Killruddery 550 years ago. In the 15th century, the King granted the manor of Kilrothery to Walter, the Abbot of St Mary's.

The first house to be built at Killruddery was destroyed during the Civil War in 1645, and was rebuilt by the 2nd Earl of Meath in 1651. He had fought, as Lord Brabazon, under Lord Ormond against the Roman Catholic rebels. Captured by the Parliamentary forces, the Earl was imprisoned in the Tower of London in 1644–45 and was exchanged seven months later for another prisoner. He later alleged that he had lost £40,000 in the Irish rebellion, having raised a force of 1,500 men, all Protestants, and armed them, at small expense to the Government. He claimed that he had been forced to sell his manor at Eastwell, which, he said, 'had descended to him in a lineal line since Edward I'.

Lord Meath was the tool of the 2nd Duke of Buckingham and 'made himself contemptible by scattering broadcast charge's against Ormond's Irish

1 The flight of stairs from the entrance hall leading up to the great hall, all demolished during the 14th Earl of Meath's 'reconstructions' between 1952 and 1956.
2 The great hall, which at 40 feet high was the largest and most impressive part of the house.
3 The ceiling of the great hall was carved by Thomas Kirk. The plasterwork was executed by Henry Pobje (d.1830), who charged £249 for his work.

Killruddery
Bray, County Wicklow

administration', but when called upon to make them good before the English Privy Council, he did not dare face that tribunal with his stories. Charles II, justly indignant, struck him off the Irish Council and forbade him the Court.' The 2nd Earl was drowned in 1675 off Holyhead, but his younger son, Edward, was rescued from the wreck.

The first illustration showing the original house dates from about 1680 and depicts a building of five bays facing east. The first gardens were laid out in about 1682, in the 3rd Earl's time, under the directions of a M. Bonet, who is supposed to have received his training at Versailles. He had already worked in Ireland for 12 years for Sir William Petty before he moved to Killruddery.

Cheney, the steward of Killruddery, wrote that Captain Edward Brabazon, who was to become the 4th Earl, was making improvements at the house – among other things, he planted a cherry garden. But the Dublin Parliament of 1689 attainted him and his estate, worth some £2000 a year, was sequestrated. Later, he commanded the garrison at Carrickfergus against James II and was wounded at the siege of Limerick. His lordship complained that the 'Glorious Revolution' had cost him £10,000 and, as a result, he sold a 35-year lease on the property at Killruddery to John Lovett the uncle of Sir Edward Lovett Pearce. In 1702, the Earl took a house on the north side of St Stephen's Green in Dublin, where the family lived during the 18th century.

The 4th Earl's wife was Dorothea Stopford. Jonathan Swift, in a letter to his beloved Stella (Esther Johnson) in 1711–12, wrote, 'Countess Doll of Meath is such an owl, that wherever I visit, people are asking me whether I know such an Irish lady, and her figure and her foppery.' He later wrote an epitaph to Dorothea and her second husband, Lieutenant General Richard Gorges, entitled 'Doll and Dicky'.

Killruddery was recovered by the 6th Earl in 1720. He married Judith Prendergast from Gort in County Galway. Mrs Delany wrote of this match, 'we had a wedding lately, Lord Meath, a man of good sense and great fortune, who was married unfortunately when he was a boy to his aunt's chambermaid. He never lived with her and she died about a month ago. Yesterday he married

Killruddery
Bray, County Wicklow

Miss Prendergast: he has been in love with her several years; she has little or no fortune and is far from handsome!'

The 9th Earl succeeded at the age of 21, but in 1797 was killed in a duel with a Mr Gore at the age of 28 (a member of the family ascribed his demise to a severe case of 'lead poisoning'). He was followed by his brother, the 10th Earl, who ruled at Killruddery until 1851. He was made a Knight of Saint Patrick in 1821 (and was one of the six Knights Extraordinary at the Coronation of George IV). Twenty years later he was created a Peer of the United Kingdom as Baron Chaworth of Eaton Hall, County Hereford, taking the surname of the first Sir William Brabazon's mother as his style. He married Lady Melosina Meade, the daughter of the 1st Earl of Clanwilliam, at her father's residence, Clanwilliam House on St Stephen's Green, Dublin. This house is now a part of University College, Dublin, and has recently been restored.

The 10th Earl decided to rebuild his seat, which was described as 'a very uninteresting residence' and 'becoming unfit for the residence of a nobleman of taste and fortune'. Accordingly, he engaged the architect Richard Morrison to design him a palatial residence in the Elizabethan Revival style (which, considering his antecedents, was perhaps the most appropriate). This 'Elizabethan Château' was given entrance gates that bore the family's motto *Vota Vita Mea* (Prayers are my Life), and are very similar to those at Fota in County Cork and Ballyfin in County Laois (both by the Morrisons).

The entrance hall had a flight of steps that led up to the most impressive space in the house – the great hall, which was 40 feet high. There was a large staircase hall with stained glass by John Millner and a splendid dining room. The plaster-work was by Henry Popje of Bray, with the assistance of Simon Gilligan. There were two drawing rooms with classical decoration; that in the small drawing room was similar to the style of the decoration at Ballyfin. The decoration of the great drawing room of this predominantly gothic house was possibly suggested by its Italian chimneypiece. The chimneypieces were ordered from Italy in 1816 and 1817 through Gaspare Gabrielli (who had executed the wall paintings at Lyons in County Kildare for Lord Cloncurry). Crimson silk damask was ordered from Spitalfields in 1820 for the large drawing room; the fabric has now faded to a delicate shade of gold.

Richard Morrison's architectural decoration seems to have been completed by 1824, and the house is reputed to have cost some £20,000 (with another £600 for the lodge). In the midst of such extravagance, it is worthwhile considering the fate of those who lived in Lord Meath's Dublin properties. Ann Plumptre visited them in 1817 and wrote, 'This jurisdiction includes some of the most ancient, which are now the poorest and worst parts of Dublin, where numbers of families are crowded together in one house to such a degree as to render them spectacles of the extremest filth and misery.'

It might have been the Meaths' purchases of French furniture in Paris that caused them to call in Matthew Wyatt Jnr. in about 1827 to give some parts of their house a 'makeover' in the Louis Revival style (although the juxtaposition of the 'Louis' and the 'Gothic' styles may be found elsewhere at this date – Belvoir Castle in England being a prime example). Among other changes, Wyatt was responsible for the wall panels and decorative pelmet cornices in the great drawing room. A few years later, local craftsman William Slater altered the upper part of this room and added an oriel window and Dutch gable. In about 1846, Daniel Robertson added the entrance to the forecourt as well as the gate-house entrance to the stable yard; he also restored the old garden.

In 1852 William Burn was called in to design a conservatory for the house. The design of the parapet for this is said to have taken its inspiration from a tiara belonging to Lady Meath. There is a story that she had already sold this in order to provide money to aid in the famine relief of the 1840s, but other accounts state that she sold the jewel to finance the conservatory. Whatever the truth, the Meaths were reported, in 1853, as 'spending largely' in 'beautifying' their house. The new addition, which opens out from the south rooms, was originally intended for growing oranges, but now acts as a sculpture gallery.

The 11th Earl voted against the Disestablishment of the Church of Ireland in 1868. Despite this, in 1877, he entertained William Ewart Gladstone (the architect of that measure) at Killruddery, during the Grand Old Man's only visit to Ireland. The 12th Earl, who established Empire Day, was made a Knight of Saint Patrick in 1905, a GBE in 1920 and a GCVO in 1923. His obituary in *The Times* described him as having 'a dry sense of humour, an unquenchable enthusiasm, and a practical knowledge of the world and its ways.' The house contains, among its other treasures, a framed address from 'The Happy Churchwardens of Bray'.

The 13th Earl rose to the rank of brigadier in the British Army and commanded the 1st battalion of the Grenadier Guards and later the Irish Guards during World War I. He was also the last Chancellor of the old Royal University (the precursor of the National University of Ireland). The 13th Earl's brother, Captain the Honourable Ernest Brabazon, was killed in action in 1915.

The 14th Earl of Meath demolished about two-thirds of Killruddery between 1953 and 1956. The entrance hall, the great hall and the dining room were among the apartments that were lost, and the small drawing room was turned into a dining room. The Honourable Claude Phillimore was the architect of this reconstruction. Whatever the reasons for this destruction, one hopes that it would not have been permitted today.

In 1883, the family estates were 14,717 acres in County Wicklow, based around Killruddery, and 36 acres in County Dublin. There were also 695 acres in

Killruddery
Bray, County Wicklow

Herefordshire, which belonged to Eaton Court – these last brought in £1,453 a year. The total rent roll of the Earls of Meath came to £9398 a year. Financial affairs have not gone too badly for the family since then either. The sale of land for development on the periphery of the demesne has brought in a handy amount of money which, when added to the sum achieved by the present, 15th, Earl for the sale of the Ballinacor estate, near Rathdrum in County Wicklow, adds up to many millions of pounds.

There is an interesting footnote to this story. About a century ago it was quite usual for the British aristocracy to allege that they were descended from Saxon princes or Norman lords, and such claims were accepted by one and all. Nowadays, however, it is rare to find a family which asserts an ancestry they cannot prove, but the Brabazons, Earls of Meath, are an exception to this rule. In the millennium edition of *Burke's Peerage*, the claims that had been made for their lineage before the 1940s are repeated (although with less exact particulars than before).

There is an account of the family which asks the supposedly rhetorical question 'did not Jacques le Brabazon land with William the Conqueror in 1066?' Well, such a gentleman may have landed at Pevensey at that date, but there is no evidence that he was in any way connected to the family that came to Ireland as the agents of Henry VIII. The genealogy given in the new *Burke's* is riddled with chronological inconsistencies.

We are told that John le Brabazon, the son of King William's companion, lived in the reigns of 'Henry I and Henry II' – from 1100 until 1189 (thereby ignoring the 19 years that Stephen occupied the throne). The next in the pedigree, Adam le Brabazon, lived at the same time as 'Richard I, John and Henry III' – in other words between 1189 and 1272. This genealogy, therefore, allows a time span of 172 years for two generations of the family. The Brabazons must have sired heirs in their dotage.

The story moves forwards in a reasonable fashion until Sir William Brabazon (with a date of 1327) is shown as having a son, Thomas, alive and well in 1299 – perhaps a misprint? This Thomas Brabazon had a son old enough to fight at Crécy in 1346 (according to an early 20th-century source), but also of an age to be around in 'Henry IV's reign (1399–1413). His son, *Burke's* informs us, was alive in 1445 – almost a century after his father had allegedly fought 'with the Black Prince'.

All of which reminds one of Oscar Wilde's quip in the play *A Woman of No Importance,* 'You should study the *Peerage*… It is the best thing in fiction that the English have ever done.'

A mid-18th-century house incorporating parts of
a 17th-century building, Kilmurry was remodelled after
1814 by Sir Richard Morrison for Charles Kendal Bushe,
later Chief Justice of the Queen's Bench in Ireland.

Kilmurry House   *Thomastown, County Kilkenny*

Kilmurry House, which is near to Thomastown in County Kilkenny, came into the ownership of the Bushe family as a result of the redistribution of Irish properties by Cromwell's commissioners. The demesne of Kilmurry had originally been seized by the Normans in the late 12th century and in 1222 a Gilbert de Kentewell possessed the lands at Kilfane, which he held from the Bishop of Ossory. His descendant, John Cantwell, was transplanted to Connacht in the Cromwellian settlement of Ireland and his land was given away to supporters of the victorious regime. In this instance, they went to Colonel John 'Fire-Away-Flanagan' Bushe.

COLONEL BUSHE HAD arrived in Ireland from Dunley in Somerset and he received a grant of Cantwell's 770 acres in County Kilkenny in the Cromwellian settlement of Ireland. In 1690, he took the side of William of Orange and, during one of the skirmishes of the so-called 'Glorious Revolution', he was sent to demand the surrender of Kilkenny Castle. A Jacobite officer, named O'Flanagan, ordered him to leave at once or he would be fired upon. The colonel's reply provided his nickname and he went on to capture the castle for the Stadtholder. The fate of O'Flanagan is not recorded.

The Colonel had two sons. The elder, Amyas Bushe of Kilfane, married Eleanor, the daughter of Sir Christopher Wandesford, in 1706. The younger son, Arthur Bushe of Kilmurry, was born in 1691 and graduated from Trinity College, Dublin, in 1711. Arthur's son, Thomas Bushe, was variously Prebendary of Inniscarra in County Cork, and chaplain to Kingston College in the same county. His wife Catherine was the granddaughter of Sir John Boyle, Solicitor General of Ireland.

Thomas Bushe was a gambler and spendthrift – a typical half-mounted Irish squireen parson, who had allegedly inherited the property now called Mount Juliet in the following romantic circumstances. It appears that some years previously an elderly gentleman had arrived at Kilmurry in a post chaise and announced that he had been robbed by highwaymen and all his papers had been taken. Mr Bushe gathered his workmen and, within a few hours, returned with the stolen goods. The next part of this tale is extraordinary: the elderly gentleman then announced that he wished to pass his remaining days at Kilmurry and, even more amazingly, the Bushes agreed. When the old man died, it transpired that he had left his estate to the Reverend Mr Bushe on the sole condition that his family should give the surname of their benefactor – Kendal – as a Christian name to each of their heirs.

Whatever the real truth, the Mount Juliet estate had to be sold eventually in order to pay the Reverend Mr Bushe's debts. The lesson thus learned was obviously lost on him since he continued to run up debts to infinity and his creditors became accordingly pressing. He 'thought it incumbent upon him to live upon a scale of expenditure more consistent with Irish notions of dignity than with English maxims of economy and good sense. He was a man of refined manners and of polished, if not prudential, habits.' His problem was that his sole remaining asset, Kilmurry, was entailed on his son and heir, young Charles Kendal Bushe, one of the most attractive characters in recent Irish history. (As a student at Trinity College, Dublin, he was defeated for the auditorship of the college Historical Society by Theobald Wolfe Tone.) On the morning of Charles's 21st birthday, his father entered his bedroom and asked him to sign some papers, telling him that he need not concern himself too much with their content. Charles did as he was bid and only then discovered that he, now legally of age, had agreed to shoulder his father's mountain of debts. Forced to sell his family home, he had to support himself by his chosen profession, the law. To make matters worse, he had a wife and a growing family to support at the time.

Kilmurry was sold in 1788 to a Dr Hoskyn for 'a good price' and the Bushe family moved to Dublin. The doctor sold it on to a Major Alcock, who was in charge of the Kilkenny Militia at the Battle of Castlebar in 1798. The rebels were aided by French troops under General Humbert at this battle and it has gone down in history as 'the Races of Castlebar' because of the speed with which the Government forces (including Major Alcock) fled the field.

Kilmurry House
Thomastown,
County Kilkenny

Kilmurry House
Thomastown,
County Kilkenny

The British Government, at war with revolutionary France, annoyed by the independent stance that had been taken by the Irish Parliament and concerned after the rebellion of 1798, decided to pass an Act of Union which would close down the Dublin legislature and move the Government of Ireland to the Westminster Parliament. The Prime Minister, William Pitt the Younger, did not intend to let either chance or unfettered democracy stand in his way with regard to this measure. Accordingly, his agents were sent out with bribes of money, titles and offices to the prospective electors, who were the members of both houses of the Irish Parliament. Charles Bushe had been elected to this body and, despite the fact that he was quite poor (although his father had died in 1795, Charles was still paying off debts) he refused to vote for the Union of Great Britain with Ireland. The government in London tried every means in their power to persuade him to change his mind. He was offered the position of Master of the Rolls, a peerage and later a very large sum of money. In consequence of his behaviour there is, in the list of members of the Irish House of Commons compiled by Sir Jonah Barrington, a single word placed against his name – 'Incorruptible'.

Charles was Solicitor General for Ireland for 17 years, from 1805 until 1822. His wife Ann (whom he called 'Nancy') was the daughter of John Crampton from Merrion Square in Dublin. Charles was devoted to her and they were an unusually close couple. He took no decisions without her advice and once he became a successful lawyer, he was in the habit of giving her handfuls of bank-notes and saying, 'There you are, buy jewels!' He returned to Kilkenny in 1814 to stay with his cousin, Gervase Parker Bushe and his wife Eliza, who lived at Kilfane, the neighbouring estate to Kilmurry. On hearing that his childhood home was up for sale, Charles rode over and found the property in a sorry state, with the trees marked for felling. He decided to buy back the estate but could raise only two-thirds of the sum required. When she heard this, Nancy took him aside and showed him her bankbook. What he saw astonished him. It transpired that every time he had given her money to buy something pretty for herself, she had banked it, providing a sum which, together with his own resources, not only enabled him to buy back Kilmurry House but also to restore and enlarge it.

The estate has been lived on from the earliest period. Bronze urns from the Middle Bronze Age, *c.*1000 BC, were found on the land. The ruins of a chapel dating from about AD 500 and dedicated to St Mary (Cill Mhuire) were shown on an 18th-century map. Part of the house is believed to date from the 17th century or earlier, but the main structure was erected in the mid-18th century. Charles Kendal Bushe added the two single-storey wings when he moved back into the house. The plasterwork and the design of the new wings suggest the hand of Sir Richard Morrison and his son, William Vitruvius – the plasterwork in the entrance hall is reminiscent of the staircase hall at Castlegar in County Galway which is by Sir Richard. Charles knew of the Morrisons' work. They had designed two houses, Lough Bray Cottage and St Valery, both in County Wicklow, for his brother-in-law Sir Philip Crampton, a distinguished physician, and in 1813 they had built Glencairn Abbey (Castle Richard) for his cousin, Amyas Bushe.

In the entrance hall of Kilmurry House, beyond which lies the blue music room, ivory-coloured Ionic columns are flanked by pilasters. The staircase hall is two storeys high and the ballroom (formed from the original entrance hall

and the rooms on either side of it) overlooks the lake. In the ceiling of the new entrance hall, placed in one of the new wings, is a central glazed lantern. Each of the wings is surmounted by a sphinx and the roof parapet is lined with carved stone urns; both wings have Wyatt windows. Off the hall are the drawing room, the dining room and the library, which has bookcases recessed under curved arches. There is a lake behind the house and a three-acre walled garden.

Charles Bushe became Lord Chief Justice of the Queen's Bench and lived at Kilmurry House until his death in 1843. There is a biography of him by his granddaughter Edith Somerville who, with her cousin Violet Martin, also wrote *Some Experiences of an Irish R. M.* (1899), about a resident magistrate in Ireland. His son, John Bushe, married Lady Louisa Hare, the daughter of the Earl of Listowel, but it was his daughter Katherine and her husband, Michael Fox, who sold the estate to Major Henry Butler, a grandson of the 11th Viscount Mountgarrett.

Major Butler had enjoyed a military career and was an excellent amateur artist. He published *South African Sketches: Illustrative of the Wildlife of a Hunter on the Frontier of Cape Colony in 1841*. His watercolours of the West Indies are creepy and atmospheric, while those which he executed during his trip to South America are now of great topographical interest. One of his daughters was Mildred Anne Butler RWS. She had two sisters, one of whom was an accomplished woodcarver – the dining room has an oak chimneypiece, 20 feet high, which was carved by her in 1896 in the Arts and Crafts style – and three brothers, who followed their father into the army. Eventually, Mildred outlived them all and inherited Kilmurry.

Mildred Anne Butler worked predominantly in watercolours. Her work was exhibited for the first time at the Dudley Gallery in London's Piccadilly in 1888, and she continued to show her work almost until her death. The recurring inspiration for her work seems to have been Kilmurry itself – she removed a wall between a drawing room and the garden in order to create her studio. There are endless views of the farmyard animals, family cats and of the lush Victorian gardens, which are designed in the style of Daniel Robertson, a Kilkenny

Kilmurry House
Thomastown,
County Kilkenny

architect, and had large herbaceous borders containing hollyhocks, camellias, tulips and roses.

One of Mildred's watercolours shows the entrance hall at Kilmurry in the full gloom and clutter that was the average Victorian's idea of interior decoration and good taste. A large Islamic carpet lies on the floor, and an over-carved octagonal centre table, in what looks suspiciously like the 'Jacobethan' style, is complemented by a 17th-century side chair covered in royal blue velvet. A hideous hexagonal lantern with insets of coloured glass is only surpassed in nastiness by the enormous fringed piece of blue-printed chintz that is draped over a curtain pole at the door to the dining room.

Mildred Anne Butler died in 1941 and left Kilmurry to her cousin Doreen Archer-Houblon who, together with her sister, Kitty Brocklebank, preserved and cared for Miss Butler's legacy with the greatest care until it was sold in 1981 and the contents were dispersed. Kilmurry House was placed on the market again in 2001.

This is a mid-18th-century house (built around the core of a much smaller 17th-century building) with later additions. Formerly the home of the Earls of Donoughmore, Knocklofty is presently a hotel.

Knocklofty *Clonmel, County Tipperary*

The name 'Knocklofty' derives from the Irish 'Cnoc Lochta', which means 'the lofted or shelving hill'. The original house dates from the late 17th century and has later additions. In the 18th century, the Clonmel architect William Tinsley, added a single-storey corridor with a domed porch to the entrance front. A pair of stone eagles surmounts the gable ends of the wings. Doric pilasters complete with wreaths are outside the ground floor corridor. Inside, there are a two-storey library (whose contents were sold in 1982 for £193,000), a drawing room, dining room, music room and study. The views from the house are towards the Comeragh foothills and the Knockmealdown mountains.

KNOCKLOFTY was the seat of the Hutchinson family who came from Alford in Lincolnshire to participate in the great government theft of Irish land that occurred in the first half of the 17th century. They received a grant of land in County Tipperary, and in 1751 their heiress, Christina Nickson, married an up-and-coming barrister named John Hely, the son of Francis Hely of Gortroe, County Cork. John Hely knew a good thing when he saw one and, in the great-niece and eventual heiress of Richard Hutchinson of Knocklofty, he saw a very good thing indeed. Eight years later (and with the brand-new surname of Hely-Hutchinson), John Hely was elected Member of Parliament for Lanesborough. He later represented Cork and Taghmon until his death.

This did not so much satisfy his ambitions as stoke them up. By 1774 he was not only Provost of Trinity College, Dublin, but also Principal Secretary of State for Ireland and Keeper of the Privy Seal, positions which he held until his death in 1794. His wife was raised to the peerage as Baroness Donoughmore of Knocklofty in 1783, together with a grand new coat of arms and a brave motto: *Fortiter Gerit Crucem* – 'He bravely bears the cross'. With his wife now a peeress and his own position secure John should have been satisfied, but his greed and unscrupulousness were infamous. In 1775, Sir John Blacquiere wrote, 'he opposed Lord Townshend – afterwards made his bargain and supported ably and zealously... he is still dissatisfied and ever will be until he engrosses the station of Primate, Chancellor, L.C.J. [Lord Chief Justice] of the King's Bench, Provost Etc, Etc, Etc, in his own person!' The Prime Minister, Lord North, commented, 'If you were to give him the whole of Gt. Britain and Ireland for an estate, he would ask for the Isle of Man for a potato garden.'

John Hely's eldest son Richard, the 2nd Baron, was created a Viscount in 1797 and in 1800 he was raised to the Earldom of Donoughmore of Knocklofty (with remainder to the heirs male of his mother), which was one of the large numbers of titles that a grateful government doled out on the day before the Act of Union came into force. The future Earl commanded the militia that was routed by General Humbert at the engagement known as 'The Races of Castlebar' because the government forces took to their heels and fled, pursued by the rebels and their French allies. Nonetheless, despite this fiasco, Richard was chosen by his Order

as one of the 28 original Representative Peers of Ireland on the abolition of the Irish House of Lords and, as if this were not enough, in 1822 George IV created him a peer of the United Kingdom as Viscount Hutchinson of Knocklofty.

His brother, John, who had followed a career in

Knocklofty
Clonmel, County Tipperary

Knocklofty
Clonmel, County Tipperary

the army (becoming a general in the process) succeeded him. He had been commander in chief during the Egyptian campaign in 1801 and was raised to the peerage as Baron Hutchinson of Alexandria. Described as having 'harsh features, jaundiced by ill-health, extreme short-sightedness, a stooping body and slouching gait, and an utter neglect of dress', he decided, in 1809, to throw in his lot with the Carlton House Party and became their chief military adviser. His attacks on the government's handling of the Peninsular War earned him this damning epitaph: 'He did not hesitate to sink his patriotism in the spirit of faction'. When he became the 2nd Earl of Donoughmore, he made some little effort to assist liberal policies by supporting a very limited amount of toleration and emancipation for Catholics.

However, as the 2nd Earl wrote in a letter to Lord Cloncurry in 1828, he was 'very glad to co-operate with you in anything, and particularly to act with you in endeavouring to settle the Catholic question, because it is the foundation on which the permanent tranquillity of Ireland can alone be erected… The fact is that the violence of O'Connell and his associates, at least in this part of Ireland, has done the Catholic cause much mischief; and it would be impossible here, and in the city and county of Cork, to get any considerable number of Protestants to affix their signatures to any document similar to that which you have in contem-

plation. In the county and city of Cork they are much more violent than in Tipperary; but even in this county, where more of the principal gentlemen are disposed to be liberal, the late proceedings of the Catholics have irritated them very much.'

The 3rd Earl was a finer sort of individual altogether. He lost his commission and spent three months in gaol in April 1816 for his part in arranging – at the request of the Princess de Vaudémont – the escape of General Count Lavalette in December 1815. Lavalette was Napoleon's Postmaster-General and one of those officers who had supported the Emperor during the Hundred Days. Marshal Ney and General de Labédoyère had already been executed – Marshal Ney's sword was eventually to find its way into the Hutchinson family's possession, as a gift from his widow. General Lavalette escaped from prison disguised as a woman, and made his way to England in the uniform of a captain of the English Guards.

The 4th Earl was the first member of the family who thought that it would be nice to call himself Viscount Suirdale – thereby completely overlooking the fact that no sovereign had thought fit to bestow such a title upon either him or his ancestors. Presumably it was some sort of romantic foolishness connected with the fact that the River Suir flows through the Knocklofty demesne; whatever the reason, it is an error the family still persists in today.

In 1883 the Earls of Donoughmore owned 11,950 acres in the counties of Tipperary, Waterford, Cork, Wexford, Kilkenny, Monaghan, Louth and Dublin. Despite this, John, the 5th Earl, managed to run into considerable financial difficulties, which did not stop him becoming for one year the Assistant Commissioner in the European Commission for the organization of Eastern Rumelia in the Balkan peninsula between 1878 and 1879.

Knocklofty
Clonmel, County Tipperary

The widow of the 7th Earl recalled that 'My husband's grandfather lost all of his money, and this house was let from some time in the late nineteenth century until the marriage of my father-in-law and my mother-in-law.' In fact, the family did not return to live at Knocklofty until 1903.

The 6th Earl was created a Knight of Saint Patrick in 1918 and was made a member of the first senate of the Irish Free State in 1921. This was not his first experience of parliamentary responsibility, since he had been Under Secretary for War between 1903 and 1905. The 7th Earl was briefly Member of Parliament for Peterborough between 1943 and 1945. He came to public attention, however, in 1974 when the IRA (after a period of putting bombs under cars and into public houses) decided that they needed a tougher subject to tackle, and they lighted upon the 7th Earl of Donoughmore, a pensioner living with his wife in County Tipperary. He proved, however, to be more of a challenge than they had bargained for and, in a form of 'political action', the brave boys had to pistol-whip the old man (and scar his head in the process) in order to persuade him to come along with them. Unfortunately, their political intelligence had failed them on this occasion. They had hoped to hold the elderly couple as bargaining chips for the release of the Price sisters, who were serving time in England for criminal activities. But the British government, as Lord Donoughmore remarked, when he was released with his wife in Dublin's Phoenix Park a week later, 'would not have given a damn' about what happened to him. His son, Richard, the present and 8th Earl, now lives in Oxfordshire, while his brother, the Honourable Mark Hely-Hutchinson, lives in Ireland.

In 1981 the family estate was put on the market and by 1983 the demesne had been sold in three lots. The bulk of the 680-acre estate was sold off at £1500 an acre, while the house and 105 acres were bought by Paddy O'Keefe, a Cork-born, businessman who had made a fortune in time-sharing schemes. He laid out a golf course, made a plan for 12 time-share apartments with a swimming pool and office facilities and offered shares in the house for 'as little as £5,000 a year (low season)... EVERY YEAR for the rest of your life'. It also promised 'a lifestyle that was once retained for only a few'. The property was opened as a luxury country house hotel in partnership with a Canadian-Irish consortium which announced that the conversions and additions would cost about £10 million

The house was later bought by Frank Murphy, a former 1500-metre champion, who had won £250,000 as part of a syndicate that had scooped over £2,500,000 in the Irish Lottery. He paid more than £2,000,000 for the estate, but in 1994 it was resold. The original guide price of £600,000 to £700,000 was brought down to a paltry £360,000 and the purchaser was Mr Denis English, who already owned Marlfield House in the same county and Castle Durrow in County Laois. The house is now owned by John and Margaret Veale who welcome you to Knocklofty House Hotel, set in 105 acres. There you will find the Donoughmore and Palatine Suites, which can seat 130 people and are 'ideal for Weddings and Conferences'. The new owners say that they have attempted to 'retain the elegance of a bygone era'. To this end there is a swimming pool to enable you to 'burn some fat' and a jacuzzi and sauna to help out as well. As one recent guest commented, 'Can't wait to come back to see the ghost!'

Mallow was constructed in the late 19th
and mid-20th centuries around the stables
of an early 17th-century Plantation castle.

Mallow Castle   *Mallow, County Cork*

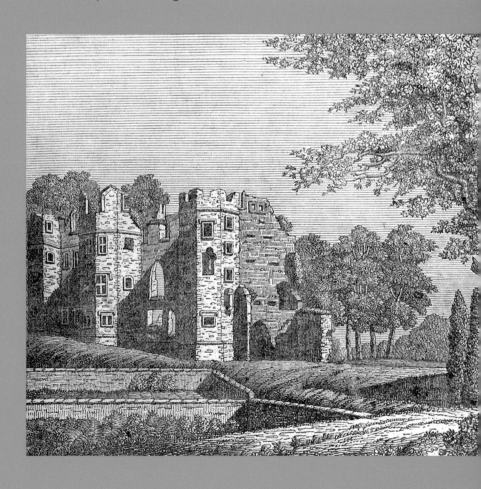

For four centuries Mallow Castle was the seat of the Norris family, one of whom met a dramatic and untimely end. In 1536 Henry VIII attended the May Day tournament in the company of his new queen, Anne Boleyn. The highlight was to have been a joust between the queen's brother, Lord Rochfort, and the King's friend and Keeper of the Privy Purse, Sir Henry Norris. Before this could take place, a message was brought to King Henry and he left at once, taking Norris with him. As they rode back, the King accused Norris of adultery with the queen, a charge that he incredulously denied. Nevertheless, Norris was taken into custody and 17 days later he was cut in two by an axe at the Tower of London, along with Lord Rochfort and three other unfortunates.

THE CHARGES AGAINST NORRIS were ridiculous and ranged from the accusation that he had slept with Queen Anne only a couple of weeks after the birth of her daughter (the future Queen Elizabeth I) to a remark that was alleged to have been made by the queen to him: 'you look to dead men's shoes for, if ought came to the King but good, you would look to have me'.

Ridiculous or not, such charges would have been enough to finish almost any other family, but Sir Henry's children were to find a friend in the daughter of Anne Boleyn, who was beheaded a few days after Norris and the others. When Elizabeth was held captive during her sister's reign, Henry, son of the beheaded Sir Henry, entertained her at his house at Rycote in Oxfordshire. Norreys (the orthography of Norris and Norreys is interchangeable – the name is pronounced as 'Norris') told her gaoler Sir Henry Bedingfield not to be so strict with the princess as he wished her to be merry while she was a guest under his roof. Elizabeth became a great friend of his family – she called his wife her 'dear black crow' on account of her dark complexion. When she became queen, Elizabeth sent Sir Henry as her Ambassador to France, and later made him a peer as Baron Norreys of Rycote.

The first fortress at Mallow, overlooking the River Blackwater, had been built by John Lackland, Earl of Morton (afterwards King John) at the end of the 12th century. The Geraldines had possession of it by 1282 – Geraldines is the collective name given to the family and followers of the Fitz Geralds, the Earls of Kildare and Desmond and the three Palatine Knights: the Black Knight (of Glin), the Green Knight (of Kerry), and the White Knight (FitzGibbon).

This state of affairs continued until 1588, when the property was forfeited as a result of the rebellion of their leader, the Earl of Desmond, in that year. Queen Elizabeth granted the Castle of Mallow and some 6000 acres to Sir Thomas Norris, a younger son of the 1st Baron Norreys. His elder brother, Sir John Norris, was already in Ireland, where he held the position of Lord President of Munster – he was praised by the poet Edmund Spenser as 'The honour of this age and Precedent of all that Arms ensue.' When Sir John died in 1597, Sir Thomas (who is described in *The Annals of the Four Masters*, the most

Previous page
A 19th-century engraving of the old castle at Mallow.

These pages
1 The lobby at the head of the staircase.
2 The anteroom with the drawing room beyond.
3 The anteroom (later the dining room). A portrait of King William III hangs on the wall.

Mallow Castle
Mallow, County Cork

1 The ruins of the old castle, built by
John Lackland, Earl of Morton, at the
end of the 12th century.
2 The chimneypiece in the anteroom.
The motto *Loyalement Je Sers* (Loyally
I serve) is carved in the stone below
the shelf.
3 The garden front, added to the
entrance front of the new castle by
Brigadier Jephson, using the designs
and stone left by Sir Denham Jephson-
Norreys.

Mallow Castle
Mallow, County Cork

comprehensive of all of the ancient histories of Ireland, as 'The Good Sir Thomas Norreys, a Knight of very great name and honour') succeeded him in the office. Sir Thomas died in 1599, as a result of a wound received in an ambush at Kilteeley, County Limerick, while he was on his way back to Mallow after meeting the Earl of Essex. His body was taken back to England for burial at Bath.

Sir Thomas's new building at Mallow was rather more of a fortified house than a castle. Made of red sandstone with limestone dressings, it was originally plastered. A rectangular block, it has two octagonal corner turrets and two centrally placed wings that project east and west from the front and rear walls. On Sir Thomas's death the property passed to his four-year-old daughter Elizabeth, who was the queen's godchild. Elizabeth I had sent her two white deer as a christening gift (so the tale goes) and the herd of white deer at Mallow today are allegedly the descendants of that first couple.

At the tender age of twelve, Elizabeth was found a husband in the person of Major General Sir John Jephson, who had received the honour of knighthood from the Lord Deputy, Sir George Cary, as a reward for his part in putting down the rebellion of Aodh Ruadh Ó Domhnall. Lady Jephson, as young Elizabeth now was, became pregnant at the age of 13 and gave birth to a son named William.

In 1606 the Attorney General of Ireland, who stayed at Mallow with Lady Norreys, described it as 'a well-built house, and stands by a fair river in a fruitful soil, but it is yet much unrepaired and bears many marks of the late rebellion.' In 1612 the manor was confirmed to Lady Jephson and she and her husband completed the building of the castle. This enabled the commissioners who reported on Mallow for the Plantation of Munster in 1622, to write that 'there was built at Mallow by Sir Thomas Norris a goodly strong and sumptuous house, upon the ruins of the old castle, with a bawn to it about 120 foot square and 18 foot in height and many convenient houses of offices.'

The next head of the family was William Jephson, MP for Stockport. A firm supporter of the Commonwealth, under whose auspices he became a major general, he urged Oliver Cromwell to take the title of king, when it was suggested in Parliament. He was also Ambassador to Sweden and Governor of Portsmouth. During the Civil War, in 1642, the Confederate forces under the command of Lord Mountgarrett attacked Mallow. A contemporary account tells us that 'the South castle was then, by its owner Captain [William] Jephson, committed to Arthur Bettesworth with a garrison of 200 arms, ammunition, one piece of iron ordnance and 2 calivers. The North Castle was bravely defended by Lt. Richard Williamson, who stood many assaults by Sgt. Major Purcell, and had several breaches made before he surrendered on honourable terms, and then most of his men were slain. When the terms were not kept he seized a sword, and fought his way to the South Castle.'

This stronghold did not surrender because there was a traitor in the Catholic camp. A certain 'Conogher Reagh Callaghans of Bellaballagh, Co. Cork, while professing to be a member of the true Catholic cause, and enjoying all of the privileges within Catholic quarters, was all his life a chief instrument to Sir Philip Percival, Sir James Cragg and other evil ministers of State and gave them continual intelligence. When Lord Mountgarrett was encamped near Mallow, Conogher Reagh repaired privately to Mr Bettesworth and by his information prevented the surrender of the Castle.'

In 1645, however, Mallow was captured by Lord Castlehaven and badly

1 A corner of the library. The portrait on
the left of the fireplace is alleged to be
of the Spanish Ambassador to the
Court of Queen Elizabeth I, painted
by Velásquez.

2 The library with its ornate, well-
stocked bookshelves.

Mallow Castle
Mallow, County Cork

damaged. William Jephson was so accomplished a soldier that Lord Inchiquin
wished to give him the command of the parliamentary forces in Munster, but
this was not permitted. Despite his love for the Cromwellian cause, Captain
William Jephson was devoted to his Irish property. His will stated that 'For
the encouragement of my wife to live in Ireland which I hope God will incline
her to do for her poor children's sake, I desire that she may live in my house at
Mallow, which I give to her for life… if she will live there until my son and heir
comes of age.' A bill survives from this period for one shilling and six pence as
payment for 'bows and arrows for Mr Jephson's son.'

Although the family was granted a charter in 1688 by James II, appointing
a provost with 26 burgesses, and the privilege of sending two members to
Parliament in Dublin, they continued in their opposition to any concept of
the 'Divine Right of Kings' and the castle was, perhaps predictably, burned by
order of that monarch in 1689. The upshot was that the Jephsons abandoned
the ruin and went to live in the old stables. From then on, thanks to James II,
they were able to treat Mallow as a pocket borough with the consequence that
from 1692 until 1800 every head of the family was also a Member of Parliament.

Major General Jephson's son, Colonel John Jephson, was Member of Parlia-
ment for Mallow between 1695 and 1698; he married the Honourable Elizabeth
Boyle, daughter of the 1st Viscount Shannon. Their son, William, married Lady
Anne Howard, the daughter of the 4th Earl of Suffolk. On William's death,
Mallow Castle passed eventually to his first cousin, Anthony, whose son Colonel
John Denham Jephson married Frances, the daughter of Sir John Aubrey.
Their son, another Denham, was followed by the colonel's cousin, Lieutenant
Colonel William Jephson, who was Judge Advocate of the King's forces in North
America between 1756 and 1761. The lieutenant colonel's second wife was the
Honourable Anne Butler, the daughter of the 10th Viscount Mountgarrett
(whose ancestor had tried to capture the castle in 1642) but it was his son by his
third wife, Louisa Kensington, who would eventually inherit Mallow Castle.

In the 18th century, Mallow was known as 'The Bath of Ireland' because of
all the social goings-on there. The gentry came from all over the country and

their wild behaviour gave them the name of 'The Rakes of Mallow'. A song bearing this title, first printed in 1740, gives a flavour of what Mallow was like in the reign of George II.

Beauing, belleing, dancing, drinking,
Breaking windows, cursing, sinking,
Ever raking, never thinking,
Live the Rakes of Mallow;
Spending faster than it comes,
Beating waiters, bailiffs, duns,
Bacchus' true begotten sons,
Live the Rakes of Mallow.

One time naught but claret drinking,
Then like politicians, thinking
To raise the 'sinking funds' when sinking.
Live the Rakes of Mallow.
When at home, with da-da dying,
Still for mellow water crying;
But, where there's good claret plying
Live the Rakes of Mallow.

Racking tenants, stewards teasing,
Swiftly spending, slowly raising,
Wishing to spend all their days in
Raking as at Mallow.
Then to end this raking life,
They get sober, take a wife,
Ever after live in strife,
And wish again for Mallow.

Another view of the society to be enjoyed in the town was given by a visitor in 1833, who reported that, 'The County of Cork abounds in handsome and populous towns, amongst these none are more worthy of the notice of the naturalist and antiquary than Mallow with its fine old castles, and salubrious waters, once held in such high esteem for the cure of diseases, and frequented accordingly ….The air of Mallow being accounted uncommonly pure, must have, both then and now, greatly contributed to its celebrity, as a chosen spot for the resort of invalids.'

The son of Lieutenant Colonel Jephson and Louisa Kensington was Sir Charles Denham Jephson-Norreys, who became the first (and last) member of his family to acquire an hereditary title when he was made a Baronet of Ireland, after a long career in Parliament. He was a friend of Daniel O'Connell and a supporter of Catholic Emancipation. Sir Denham looked into the possibility of restoring the old castle but decided that it would be prohibitively expensive. Accordingly, he extended the old stables in order to create the present Mallow Castle. To a great extent he was his own architect, although he is supposed to have drawn inspiration from Ockwells Manor in Berkshire, which had belonged to his family.

The baronet had intended to extend the house but never got around to it. He did, however, leave his plans and designs, as well as all of the stone cut and

Mallow Castle
Mallow, County Cork

ready for the task. It took 100 years, but in 1954 his eventual heir, Brigadier Jephson, added on the present entrance front, using the materials that Sir Denham had left for the purpose. Inside the castle, the drawing room and dining room open off each other and are panelled in elm of a striking orange colour. The staircase, in the best 'Jacobethan' 19th-century taste, is supposedly copied from the one at Ockwells. The carved oak chimneypieces were made by the estate carpenter and were designed by Sir Denham. There is a full-length portrait of William III, whose private secretary was William Jephson (the younger son of Cromwell's friend). The library has an oriel window, which looks out over the river and in the park is the famous herd of white deer.

Sir Denham Jephson lived to be almost 90 and died two months after his only son and heir, who was unmarried. His daughter inherited the estate and, on her death in 1911, she left it to her seventh cousin, Arthur Mounteney Jephson-Norreys, who descended from the younger brother of Oliver Cromwell's friend. In 1938, Arthur was killed in an accident on the London underground and was followed by his first cousin Brigadier Maurice Jephson, although Arthur's mother, Anna, was allowed to live in the castle until her death in 1954. Brigadier Jephson and his wife were killed in an air accident in 1968, and the estate passed to his first cousin once removed, Lieutenant Commander Maurice Jephson who had taken part in the sinking of the great German battleship *Bismarck*. In 1982, the naval gentleman quietly sold up his Castle with its 21 bedrooms and much reduced acreage (as well as 55 white deer) and left Mallow. It had taken nearly four centuries for the adventure to come to an end.

A early 17th-century house which was the first to be gothicized in Ireland. Once the home of the Earls and Marquesses of Drogheda, Moore Abbey is now owned by a religious order. They participate in an annual school to celebrate the life and works of the Jesuit poet Gerard Manley Hopkins.

Moore Abbey   *Monasterevin, County Kildare*

The Moore Abbey shown in these photographs is a house of three storeys high and 15 bays long. The windows on all the floors are exactly the same and have pointed glazing bars. The alterations to the porch and the front steps are the only real external changes since 1767, apart from the balustrade around the area. The gothic work added at this time gives a monumental appearance to what is still, essentially, a classical façade. Off the great hall are the staircase and the library, the latter has a set of fitted bookcases. The carved chimneypiece in the library came originally from the dining room.

MONASTEREVIN is on the River Barrow – an important strategic position because the river separated English- from Irish-held territories. Reserved, like the castles of Roscommon and Athlone, for the use of the Lord Deputy, the original house at Monasterevin was built on the site of a monastery, which, in various foundations, had stood there since at least the 10th century. The place was called after Saint Evin, a Munster man, who founded a monastery that was originally called Ros-Glaise (The Green Wood). This foundation acquired the nickname of 'Ros-Glaise na Muimhneach' (Ros Glas of the Men of Munster) because of the large number of monks from that province, who followed the saint to Kildare.

Diarmuid Ó Díomusaigh (Diarmuid O'Dempsey), the King of Offaly, became the Chief of Clann Molughra on his father's death in 1162 and he re-founded the Ros–Glaise monastery towards the end of the 12th century. This foundation became a mitred abbey with its abbot sitting as a baron in the Irish Parliament. In 1563, Owen O'Dempsey 'Chief Captain of his Nation' submitted to Elizabeth and surrendered his lands to the Crown. These were largely re-granted but were forfeited in 1641 and not restored by Charles II. In 1631, the O'Dempsey chief accepted the title of Viscount Clanmalier, the second and last of whom died in 1690.

At the Dissolution of the Monasteries the property passed to the Crown, and between 1556 and 1558 was converted to secular use. In 1596 Moore was described as having a 'fair hall, a stable, kitchens and other rooms'. In this year it was demised to the Earl of Essex who agreed to 'keep up

Previous page
Moore Abbey seen from the formal gardens

These pages
1 The great hall with its ornate wall panelling and decorative ceiling.
2 The gracious steps and entrance door of Moore Abbey.
3 The entrance front of the house.
4 A font in the gardens is a relic of the Cistercian monastery that once stood on this site.

Moore Abbey
*Monasterevin,
County Kildare*

and maintain the house of Evon with slate, thatching, and mud-walls, and other necessary repairs.' He also agreed to let the Lord Deputy use the house and 'its great stable, whenever he chose to live there', reserving only his own lodging for himself. The actual resident was probably Captain Warham St Leger, who received the Lord Deputy Russell there in the same year. As for Essex, he did not have much time left to enjoy his new property since he was beheaded for treason in 1601. Lord Mountjoy, the Lord Deputy, stayed there in 1600–1 during his winter campaign against the rebellious Irish.

In the meantime, the English had not been idle. Adam Loftus, who had arrived in Ireland as chaplain to the Earl of Sussex, became Archbishop of Dublin in 1567; by 1578, he was Lord Chancellor of Ireland. His daughter, Dorothy, married Sir John Moore, the scion of another family of English adventurers and soldiers of fortune, who arrived in Ireland during the reign of Elizabeth I. The fortunes of the Loftus and Moore families would intersect during the next hundred years, eventually leading to the lands of Monasterevin passing to the Moores.

The first Adam Loftus died in 1605. He was followed by his nephew, another Adam, who was created Viscount Loftus of Ely in 1622 and served as Lord

1 The view from the entrance hall into the great hall.
2 The library.
3 The library chimneypiece which was originally in the dining room.

Moore Abbey
Monasterevin,
County Kildare

1

Chancellor of Ireland between 1619 and 1638. He received the abbey and lands of Monasterevin from the Crown in 1613, but may have leased the property before that date since there is a stone with the date 1607 in one of the walls. There is also a series of strange carvings inserted into the walls of the present house that combine native Irish designs with early 16th-century Italian engravings. Lord Loftus built the house on the abbey site where he lived until Lord Wentworth's legislation forced him to pay a large sum of money in settlement of a very dubious claim. Wentworth is said to have held court in the present Great Hall. Loftus fell foul of Strafford and was imprisoned in Dublin Castle. On his release he left Ireland and died in York-

shire. His daughter married Charles Moore, later the 1st Earl of Drogheda.

Charles's great-grandfather, Sir Edward Moore, had came over from Kent with his brother, Sir Thomas. Sir Edward received a grant of Mellefont Abbey in County Louth in 1566 from Queen Elizabeth as part of the ongoing redistribution (or theft) of the Monastic lands in Ireland. His son Gerald was knighted by the Earl of Essex in 1599 for his part in smashing the attempt of Aodh Ó Néill – the Earl of Tyrone – to achieve an independent Gaelic Ireland. In 1616 Gerald was created Baron Moore of Mellefont by James I and in 1621–2 was raised a step in the peerage to become Viscount Moore of Drogheda.

A cannon shot in 1643 killed his son, the 2nd Viscount, who fought for the Parliament in the Civil War. In 1634, Lord Wentworth wrote about the Viscount's wife, a daughter of Lord Loftus of Ely, 'that unclean mouthed daughter of his busieth herself up and down the Court.' She conspired to betray Drogheda and Dundalk to the Parliamentary forces and was imprisoned in Dublin Castle in 1645. She died in 1649 'of a gangreene' as a result of breaking her leg in a fall from her horse. The 3rd Viscount was made Earl of Drogheda in 1661. He decided to develop the land that he owned in Dublin and named the new streets after himself and his countess. These names are mostly still with

us. He was Henry Moore, Earl of Drogheda, and his wife was called Mary; thus we have Henry Street, Moore Street, North and South Earl Streets as well as Mary Street.

The 3rd Earl was attainted by James II and fought at the Boyne on the side of William of Orange. Obviously fond of the bottle, the Earl is described, in 1701 during

1 The dining room.
2 The drawing room.

Moore Abbey
Monasterevin,
County Kildare

the proclamation of Queen Anne, by Ulster King of Arms, as being so bad with the gout that he was unable to get out of his coach. His grandson Henry Moore, the 4th Earl, inherited the property at Monasterevin and changed its name to Moore Abbey. The estate came to him because his mother, Jane, was the heiress of the 3rd, and last, Viscount Loftus of Ely. Profligate, the 4th Earl managed to amass £180,000 in debts before his death at the age of 27.

The heir to the title was his brother, who was married to Lady Sarah Ponsonby, daughter of the 1st Earl of Bessborough. In 1758, the earl and his son Edward were drowned on their way back to Dublin from England. Mrs Delaney wrote to a friend that the victims of this disaster included 'Lord Drogheda and his third son, a clergyman... a linen draper... a milliner who has left a necessitous family of six children... Mr Maddocks and Miss Wilkinson, the wire dancers... a great consolation that none of one's particular acquaintance have suffered'.

Lord Drogheda's heir was his second son, Charles. This nobleman was a founder Knight of the Most Illustrious Order of Saint Patrick. He was created Marquess of Drogheda in 1791 and even became a field marshal in 1821. He gothicized Moore Abbey in 1767 and, in so doing, created the first Gothic

Revival house in Ireland. It is worth mentioning that the abbey became so cold as a result of his second remodelling of the place in 1823, that on one occasion a heavy trunk belonging to a visitor fell open and several hundredweight of coal fell out. The cautious guest was John Scott, Earl of Clonmell and Lord Chief Justice of Ireland, who was notoriously venal and incompetent. When he had been Lord Chief Justice of Ireland for six years he wrote in his diary 'Resolved seriously to set about learning my profession'.

The *Anthologia Hibernica* magazine reported that 'Charles, the 6th Earl of Drogheda, in 1767, beautifully repaired the ancient abbey by enlarging the windows, placing a new roof and repartitioning the whole; preserving, however, the external walls and original form, except somewhat lengthening the eastern front. The great hall and the ancient door of the southern front still retain their primitive state, and the whole has the venerable appearance of all the Gothic structures. His Lordship also pulled down the old church, which stood near the monastery on the right side of the east front, and rebuilt it in a neat Gothic style at the other end of the town. He walled in the demesne with a high wall, except on the side near the river. This demesne contains about 1000 acres, nearly in the centre of which rises a large conical hill of 200 acres, well planted and

1   The gate lodge.
2   The formal gardens.

Moore Abbey
Monasterevin,
County Kildare

commanding an extensive and beautiful view of the country. Near the deer park, on the north side of the hill, are some remains of an ancient wood last occupied by one James O'Dempsey, commonly called Shamus na-Coppuil (Séamus na gCapall – 'James of the horses'), the highwayman'.

There was another side to the 1st Marquess's character. He was described, in retrospect (and with the shade of his uncle lurking in the background) as 'a very eccentric character, passionately fond of play, to which he was a victim all his life, and subjected to great pecuniary embarrassments. In his latter years his estates were put out to nurse and a moderate pension was allowed to him by his creditors'. Worse was to follow, for the 2nd Marquess was insane for the last 45 years of his life. He died in 1837 and, on the death of his undistinguished nephew in 1892, the marquessate became extinct. The earldom, however, passed to a cousin who, as the 9th Earl, was a Representative Peer for Ireland between 1899 and his death in 1909.

In 1883, the family estates consisted of 16,609 acres in County Kildare, centred on Moore Abbey, and 2688 acres in Queen's County (Laois). The Prince of Wales, later Edward VII, was entertained at Moore Abbey in 1861 at about the time that he was discovering the pleasures of the fair sex (in the form of Nellie Clifden) at the nearby Curragh Camp. Edward planted a tree in the grounds to commemorate the event. .

In 1927, the tenor John MacCormack leased Moore Abbey and remained there until 1938. He was created a Papal Count in 1928 in recognition of his services to Catholic charities. Lily, Countess MacCormack, related in her memoirs *I Hear You Calling Me* that the family and servants would gather in the 'truly baronial hall' after Midnight Mass and would be led by her husband in a rendition of 'Adeste Fideles'. '…I can see the Great Hall now, lighted by candles on the tree and in the sconces, with John playing heavenly music…'. His grandson, John, is the present Count MacCormack and is a successful restaurateur in Dublin.

After MacCormack left, Lord Drogheda sold the house to an order of Belgian nuns – the Sisters of Charity of Jesus and Mary – who still own and maintain the house, which they run as a hospital. Of all the houses featured in this book, this is the one that has found the most useful purpose, although the demesne is disfigured by a series of, doubtless practical but otherwise, horrendous new buildings. The 10th Earl of Drogheda, who sold the house, was created Baron Moore of Cobham, Surrey in 1954 as a reward for a long life of political service, during which he served from 1913 until his death in 1957 as one of the last Representative Peers for Ireland.

A magnificent mid-18th century mansion with early 20th-century additions, Mount Juliet was originally the home of the Earls of Carrick and more recently the McCalmont family. It is now a prestigious hotel with a world-class golf course.

Mount Juliet   *Thomastown, County Kilkenny*

In July 1776, traveller and writer Arthur Young wrote, 'viewed Mount Juliet, Lord Carrick's seat, which is beautifully situated on a fine declivity on the banks of the Nore, commanding some extensive plantations that spread over the hills, which rise in a various manner on the other side of the river: a knole of lawn rises among them, with artificial ruins upon it'. Almost 50 years later, J.N.Brewer commented that 'the mansion, which is spacious and of a very respectable character, is placed on rising ground, adorned in every direction with venerable wood or thriving plantations… the first Earl of Carrick erected the mansion of Mount Juliet… and gave it the appellation it now bears, in compliment to his wife Juliana, the daughter of Henry Boyle, first Earl of Shannon'.

AT ABOUT THE SAME TIME, the *Irish Tourist* wrote that 'Mount Juliet, the seat of the Earl of Carrick... is one of those grand objects which enrich and ornament the surface of this country, now (in common with some other districts of the island) steadily, though slowly elevating itself in the scale of British improvement. The plantations of this splendid demesne are composed of ash, elm and beech trees, many of which are full grown, and are as beautifully distributed, as they are valuable in their qualities.'

Mount Juliet was originally not one estate but two. The present demesne comprises the former estates of Ballylinch and Waton's Grove. The name of the latter was changed when Somerset Butler, 1st Earl of Carrick, bought the estate in 1750 and renamed it after his wife Juliana.

The Butlers first came to Ireland in the person of James le Botiller in 1290. For his support against the invasion of Edward Bruce in 1315, he was supposedly made Earl of Carrick, one of only 11 known Irish peerages that were created before 1500 but, for some reason, the title was never used. His son, James, was created Earl of Ormond in 1328 and his direct descendant, Sir Piers Butler, was made the 1st Viscount Ikerrin.

A century before the Butlers decided to come and live in Ireland, the Normans had arrived with Richard de Clare, Earl of Pembroke, at their head, ably assisted by his lieutenants Hugh de Lacy, John de Courcy and Raymond le Gros (the 'great' or the 'fat', depending on whether one claims to be descended from him or not). Ballylinch and the town land of Legan were part of the possessions of Jerpoint Abbey. After the dissolution of the monasteries, these lands came to Henry VIII, who granted

Previous page
The entrance hall with an equestrian bronze of Vinegar Hill in the foreground.

These pages
1   The long gallery.
2   The forecourt and entrance front of the house.
3   The garden façade overlooking the River Nore. This was originally the entrance front before changes made in the early 20th century.

Mount Juliet
Thomastown,
County Kilkenny.

Mount Juliet
Thomastown,
County Kilkenny.

them to his supporter, the Earl of Ormond. The Earl, in his turn, re-granted them to the Graces, who claimed descent from Raymond le Gros. They forfeited the property in the 1650s, and the lands passed into the possession of the Cromwellian Colonel Redman, whose daughter, Elinor, married the 3rd Viscount Ikerrin.

The original owners of the Waton's Grove estate were the Waton family. Like so many others, William Waton was dispossessed by Oliver Cromwell, and at the Restoration his family did not regain their lands, which were given to the King's brother, James, Duke of York. After the Glorious Revolution (as the treason of 1688 is known) the estate was sold and passed to a Mr Sweet who resold it in 1719 to a Mr Kendall. This gentleman bequeathed it, under very peculiar conditions (see p.145) to the Reverend Thomas Bushe, who sold it to Lord Carrick in 1750 to pay some of his mounting pile of debts.

The building of the new house commenced in 1760 and the earliest interiors have stucco work in the style of Patrick Osborne, an Irish stuccodore from Waterford; the anteroom to the right of the entrance hall has particularly fine rococo plasterwork. In 1774, the year he married, the 2nd Earl (Somerset Butler's son) decorated the principal rooms in the style of stuccodore Michael Stapleton. An imperial staircase rises up through arches in the entrance hall and all of the main rooms have superb plasterwork. It has been suggested that it was the stuccodore who decorated the town house of the Butlers in Patrick Street, Kilkenny who should be credited with the stucco work in the dining room at Mount Juliet, which was 'rich but less delicate' than Stapleton's usual manner. The house was finished in 1785.

The 7th Earl, Charles Butler, was created a peer of the United Kingdom in 1912 as Baron Butler of Mount Juliet. Despite this advancement, he decided, because of the cost of his children's education and other factors, to sell his family seat to General Sir Hugh McCalmont from County Antrim. Two of Sir Hugh's uncles had made fortunes in the City and he had been the tenant at Mount Juliet for some years. His son, Major Dermot McCalmont, founded the

Ballylinch stud, on that section of the estate, with the great 'spotted wonder' Tetrarch as its first stallion. As a two-year-old, Tetrarch failed to stand training and was brought to stud in 1915.

Mount Juliet now underwent some major surgery. The house was turned back to front so that the original entrance front, which overlooks the river Nore, became the garden façade, and a large ballroom was built (on the site of an 18th-century mock 'ruin') with plasterwork that was copied by a Dublin firm of plasterers in low relief from designs in the dining room.

The ballroom, which was reached by a curving gallery, was decorated in Wedgwood blue, while the dining room was pink and white. An impressive series of Adam-style chimneypieces was accumulated by the Honourable Lady McCalmont, so many in fact that there is one in almost every room (with some rooms having two). The library was later remodelled for the family by Don O'Neill Flanagan.

By the 1980s, despite being the largest employer in the Thomastown area, Major Victor McCalmont, Sir Hugh's grandson, who was Master of the

Mount Juliet
Thomastown,
County Kilkenny.

Kilkenny Hounds, was in financial trouble. He complained to a newspaper 'I can't keep going like this. I'm afraid I've got my back to the wall now. I'm living on a day to day basis at the moment.'

The house and estate were put on the market and, amid rumours that it was going to be bought by Robert Sangster, the racehorse owner and pools million-aire, it was sold in 1989 to Tim O'Mahony of Toyota Ireland, whose consortium, Kileen Investments, paid £2.5 million for the estate and then spent £25 million on turning it into a luxury hotel. But it was the decision to engage Jack Nicklaus to design an 18-hole, par 72, championship golf course that proved to be the winning stroke in their calculations. The estate has since hosted the Irish Open Golf Championship and the course is one of the finest in the world. Nicklaus remarked when he arrived to look at the estate, 'I think Mount Juliet gets high marks… it's just a beautiful piece of property on which to build a golf course.' Tim O'Mahony put it rather more succinctly when he remarked 'it's like having a Picasso in the basement'.

An ancillary development, The 'Hunter's Yard', was designed to be as 'a deliberate foil' to the main house – a place where one could remove 'muddy shoes, wellies or dripping rain gear'. It is situated in the old stable block, about a quarter of a mile from the main house. An article on this project admitted that 'by now virtually nothing remains of these old buildings, apart from an odd wall which is carefully identified in its design'. It continued, 'The instant "aging" of the building is quite deliberate and unashamed… we wanted to make buildings … slightly worn and shabby, like old but well-made clothes in which one feels at ease.'

The sale of the contents of the house took place in September 1986 and was handled by Sotheby's. Everybody has an off-day at one time or another, and this was Sotheby's. They sold a picture of Captain James Cook, which had a pre-sale estimate of £350–£450, to The Leger Gallery in London for £29,700. Everyone was happy about this, until it was discovered that the purchasers had sold it on, less than two years later, for a sum 'in excess' of £600,000. It turned out that the oil was by William Hodges and was the very portrait that had been executed during Cook's journey to the South Seas between 1772 and 1775 on board his ship *Resolution*. The work had been engraved in 1777 by James Basire and was presumed to have been lost. In fact, it had passed to Cook's commander in the *Eagle,* Admiral Sir Hugh Palliser of Chalfont St Giles in Buckinghamshire, and had been bought by Major McCalmont from the Admiral's heirs in 1902. When he heard this, Major Victor McCalmont and his wife, Bunny, were sanguine about the situation. He stated, as so many others might not have done in his position, 'I'm very disappointed that the money is not in my pocket. But it's no good crying over spilt milk.'

Rockfleet *Newport, County Mayo*

A late 18th-century house with 19th- and 20th-century additions, Rockfleet stands near the shore of Clew Bay. It has been home to the only woman alleged to have held the position of an Irish Chief, as well as to two distinguished diplomatists and their families.

Carrigahowley is a small, 16th-century tower house on the shore of Clew Bay, four storeys high with box machicolations (projecting galleries) on two opposing corners of the parapet. There are very few windows, but there are a number of narrow loops. Carrigahowley, or 'Carraig an Chabhlaigh' ('Rock of the Fleet of Ships') is the only residence that can be connected with certainty to Grace O'Malley. Grace, Gráinne Uaille or, more correctly, Gráinne Ní Mháille, is known to Irish history and folklore (the two tend to be intertwined) as 'The Queen of Clew Bay'. In point of fact, she was nothing of the sort, and, unfortunately, most of the tales that concern her are based more on fiction than on fact. The house known as Rockfleet stands near the tower house.

GRACE WAS BORN between 1530 and 1540, the daughter of Eoghan Dubhdara ('Black Oak') Ó Mháille, the Lord of Umhall Uachtarach (Upper Umhall) or the barony of Murrisk. Her father's people were described as 'manannáin' (sea gods) of the western ocean by the inhabitants of Mayo. To everybody else they were known as dangerous pirates. As a child, Grace accompanied her father on his marauding expeditions, and on his death she took over the leadership of the Murrisk O'Malley clan, since her brother was still a child. This was an extraordinary achievement for, despite its logic, it was completely contrary to the Brehon laws of succession in Gaelic Ireland.

In about 1546, Grace married Domhnall an Chogaidh (Donal 'of the Strife'), the son of Giolla Dubh Ó Flaithbheartaigh (O'Flaherty), the Lord of Iar Chonnacht and Connemara. This marriage lasted for about 15 years – the Joyces (the descendants of Cambro-Normans, who controlled a large part of County Galway, butchered him before 1561. Grace then married Sir Richard Fitz-David Bourke, The Mac William Uachtar, who was known in Irish as Riocard an Iarainn ('Richard of the Iron' or, less felicitously, 'Iron Dick'). Thanks to this match, she became Lady Bourke. Her eldest son by 'Iron Dick', Tióbóid na Long (Theobald of the Ships), would become the 1st Viscount Mayo.

Grace now turned to open piracy, which she called her 'trade of maintenance'. An old manuscript described her as 'a great pirate and plunderer from her youth'. She was finally proclaimed an outlaw and a reward of £500 was offered for the capture of – 'Grany O'Mayle, a woman that hath impudently passed the part of womanhood, and been a great spoiler and chief commander and director of thieves and murtherers at sea.' An attempt to capture her at Carrigahowly Castle failed after a siege that lasted for a fortnight.

Another tale has it that Grace acquired the castle by marrying her second husband Sir Richard Bourke on a trial basis for a year. At the end of which, having filled the place with her own people and got herself an heir, she dismissed him.

In 1576, Grace approached The Lord Deputy, Sir Henry Sidney, in an attempt at a *rapprochement* with Dublin Castle, but he rejected her overtures and wrote that 'she brought with her, her husband; for she was, as well by sea as by land, more than master-mate with him.' The unfortunate Sir Richard Bourke died in 1583, leaving Grace a widow for the second time. She now decided to cast her net wider than before and led a raiding party against the Geraldines in County Kerry. It was a disastrous undertaking. Captured by the Earl of Desmond and imprisoned for 18 months, no sooner was she released than she took to piracy once again. Her conduct led Sir Richard Bingham to write that she was 'a notable traitress and nurse to all the rebellions in Connacht for forty years.' Her son, Murchadh Ó Flaithbheartaigh (Murrough O'Flaherty), had made submission to the Crown and was never forgiven by his mother. Bingham recalled that 'she fell out of charity with Murrough, and having manned her navy of galleys, she landed at Ballynahinch, where he dwelt, burnt the town, destroyed his people's cattle and goods, and killed three or four of his men who resisted.'

Then she retired to Carrigahowley with 'all her own followers and one thousand head of cows and mares'. Grace did not take sides in the political conflicts of the age in which she lived. All were considered as fair game. Consequently, in 1558, when those ships that had escaped from the disastrous defeat of the Spanish Armada sailed into Clew Bay, she made short work of them, and their crews were summarily dealt with, an action which won the approbation of Queen Elizabeth. Seeing her opportunity, Grace decided that now was the time to make her

Previous page
The entrance front of Rockfleet, also known as Rossyvera.

Facing page
Carrigahowley (Carraig an Chabhlaigh) Castle.

Rockfleet
Newport, County Mayo

Rockfleet
Newport, County Mayo

1

submission to the queen but, being Grace O'Malley, she did not submit to Elizabeth's representative but went in person to the court in London in 1593. However, despite the stories, there is no evidence that Grace ever actually met the queen. When she was in London, she petitioned for the release of her sons , which was granted, and asked for her entitlement from her husband's lands, but this was refused. The Queen did, however, instruct Bingham to give her 'some maintenance for her living the rest of her old years.'

There is a famous tale that on her way back from the Queen, Grace was refused hospitality by Lord Howth. In revenge, she seized his infant son, taking him back to Mayo with her and only returning him after she was given a promise that a place would be laid at Howth Castle from that day forwards for the O'Malleys – just in case a member of that family might happen to be passing and be in need of refreshment. There are serious flaws in this account of events. For one thing, the Lord Howth in the 1590s had no infant son to be kidnapped by anyone. But the legend is so well known (and a place is still laid at Howth Castle) that it is not impossible she might have kidnapped some member of Lord Howth's family.

Interestingly, a similar legend concerns Ricard Ó Cuairsge Bourke, Lord of the macWilliams from 1469 until 1479 (and a collateral ancestor of Grace's late husband). This version has it that it was this Risteárd (or Richard) Bourke who seized Lord Howth and, as part of his ransom, insisted that the head of the St Lawrence family should always 'keep the door of his Court open at dinner time'. Perhaps the facts and the legend have become so mixed that it will never be possible to know the truth of the story.

Grace made a second trip to London in 1595 and died at some date after 1601 for, in that year, one of her galleys was captured with 100 musketeers on board by an English ship. She is allegedly buried on Clare Island in Clew Bay.

Rossyvera House, or Rockfleet, is near to the tower house of Carrigahowly. It has been suggested that it was originally a dower-house or an estate agent's house for the O'Donel family, who lived at Newport House. (Newport is a small village, ten miles west of Castlebar in the northeast corner of Clew Bay.)

However, there is an account that it was built as 'a nice neat house' by a family by the name of Arbuthnot.

In the 19th century the house came into the possession of the Stoney family. They had come from England in the 17th century and in the 19th century, James Stoney (1814–97), a Justice of the Peace, is known to have lived at Ross-y-Vera (as it was spelt). His family cannot have owned the house after his time because James's elder son, Robert, lived at Rosturk Castle, near Mulrany in County Mayo and at Knockadoo in County Roscommon (which was his mother's estate), while the younger son, Thomas, resided at Oakfield Park, near Raphoe in County Donegal.

The next name that is associated with Rossyvera is that of Sir Owen St Clair O'Malley. Sir Owen described himself as 'an autochthonous Irishman' and was one of the O'Malleys of Belclare. This branch of the family lived at Hawthorn Lodge (or 'Tallyho' as it was originally named), near Castlebar in County Mayo. One of this family was created a Count of the Holy Roman Empire and another, Loughlin O'Malley, conformed to the Established Church in 1718. His great-grandson, Peter O'Malley QC, moved to England in the mid-19th century and became the Recorder of Norwich. His son, Sir Edward, was variously Attorney General of Jamaica and Hong Kong and eventually Chief Judge of H.M. Supreme Consular Court for the Ottoman Empire. Sir Owen O'Malley was Sir Edward's son. He entered the diplomatic service in 1911 and the next year married Mary Saunders. During a long career, he was accredited to Peking, Mexico, Spain and Hungary and, as the Ambassador to the Polish government in exile during the latter part of World War II, he was responsible for compiling the damning report that finally placed the blame for the murder of over 10,000 Polish officers in Katyn Forest at the door of the Soviet Union. Sir Owen was finally appointed as Ambassador to Portugal, a posting he held until he retired in 1947.

On Sir Owen's retirement, he and Lady O'Malley began remodelling and enlarging Rossyvera – it is recorded that Sir Owen built the additions with his own hands. They added a two-bay wing to the original three-bay house, an extra storey with a flat roof, as well as a cupola on the top of the staircase hall. There

[*181*]

1 The octagonal drawing room, added during Sir Owen O'Malley's 20th-century renovations.
2 The oval hall, with a portrait by Gainsborough Dupont (1754–1797).

Rockfleet
Newport, County Mayo

is an elliptical hall and a spiral staircase, the three original reception rooms are now four – one of which is an octagon shape – and there are nine bedrooms. The library bookcases and the dining room chimneypiece are made out of macacauba wood, an exotic oriental timber used by Sir Owen to make cases for his possessions when he moved from Portugal to Ireland. With a view to reusing the timber, he instructed his packers to employ screws rather than nails when fastening the timber.

In the 1950s, Sir Owen O'Malley and the O'Malley Clan Association restored Carrigahowley Castle (which had been used, at one period, by a family called Flynn for storing hay) and it is now a National Monument. He wrote a history of the O'Malley lordship in the 16th century in *The Galway Archaeological and Historical Journal* (1950).

Sir Owen sold Rockfleet (the name is a contraction of the anglicization of Carrigahowley) in 1955, and moved to Oxford, where he died in 1974, a month after his wife. The new owner of the house was Carmel Snow, the editor-in-chief of *Harper's Bazaar* and the doyenne of fashion writers during the 1930s and 40s – Diana Vreeland was her fashion editor. It was she who made the pronouncement that 'elegance is good taste plus a dash of daring.' No sooner had Carmel Snow moved to her new home in County Mayo than she restored its original name of Rossyvera.

In 1957, Rossyvera was bought by Walter P. Curley and his wife, Mary. After a successful career in venture capital, Walter Curley served as the Ambassador of the United States of America to Ireland from 1975 to 1977 (under Presidents Ford and Carter), and later, from 1989 to 1993, as his country's Ambassador to France (under President Bush). Ambassador Curley is of Irish ancestry – his name is, more properly, spelt as Mac Thoirdealbhaigh. The author of *Letters from the Pacific* and *Monarchs in Waiting*, he is currently involved in writing a book on the Clan Chiefs of Ireland. Ambassador and Mrs Curley now live at Rossyvera for several months a year.

1 | 2

Rockingham
near Boyle, County Roscommon

As originally designed, Rockingham was the most
beautiful neoclassical house in Ireland, set in parkland
of unsurpassed loveliness, but it was later altered
and twice burnt out. The house was taken over by
the Irish State and demolished and a national
park established in the demesne.

Carraig Locha Cé (Rockingham) was originally a part of the lands of Moylurg, the seat of the MacDermot, but centuries of undisputed rule and patronage ended with the arrival of the Normans in Connacht. The MacDermot family was eventually reduced to the possession of a small tract of land beside Lough Gara. There, in a little house called Coolavin, The MacDermot, formerly the king of the great Territory of Moylurg (Mac Diarmada Mhaighe Luirg), made his home. In 1780, the writer and traveller Arthur Young went to see him and recalled that he was 'making the best of his affairs', called himself 'Prince of Coolavin', and 'though he has not even £100 a year will not permit his children to sit down in his presence.'

THE KING FAMILY were traditional English adventurers, anglicized versions of the 'Mick on the Make'. With the exception of a single member, Edward King, they were almost universally objectionable during their time in Ireland. Their blood was somewhat improved when it started to flow through female lines of descent, but even this would not be enough to save them. The first of the gang to arrive in Ireland was John King, who obtained a lease on the Abbey of Boyle from Elizabeth I. The family climbed the greasy pole up to a baronetcy and in 1764 the head of the family, Edward King of Rockingham, the second son of Henry King, the 3rd Baronet, became Baron Kingston of Rockingham. Two years later he rose a step in the peerage to Viscount Kingston and in 1768 he was created Earl of Kingston.

The family lived in their splendid (and recently restored) town house at Boyle, but it was the 1st Earl who decided to build a residence on his demesne at Rockingham. Robert, the 2nd Earl, was tried for the murder of Colonel Fitzgerald, the illegitimate son of his brother-in-law who 'with circumstances that were particularly dishonourable' seduced and then eloped with his daughter.

The Earl was tried by his peers in Dublin and had the sympathy of their lordships from the start. The full panoply of state was trotted out for this, only the third trial of a peer in Ireland. There was, of course, a full house with all the other peers decked out in their parliamentary robes for the occasion. A member of the public, dressed up to look like the public executioner, stood beside the accused throughout the trial armed with an axe, the blade held raised during the whole of the proceedings. If the verdict were guilty, then the axe would be turned towards his Lordship's neck, in order to indicate the inescapable sentence – although at this date (following the splendid example set by the late Earl Ferrers) it would probably have ended in a hanging with a silken rope rather than a beheading. As it turned out, no witnesses appeared for the prosecution and so each of the peers declared that Robert, Earl of Kingston, was 'Not Guilty, upon mine honour.' The Lord Chancellor then broke his wand of office and the peer was declared to be acquitted.

This Lord Kingston was the public-spirited individual who is credited with the invention of the 'pitch cap', a diabolic form of torture whereby the victim's head is liberally covered in pitch which is then set alight. It was much used immediately before and during the 1798 rebellion (cynics have even suggested that its use might have contributed, in some small way, to the outbreak of that unfortunate incident). With an eye to a fortune, he had married the heiress of the Fitzgibbons, the head of which family was known as the White Knight. She had brought as her dowry the vast estates in County Cork that became the seat of the future earls. Rockingham passed to their second son, Robert King, who had been jointly charged with his father for the murder of Colonel Fitzgerald and, like his father, found innocent of the charge.

The Act of Union brought Robert King an Irish barony as Lord Erris of Boyle. This was improved on six years later when the Viscountcy of Lorton was bestowed on him, and in 1810 he engaged John Nash to build him a grand neoclassical mansion on the shores of Lough Key. The house was originally of two storeys over a basement, which was underground, roofed over by lawns. Fuel was brought in boats across Lough Key and taken into the house through one of several tunnels; another tunnel was used for delivering other goods by land, while the servants used a third to reach the stable yard where they slept.

Previous page
The south front seen from across the parkland.

Facing page
The north front overlooking Lough Key. The third storey was added in 1822 by the 1st Viscount Lorton.

Rockingham
near Boyle,
County Roscommon

1 The elegant entrance hall with its
   screen of Corinthian columns.
2 John Nash's original design for the
   house had a curved central bow and a
   colonnade of Ionic columns. The dome
   over this section was removed in the
   alterations to the house in 1822.

Rockingham
near Boyle,
County Roscommon

In *The Statistical Survey of Roscommon* of 1832, Isaac Weld wrote about the landscape 'No office of any kind being visible, but the whole being surrounded by smooth, shorn grass interspersed with beds of flowers and ornamental walks … subterranean passages carried from underneath the eminence on which the house stands towards the stables, which stand at a considerable distance screened by trees; the covered passage… does not reach the whole way to the latter, but merely far enough to prevent the appearance of movement near the mansion.' When the house was burned down in 1863, the tunnels were retained.

The garden, or lake, front had a curved central bow with a colonnade of Ionic columns. On either side of the bow, at ground floor level, were three windows with curved tops flanked by statues placed in niches. These three windows were framed by four recessed Ionic pilasters and over them was a pair of sphinxes. A dome surmounted the central section of this elevation, but in 1822 the 1st Viscount removed the dome and added an extra storey to provide more bedrooms. It may have been a practical solution for the problems of sleeping accommodation, but it destroyed the beauty of Nash's design. On the entrance front, an Ionic porte-cochère was added at about this time. The sphinxes, the pilasters and the statues disappeared in either 1822 or 1863. A conservatory was built at

the opposite end to the entrance, and plate glass was introduced into the windows. The most impressive room was the entrance hall, which had a coved ceiling. This apartment was divided from an imperial staircase by a screen of Corinthian columns. A fire in 1863 led to further alterations, which did nothing to improve the look of the house.

Robert, 1st Viscount Lorton, served as a Representative Peer for Ireland between 1823 and 1854. By this time it had become obvious that the senior branch of the family going to die out and that, in consequence, the Earldom of Kingston would pass to the Lortons. The 2nd Viscount accordingly arranged that Rockingham would pass to his second son, Laurence, who took the additional surname of Harman (when he married the heiress of that family from County Longford). Under this settlement Lord Lorton's heir Robert retained the right to reside in the mansion, and he arrived one day bringing his mother, who was estranged from her husband. Lord Lorton was informed and he attempted to prevent his wife from getting into the house. Nonetheless, she arrived with Robert and her youngest son Henry and pushed her way into the house to take possession. Lorton ordered that his wife and sons should be ejected by force if necessary and locked the gates. He tried to starve them out and, although some of the workers did side with her ladyship (as well as the

local curate, a Mr Ward), the siege of Rockingham lasted for almost three months before the party decamped from the house.

The Earldom had been through awkward times since it had been created. The 3rd Earl, Robert's older brother and known as 'Big George', was unintentionally the cause of the death of his son and heir. This gentleman, Lord Kingsborough, had stood surety for some of his father's debts and, since they were unpaid, he was committed to the Sheriff's prison in

Dublin. As a result of drinking the water there, he contracted typhus fever and died in the gaol. His father, jealous of his younger brother Robert's palatial home at Rockingham, had engaged the Pain brothers (who had come to Ireland to assist John Nash) to build him a new castle at Mitchelstown in order to outdo his brother's mansion, his only instruction to his architects being that it was to be bigger than any other house in Ireland. He eventually went mad after his tenants rejected his candidate in an election. 'They are coming to tear me in pieces!' he is said to have shrieked. After that, it was off to a lunatic asylum in London for the rest of his life.

Affairs did not improve for the family. The 4th Earl, Robert King, (described as 'a very weak minded man, wholly governed by whatever may be his favourite at the moment… he generally selects from the most vulgar of people') was charged in 1848 with sodomy, but failed to appear for his trial. He had been bankrupted four years earlier; his castle had been under siege from his creditors and the great doors had to be forced. By 1860 he was making a series of court appearances charged with drunkenness, assaulting the police and even failing to pay his cab fares. The family, and the establishment, decided to put him safely out of harm's way and in 1860 had him declared to be of unsound mind. He was followed as 5th Earl, for a brief two years, by his younger brother, on whose death the peerage passed to his cousin, the 2nd Viscount Lorton, who died a mere six weeks after becoming the 6th Earl.

Laurence King-Harman (the son of the 6th Earl, who inherited Rockingham) was followed by his son Colonel Edward. Of imposing stature, Edward was known as 'The King'. A brawler, who nearly died when he was stabbed in a public house in Sligo, he was a member of parliament for the Home Rule Party at a time when popular representation was passing out of the hands of the landed classes. He received about £8000 a year from rents which, but for encumbrances, would have brought him nearer to £40,000. Despite the drastic fall in his rents, he was a kind-hearted man who would forgo rents if he knew that his tenants were in difficulties. By 1882, however, the Land War had forced a drop in his rent roll of some 20 per cent, which removed, at a stroke, the remaining £8000 per annum that his rents gave him. Despite this setback, which would have finished lesser men, the Colonel determined to keep going. An opinion of him was expressed by the journalist Jasper Tully, who wrote 'breeding may confer titles, but it cannot confer brains'.

In 1883, the King family estates consisted of 24,421 acres in County Cork, based around Mitchelstown Castle, and 250 acres in County Limerick – these brought in an annual income of £17,950. In addition, there were 17,726 acres in County Roscommon, with Rockingham at their heart; 1783 acres in County Sligo; 1554 acres in County Leitrim; 196 acres in Dublin and 48 acres in County Westmeath, which had an accumulated rent roll of some £9064 a year.

The 'King's' daughter married Dr Thomas Stafford, a Catholic gentleman who nonetheless agreed to their children being brought up as Protestants. He eventually received a baronetcy (although for his medical services rather than for his ecumenism). The house was let to the Viceroy Lord Dudley among others at the turn of the 20th century. It was even suggested as a suitable residence for a member of the royal family, which, in the mood of the early 20th century was wishful thinking indeed.

There is a story told about the time that Sir Thomas Stafford's sons, Edward and Cecil Stafford-King-Harman, went to stay with their neighbours, the Gore-Booth family, at their home, Lissadell. They arrived rather late and then, to make matters worse, Edward mistook Sir Josslyn Gore-Booth for the butler and handed him his hat and coat. There was a ball after dinner and the young men got to bed not so much late as early. They were awakened before dawn by the real butler, Kilgallon, who told them that they had to go. They protested

Rockingham
near Boyle,
County Roscommon

that they had, in fact, only just arrived, but the butler said that they had to leave at once, 'those are my orders.' And so it was that, at 8 o'clock in the morning, the brothers found themselves on the Sligo train bound for Rockingham. They felt very insulted until they discovered that Sir Josslyn was also offended by their behaviour. It transpired that the butler Kilgallon had taken a dislike to the manners of the two young men and decided to take matters into his own hands and send them away.

When Edward Stafford-King-Harman came of age in 1912, 5000 people gathered for tea, sports and fireworks in the demesne. He married Olive Pakenham-Mahon in July 1914. Mercifully, they were not tempted to follow his family's practice and hyphenate her surname with his. He was the heir to Rockingham and she was the heiress of Strokestown Park in the same county. The tenanted farms however had been sold as a result of the Wyndham Act and these large properties were expensive to run. World War I began less than a month later, and in November, Edward was killed in the trenches. His brother Cecil inherited the estate and the title and came to live at Rockingham in 1929.

During 'The Troubles' (as the bloody internecine Irish Civil war of the 1920s is now euphemistically called), the future president, Eamon de Valera hid in a bog beside Lough Key, and the house survived the burnings of those years. Sir Cecil's son, Thomas, came of age in 1942 and 200 people came to his party – he was killed less than two years later. The family stayed on and employed the architect Philip Tilden to make the house more manageable. Tilden closed off the basement and the top floor and brought the kitchen upstairs. In a strange twist of fate, Sir Cecil agreed to serve on President de Valera's Council of State. In 1957 the house was burnt out again, and Sir Cecil sold the estate to the Department of Lands.

When the state took over the demesne in 1958, the house was unroofed but otherwise intact; even the glass was still in the windows of the conservatory. The church still had its pews and the lodges were in good shape, as were the bridges. But government mandarins had their own vision of what should be done with a great country house demesne in the new Republic. Consequently, the house was demolished, nothing was done to prevent the vandalizing of the bridges in the demesne (they had not been harmed when the King family were the owners) and the red cedars were cut down. The powers that be did provide a huge ugly concrete viewing tower – the 'Moylug' Tower – on the site of what had once been one of the most extraordinarily beautiful houses in Ireland. This erection has been correctly described by Jeremy Williams, as 'triumphant brutalism'.

The beech walk at Rockingham, which was three-quarters of a mile long.

Rockingham
near Boyle,
County Roscommon

Further to emphasise their plans for the demesne, they built this edifice in concrete rather than in stone, and provided new 'Scandinavian style' wooden reception buildings (instead of converting the old stone ones that had survived). There was talk of massive development of the area (in conjunction with private enterprise) and, just to show that they hadn't missed a trick, the civil servants built large tarmac car parks, as well as a huge caravan site, in the demesne.

The King family and the Irish government do not come well out of this story. Only the house was important – and that has gone. The 11th Earl of Kingston now lives in a flat in North London and, just before Christmas 2000, he married for a fourth time.

The largest of John Nash's four Irish castles, Shanbally was in excellent condition when the protectors of Ireland's heritage in the Irish civil service decided to allow its demolition. Roofed and in good repair at the time it was pulled down, Shanbally's destruction was one of the most pointless acts of official vandalism in the history of the Irish State.

Shanbally Castle   *Clogheen, County Tipperary*

Of all the 'lost' houses in this collection, Shanbally Castle is the most tragic. Not only was the building of the first importance in the history of Irish domestic architecture but it was also in good and complete condition before it fell foul of the crass ignorance and prejudice of the bureaucrats who decided to destroy it. It was the largest castle that John Nash ever built in Ireland – Nash was the Prince Regent's architect, and his white terraces and wide thoroughfares, such as Regent Street, may still be seen in London. Nash's other castles in Ireland were Ravensworth, Caerhays and Aqualate. Shanbally also had the distinction that it was built, not for the descendant of some Cromwellian carpetbagger, but for the scion of an old Irish family, Cornelius O'Callaghan.

THE O'CALLAGHANS held the lands at Shanbally (Seanbhaile or 'the old town') for as long as written records go back. Thomas O'Callaghan of Shanbally married Sarah, the daughter of John Davis and his wife, the Honourable Ann Caulfield, daughter of the 2nd Viscount Caulfield. Thomas and Sarah's son, Cornelius O'Callaghan was the member for Fethard in four parliaments in Dublin from 1761 until 1785, when he was raised to the peerage as Baron Lismore of Shanbally. In true parliamentary fashion, he married Frances Ponsonby, daughter of the Right Honourable John Ponsonby, Speaker of the Irish House of Commons in Grattan's parliament.

Their heir was Cornelius O'Callaghan, 2nd Baron Lismore, who was raised to a viscountcy in 1806. He engaged John Nash to design Shanbally Castle, which was situated in a Reptonian landscape, bounded by the Galtee and Knockmealdown mountain ranges and overlooking a lake. In 1807, Cornelius made an unsuccessful attempt to be elected as a Representative Peer of Ireland. He eventually got to parliament in 1838, when he was created Baron Lismore of Shanbally Castle in the peerage of the United Kingdom – one of Queen Victoria's coronation peerages. Cornelius was Lord Lieutenant of County Tipperary in 1851, but scandal followed in 1856 when he divorced his wife Lady Eleanor Butler, the daughter of the Earl of Ormond and Ossory. Cornelius died at Shanbally Castle, the house he had commissioned.

His son, George Ponsonby O'Callaghan, 2nd Viscount Lismore, married Mary Norbury in 1839. He was Sheriff of County Tipperary in 1853 and Lord Lieutenant of the county between 1857 and 1885. His only son, the Honourable George Cornelius O'Callaghan, married Rosina, the widow of Edward Follett, at Umballa in India in 1874, but died childless at only 39. The 2nd Viscount was a Liberal until 1886 in which year, and in opposition to Gladstone's attempts to introduce Home Rule for Ireland, he left the party, but he remained a Unionist. The Government offered him the Order of Saint Patrick in 1864 but he declined the honour and the peerages died with him in 1898. His will was proved at £20,000. His lordship was a victim of the Land War that took place during the 1880s, and he had a lot of land to be worried about. In 1883, his

Previous page
The castle seen from its extensive park.

These pages
1   The garden front.
2   The summerhouse, near the lake in the park. This is now all that remains of Shanbally.
3   The garden front.

Shanbally Castle
Clogheen, County Tipperary

estates comprised 34,945 acres in County Tipperary, together with Shanbally Castle (1000 acres were all that was left in 1954 to be sold to the Land Commission), 6067 acres in County Cork and 1194 acres in County Limerick – making a total of 42,206 acres with an annual rent roll of £16,354.

The castle then passed through the female line. It escaped the mad phase of house burnings that took place during the War of Independence, although the IRA did use it in 1921 as a training centre. When peace returned, two daughters of the Marquess of Ormonde, Lady Constance Butler and her sister, Lady Beatrice Pole-Carew, occupied the castle almost until the time of its destruction. After Lady Beatrice died, there was a five-day sale of the contents of the house, but Lady Constance continued to live in a wing of Shanbally until well after World War II.

In 1954, the Land Commission acquired 750 acres of arable land and 250 acres of woodland, as well as Shanbally Castle and by 1957 it had been decided that Nash's fine house should be levelled to the ground. It was not dangerous – not yet. First the civil servants gave instructions to remove the roof and the fitments. Then, in a wicked act of destruction the battlements were hacked down. This drew a protest from Professor Denis Gwynn, Chairman of the Cork Advisory

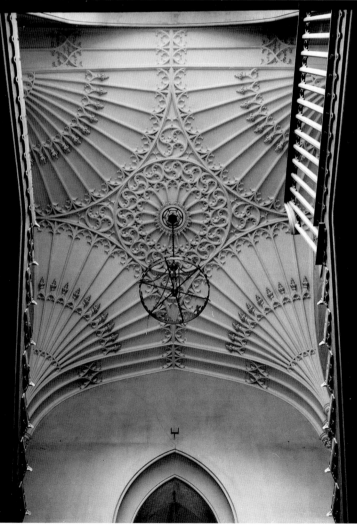

Group of the Arts Council, to the Minister of Lands, Erskine Childers. He received a reply stating that the Minister would be unavailable until mid-October, but would give the matter his fullest attention when he returned to work.

The demolition started in September. The beautiful lawn trees at Shanbally were cut down and 'rapidly carted away.' Despite the attempts of a religious community (and of Edward Sackville, 5th Lord Sackville of Knole) to buy it, the Land Commission sold the castle to a Limerick firm who razed it to the ground in order to salvage materials from the ruins. A Limerick auctioneer sold these at public auction. The philistines who did this were merely symptomatic of the general attitude of the population at the time. The Land Commission issued the following notice: 'The beautiful cut stone of the Castle will no doubt be put to practical use.'

The Government Information Bureau, in an attempt to defend the vandalism, issued the following lie, 'apart from periods of military occupation the castle has remained wholly unoccupied for 40 years.' This attempt at deception was shown up for what it was when letters arrived at the newspapers from people who had bought items at the sale of the castle's contents less than 20 years before. Indeed, a part of it had been lived in until a few years before its destruction. Undaunted by the truth, the government decided to press ahead with the demolition and the breaking up of the cut stone for the 'practical use' of surfacing roads.

Finally, in 1960, explosives had to be used to demolish what remained of the castle, so well had it been built. According to one newspaper report, the stone walls were demolished with 'one big bang' by charges of gelignite after demolition experts had bored no fewer than 1400 holes into the walls about 18 inches from the ground.

When the government apologists wrote that that the castle was in a dangerous state, Professor Gwynn: replied that 'Shanbally Castle would not even have been a ruin if the Government had not authorised the removal of its roof and interior fittings.' He went on about this wanton destruction 'the slate and finely cut stone and the beautiful ornamented ceilings are already littering the ground,' and reminded his readers that it could have been restored for a fraction of the cost

1 The staircase leading from the gallery.
2 The splendid fan-vaulted ceiling of the staircase.
3 The top-lit gallery, which occupied the same position at Shanbally as the one built by Nash at Rockingham.
4 The dining room which was in the great round tower and was lit by three lancet windows.

Shanbally Castle
Clogheen, County Tipperary

1 The view from the terrace across the parkland.
2 The garden front of the castle during its demolition.
3 The view across the drawing room to the library.
4 The library, a gracious room lit by three gothic windows.

Shanbally Castle
Clogheen, County Tipperary

of its destruction. The *Cork Examiner* commented, in 1957, 'Unless the present trends of the Department of Lands are stayed, there will be nothing in fifty years left to link the age of the Norman castle tower as a habitation, and the latest concrete semi-detached council house.'

In its heyday, Shanbally Castle was entered under a porte-cochère, which led into the entrance hall. This was divided from the billiard room by a gothic arch. Directly beyond this lay a great top-lit gallery, at one end of which (and separated from it by another gothic arch) was an imperial staircase. Both these rooms had fan-vaulted ceilings, while the ceilings in the other main rooms of the castle had excellent gothic plasterwork. To the right of the entrance hall was the dining room, while the garden front of the castle had, from left to right, the following; a dining room in the great round tower, lit by three lancet windows; a library, which occupied the central section of this front (also lit by three gothic windows); and, farther on, there was a conservatory of six bays with pointed windows. All of this has gone, a victim of an ignorant mentality. A two-storey summerhouse down by the lake is all that remains of a house and a demesne which, if the government had allowed it to survive, would today be one of the treasures of Ireland's heritage.

Shelton Abbey   *Arklow, County Wicklow*

A superb house in a magical setting, Shelton
was designed by the Morrisons for the 4th
Earl of Wicklow. It was sold to the Irish
State in 1951 and is presently an open prison.
The interiors have been mostly gutted and
more than half of the structure, including
the original 17th-century house,
has been demolished.

'The monstrous practice of castle-building' was the phrase applied by Sir George Gilbert Scott, in his *Remarks on Secular and Domestic Architecture* to the fashion in the middle of the 19th century for erecting mock castles. This opinion was a reaction to the plethora of gothic residences that had sprung up over the preceding 60 years in Great Britain and Ireland, with the latter kingdom proving to be an especially fertile ground for such creations. Castles conjured up the idea of security, so useful after the French Revolution, the Napoleonic Wars and, closer to home, the rebellion of 1798. They also suited the Irish temperament with its love of antiquity and show. To live in one implied an ancient ancestry, even if the stucco inside the building and the paint upon one's newly acquired coat of arms were scarcely dry.

ONE SUCH CASTELLATED MANSION was Shelton Abbey, the home of the Howard family. It is alleged that Ralph Howard, who became a physician in Dublin, was the first of the Howard family to arrive in Ireland and that he married a Mrs Hazells, the widow of a Cromwellian adventurer who had acquired a lease on the Shelton and North Arklow estates of the Duke of Ormonde. John O'Donovan, however, states that there was a marble headstone in Kilbride churchyard that recorded the burial in 1684 of Dorothea Howard, the widow of Mr 'Hasells', and the relict of John Howard. If accurate, this would imply that it was Dr Ralph's father John, who died in 1643, who first came to Ireland and would explain how his son Ralph came to study medicine at the University of Dublin. Whatever the truth of the matter, it was Dr Ralph who secured the Wicklow lands in either 1658 or 1665 by means of a renewed lease. Despite owning estates in County Wicklow, he chose to reside in town at his house in Great Ship Street, beside Dublin Castle. As an opponent of James II, he was attainted in 1688 and fled to England with his family.

In his absence, his estate was given to a Mr Hacket. There is a tradition that James II stopped at Shelton as a guest of this Mr Hacket after the Battle of the Boyne and during his flight to Waterford. There is a path in the demesne that is still known as 'King James Road'. The story claiming that James visited the

house also alleges that his nose bled as he leaned against the front door of the house; that the piece of wood was then cut out and was kept as a relic until a servant girl, mistaking it for a piece of kindling, consigned it to the fire. There are, however, as many tales concerning James II and his nosebleeds as there are locks of hair allegedly given away by his grandson, Prince Charles Edward. In 1697, Dr Ralph Howard acquired the freehold of the Shelton estate.

The family were in ignorance of their antecedents before the lifetime of Dr Howard's father, John Howard. This little detail did not stop them buying from Ulster King of Arms, the Principal Herald of All Ireland, the coat of arms (without the Flodden augmentation) of the Duke of Norfolk, who surname is also Howard, in order to pretend that they were in some way or other related to the illustrious family of the Earls Marshal of England. It was a fraudulent transaction and Ulster should have known better. He had no more right to dispose of the duke's arms to strangers than he could have sold to them His Grace's Castle at Arundel. These false arms were later amended in 1780 when the future 3rd Earl of Wicklow inherited the Forward estates in Donegal and, as a condition of the inheritance, quartered the Forward and Howard Arms on his coat. He also, at this date, changed his surname by Royal Licence to Forward, although in 1815 he hyphenated this with his original surname, thus becoming Forward-Howard.

Previous page
The small drawing room, which opens into the large drawing room. Both are on the garden front of the Abbey.

These pages
1 The entrance front seen from the southeast with the crenellations and pinnacles commissioned by the 4th Earl of Wicklow in 1818. The conical tower on the left has been demolished.
2 The library – this has been gutted and the plasterwork and bookcases destroyed. The room is now divided into offices.

Shelton Abbey
Arklow, County Wicklow

Shelton Abbey
Arklow, County Wicklow

Dr Ralph's eldest son, Hugh, was the Paymaster of the Board of Works in England; he died unmarried in London in 1726. William, the doctor's youngest son, was elected a Member of Parliament for Dublin in 1727, but did not live long to enjoy the position, since he died in the following year. He bequeathed his library of books to his surviving brother, Bishop Robert. They had belonged to Lord Chancellor West and, until their sale by the last Earl of Wicklow, they formed at Shelton the nucleus of one of the great private libraries in Ireland.

In 1729, Dr Howard's remaining son, Robert, until then the Bishop of Killala, was translated to the Bishopric of Elphin. It was Robert's son who was elevated to the Barony of Clonmore in 1776 and to the Viscountcy of Wicklow in 1785. After his demise in 1793, his widow, formerly Alice Forward from County Donegal, was created Countess of Wicklow in her own right. The 2nd Earl, William, a man fond of his drink was described as 'quite imbibed with such a strong sense of religion as enabled him to bear up against a most serious indisposition [the gout]… [which] deprived him of the pleasures of society'.

The 4th Earl of Wicklow inherited the lands of Shelton, near Arklow in County Wicklow, in 1818. With the demesne he also acquired a large, plain, 11-bay Georgian house, built in 1770 by Ralph Howard, 1st Viscount Wicklow, which had replaced a 17th-century residence on approximately the same site. The new earl immediately commissioned the architect William Vitruvius Morrison to turn the Georgian house into a castellated mansion. In 1811 the Howard family had engaged William's father, Richard Morrison, to adapt and enlarge a modest building in the same county for Lord Wicklow's uncle, Colonel Robert Howard. This is Castle Howard, which overlooks the 'Meeting of the Waters' in the Vale of Avoca. For this residence, due to its location perched high on a wooded hill, Richard Morrison had chosen the 'medieval' style as being the most appropriate.

Writing in 1839 about Castle Howard, Hughes stated that 'The Architecture of it is designed on the principle of uniting the characters of a castellated place of defence and a monastic structure – a combination difficult of attainment, but of striking effect when, as in the present instance, it has been well conceived and skillfully executed', while J.P. Neale, writing about Shelton Abbey, stated that it was built in the style 'of an Abbey erected in the fourteenth century and formed into a baronial residence shortly after the Reformation.' O'Neil-Fielding, taking his cue from Neale, wrote of Shelton that 'The architects who designed the mansion proposed to themselves to represent a monastic structure of the fourteenth century, converted into a baronial residence of a date shortly subsequent to the Reformation.'

The similarity of the architectural intentions for both houses – Castle Howard and Shelton – coupled with the use of the plural in the latter quotation, suggests that William Vitruvius's father may have been his partner in Shelton's design. This hypothesis is supported by the fact that John Morrison, in his biography of his brother, stated that William had worked with their father from about 1809 until the mid-1820s. The use of classical themes in the library and the dining room also suggests the collaboration of Richard Morrison in the design of Shelton Abbey.

The Morrisons, father and son, had the most extensive architectural practice in Ireland during the first 30 years of the 19th century. They built, or altered,

3

1 The staircase – the plasterwork has
   now been removed.
2 The 'prayer' hall – the plasterwork
   has been cut down and a lower plain
   ceiling inserted.
3 The entrance hall – the niches have
   been filled in, the dado is gone and the
   plasterwork on the ceiling has been
   knocked down.

Shelton Abbey
Arklow, County Wicklow

such mansions as Castlegar, Carton, Killruddery and Thomastown Castle as well as Ballyfin, the most opulent neoclassical house in Ireland. Richard Morrison was the moving spirit behind the formation of the Royal Institute of Architects in Ireland, for which he was awarded a knighthood in 1841.

The gothic taste was also deemed to be particularly suitable for the new house at Shelton due to its sequestered situation in the 'Garden of Ireland'. Unfortunately, Lord Wicklow insisted that most of the original structure should be retained, a circumstance that led John Morrison to complain that 'the architect was much fettered, his design and the building rendered less perfect than it would otherwise have been'. In a sort of cross-fertilization, when Castle Howard was extended some years later the crenellations that were added to the gable end of the building were copied from those on the central pediment of Shelton Abbey.

The 4th Earl of Wicklow, who became a Knight of the Most Illustrious Order of Saint Patrick in 1842, had no son – his nephew succeeded him in the peerage – but he did have seven daughters. Accordingly, in about 1840, he instructed Richard Morrison, William Vitruvius having died in 1838, to build a new wing to house them all. This structure came to be known as 'the nunnery' and, such

must have been the power of suggestion, three of the Howard ladies eventually turned Roman Catholic and did, indeed, become nuns.

After the Morrisons' alterations, Shelton was one of the most splendid and romantic houses and demesnes in Ireland. Externally, it has two principal elevations in the Tudor-Gothic style, with a roofline filled with crenellations and spiky pinnacles that rise up on octagonal shafts. The abbey is entered through a large single-storey gothic portico, over which is placed the Wicklow coat of arms. At the junction of the garden and entrance fronts, there is an octagonal tower which contained the earl's study and serves to disguise the difference in the heights of these two façades. This tower was once crowned by a conical copper roof, which the present owners have seen fit to demolish and not to reinstate.

The interior of the abbey was an eclectic mixture of classical (the library and the dining room) and gothic (the remaining principal rooms). The interiors were embellished with rich and splendid plasterwork. There are two gothic drawing rooms, their ceilings filled with pendants (one of which, according to the late Lady Wicklow, resembled nothing so much as rows of cow's udders); an entrance hall with gilt pendants; a 'prayer' hall; a grand staircase and a monastic cloister. The

The corridor outside the drawing
rooms – the plasterwork has been
completely sliced from the ceiling and
the walls, while the windows have been
removed and replaced with cheap
modern ones.

Shelton Abbey
Arklow, County Wicklow

ornate plasterwork that adorned these rooms has been completely destroyed by
its current owners.

The approach to the residence is by an avenue fully two miles in length, which
was once lined with rhododendrons. The end of the 19th century saw the Victorian parterres beside the house joined by wild and subtropical gardens planted
by the 7th, and penultimate, Earl and his countess. The last earl claimed that the
rhododendrons had been gathered from seed by his father from as far away as
the Himalayas and Tibet. He wrote in 1951 that 'the plants are only just coming
to flower and should be of great interest and beauty in the future'. Unfortunately,
the fumes emanating from the nearby fertilizer factory have since destroyed
them all.

Like the 4th Earl, the 5th Earl was elected by his order to represent the Irish
peerage in parliament. He was faced by a legal challenge to his inheritance when
a certain William Howard claimed to be the son of the 5th Earl's older brother,
who had married but had died childless in 1864. Eventually, in 1892, judgement
was given against the pretender at the High Court in Dublin.

The 6th and 7th Earls also represented the Irish peerage in parliament, while
the 7th Earl was, additionally, a member of the first Senate of the Irish Free
State. He married, as his second wife, Lady Beatrix Herbert, Lord Pembroke's
daughter and the widow of Sir Nevil Wilkinson, the last Ulster King of Arms
to have authority over the whole island of Ireland. The 7th Earl's son, William,
the last Lord Wicklow, chose the life of a curate in the Church of England after
he came down from Oxford, and was sent to Somers Town in a very poor area
of London. Three years later he followed the 4th Earl's three daughters and converted to Roman Catholicism. He then petitioned to join the Sovereign Military
Order of St John of Malta but, according to the 'Pope' O'Mahony, when he was
asked to produce his proofs of nobility, he refused and just said 'Look me up in
Burke's!' The consequence was that he became a Knight of Magistral Grace,
instead of the higher rank to which he would have been entitled.

On his father's death, William inherited a residence complete with, among
other things, 21 indoor servants. He also acquired crippling tax bills and, in
a vain attempt to save the situation, opened his home as an hotel in 1947. The
next three and a half years were an unmitigated disaster. From the fastness of
his Tuscan retreat, Harold Acton remarked that Lord Wicklow had tried to
save the family fortune but had lost instead the family silver. The future of the
abbey looked bleak; a situation that was not helped by the fact that Wicklow's
future brother-in-law was an architect known as Johnny 'knock it down' Butler.
He had acquired this epithet, as it was, apparently, the principal advice that he
gave to his clients when he was asked to cast his professional eye over their properties with a view to adapting them to meet the exigencies of the 20th century.
However, Shelton Abbey escaped Mr Butler's possible plans for it and was sold,
together with its demesne, to the Department of Forestry in 1951.

Its future now rested with that particular breed of Irish civil servants who,
until quite recently, were not known for their aesthetic sensibilities as well as
their overriding concern for the nation's heritage. The fate of the abbey was,
consequently, rather predictable. A very large and nasty fertilizer plant was
built in the demesne and the house was turned into an open prison – so open in
fact that, as Jeremy Williams has pointed out, the authorities have removed the
wrought-iron gates from the entrance and demolished them. The roof of the
conical tower, at the junction of the two main fronts, has gone, as have the

panelling and bookcases. Inside the house all the plasterwork has been turned into rubble; only that in the two drawing rooms has been spared. The original 17th-century house was knocked down, as well as the coach house and the stable yard. In an article on his home, Lord Wicklow had written that he hoped its future would be 'a propitious one'. It would prove to be a vain hope.

'Billy' Wicklow shared his ancestor, the 4th Earl's, fondness for the bottle. In his old age, the staff at the Gresham Hotel in Dublin would approach him, as he lay slumped in a chair at the end of an evening's entertainment, armed with the bill and the query 'Would your lordship like to make your mark now?' Having abandoned Shelton to its awful fate, Lord Wicklow retired to a tasteful modern villa in a salubrious suburb of County Dublin. Eleanor Wicklow was a member of both the Irish Labour Party and the Irish Senate; despite her strong socialist convictions she was also a fervent admirer of Richard Nixon. Lord Wicklow had married her in 1959, after a 13-year courtship. On his death in 1978, the Earldom of Wicklow became extinct. Lady Wicklow died in 1997. Of the family estates which extended in 1883 to 22,103 acres in County Wicklow with Shelton Abbey at their heart, as well as 6440 acres, together with Castle Forward in County Donegal, nothing now remains.

The view from the Abbey towards the south – a large and ugly fertilizer factory has now been built just beyond the tree in the middle distance. Fumes from the factory have destroyed most of the rare trees and plants that the Wicklow family spent many generations cultivating in the demesne.

Shelton Abbey
Arklow, County Wicklow

Stradbally Hall *Stradbally, County Laois*

A mid-Victorian remodelling of an earlier house for one of the most important families among the Irish landed gentry. The Cosbys arrived in the 16th century and are here still. The present owner now farms the land and the estate has hosted the National Traction Engine Steam Rally.

Three miles from the Rock of Dunamase in County Laois is the Victorian pile that is Stradbally Hall. *Anthologia Hibernica* tells us that 'In the 12th century O'Mara, chief of the district, granted the lands to conventual Franciscans, and founded a monastery, called Mon-a-beallin, some remains of which are still visible.' Later on, the lands of Stradbally became the principal seat of the O'Mores, Lords of Laois. However, as the *Anthologia Hibernica* continues, 'on the dissolution of the religious houses, the monastery with its mill, castles and lands, consisting of 345 acres, was granted August 18th, 1592, in capite, by knight's service, to hold of the castle of Maryborough, to Francis Cosby, his heirs and assigns, at the annual rent of £17.6s.3d Irish money; they to find yearly nine English horsemen'.

2

THIS ACCOUNT is somewhat at variance with the confused accounts that the family have given about the exact date of their arrival in this part of Ireland. Major Errold Cosby claimed in the *Irish Tatler and Sketch* that Stradbally had been the seat of the family since the reign of Edward VI, while *Burke's Irish Family Records* (1976) states that Francis Cosby, who had married the sister of the 1st Duke of Somerset (the Protector of the Realm for his nephew Edward VI), came to Ireland in the reign of Mary Tudor, had been appointed General of the Kern of Laois in 1588 and was only granted the site of the suppressed Abbey of Strad-Bally in 1562 – in the reign of Queen Elizabeth I.

In a petition by his son, Francis Cosby was stated to have been one of the first English gentlemen at the winning of the Queen's County. He was slain in Glenmalure in County Wicklow in 1580 by Fiach mac Aoidh Ó Broin; Cosby had warned against attacking the O'Byrnes but his advice was not heeded. Francis's heir was his son Alexander, whose wife, Dorcas, wrote to Queen Elizabeth requesting that her husband should have the keeping of 12 horsemen 'the better to enable him to keep house in the waste country he inhabits in Leix'. This suggests that the Cosby family realized the perils of living beyond the pale among the native Irish, but in 1596 Alexander Cosby made the mistake of his life. Not content with taking over the property of the O'Mores (he had by then received even more of their former lands from the government), he then denied them the use of the bridge to cross the river. A skirmish followed (rather grandly known as 'The Battle of Stradbally Bridge'), during the course of which both Alexander Cosby and his son, another Francis, were hacked to death.

Their heir to the estate was Alexander's nine-week-old baby son and next in line was the baby's uncle, Richard. Doubtless coincidentally, baby Cosby did not live to see three months. Richard inherited the property, or what was left of it, for the O'Mores burned down the house that Francis Cosby had built using the stones of the friary and many 'records and Curious Antiquities' were destroyed in the blaze. Richard Cosby was not a man to forgive or forget. It took him ten years but, in 1606, he destroyed the power of the O'Mores at a battle in the Glen of Aughnahelly near the Rock of Dunamase. Cosby was so

Previous page
The study with a portrait of Colonel Cosby over the chimneypiece.

These pages
1   The dining room.
2   The south front of the hall.

Stradbally Hall
Stradbally, County Laois

3 | 4

badly wounded that he could not be brought back to Stradbally for medical treatment, but was nursed at the site of his victory. Despite this, he survived the attention of his doctors and lived for another quarter of a century.

The next house at Stradbally was built by Colonel Dudley Pole Cosby immediately after the 'Glorious Revolution' of 1688–89. It is said that 'The Ascendancy built in order to convince themselves not only that they had arrived, but that they would remain'. As a consequence of this way of thinking, the Cosbys were soon in debt. In 1703, the Colonel's son wrote 'my father's circumstances were so bad that it was thought that he sho'd go into the army'. His father decided to go abroad instead. Unfortunately, ten years of exile did not teach him thrift. On his return he added to the house and was soon, according to his son, living in a higher state than any of his neighbours. The gout was his undoing. His son wrote that 'he wo'd follow… a pack of fleet Hounds from morning till night and keep closer in with ye hounds than anyone on horseback, he danced on the roaps as well as any roap dancer that ever was, he was a fine Tennis and five player, a most extraordinary fine Hurler… it was to those violent exercises that his violent gout was attributed for he strained his joints and his whole body so much that ye gout was knotted more in knobs with him than it would other-wise have done.'

A charitable couple, Colonel Dudley and his wife never sent the poor away hungry from their door. As the economy of the country improved, so did the fortunes of the Cosbys. Despite eventually marrying an heiress, and having the example of his sire constantly before him, young Pole Cosby was soon emulating his father and living beyond his means. In 1729 the Colonel was at last carried off by the gout, a painful if appropriate end for a man with a kind heart who had lived entirely for pleasure. At his funeral, '100 poor were served at the door with bread and ale and great quantatyes of victuals of all sorts within, with plenty of wine.'

The new master of Stradbally was forced 'to live some years in England cheaper than Stradbally.' Unfortunately Mrs Cosby miscarried while there and the whole family returned home 'not all of us liking England.'

1 The drawing room.
2 The staircase hall.
3 The library.
4 The ceiling of the ballroom with wallpaper showing the story of Cupid and Psyche.

Stradbally Hall
Stradbally, County Laois

Stradbally Hall
Stradbally, County Laois

One of Pole Cosby's brothers, General William Cosby, was Governor of New York in 1731, while another, Alexander, was Lieutenant Governor of Nova Scotia and Lieutenant Governor of Annapolis Royal, where his son, later Admiral Philip Cosby, was born. The Admiral was eventually to inherit Stradbally but, after Pole Cosby's death in 1766, it went first to his own son, Dudley. This gentleman, who had been His Britannic Majesty's Ambassador to the Court of Denmark, was raised in 1768 to the peerage as the 1st (and last) Baron Sydney and Stradbally. Prompted perhaps by his elevation to the peerage Lord Sydney began to rebuild his family home under the watchful eye of Arthur Roberts his overseer. It has been stated that work began on the new house in 1772; however, an account from 1794, states that 'in 1771 – Cosby, the late lord Sydney, began a noble house a little without the town… but lived to finish only the offices and one wing. The demesne is highly ornamented and now

belongs to admiral Cosby. The town is a manor, to which appertain a court baron and a court leet. In 1771 it contained 100 houses, but at present in 1794 it has 214, most of which are neat and well built.' Lord Sydney married Lady Isabella St Lawrence, daughter of the 1st Earl of Howth, but managed to die childless. As a consequence, his peerages became extinct and his estates passed to his second cousin once removed, Admiral Philip Cosby.

Admiral Cosby was beside General Wolfe at the taking of Quebec, and it was on his ship that Lord Cornwallis and the English officers were taken back to England after their defeat at the hands of George Washington. But, like the baron, the admiral left no children. He was buried in Bath Cathedral in 1808 and his heir was his second cousin Thomas Cosby of Vicarstown. Tragedy struck Thomas's family when his two elder sons were drowned in 1789 and 1791 and the current owner of the demesne descends from his surviving son.

During the years of the great famine (1845–49), this account of the estate was given by a visitor who stated that there were in Laois 'numerous tasteful residences of the gentry, amongst these, Stradbally Hall, seat of Mrs. Cosby, is a lovely spot, embellished with wood and water and charming diversity.'

Between 1866 and 1869 the house was remodelled and extended by Charles Lanyon in an Italianate style that disguises all traces of the earlier building. The main rooms were elevated and treated as a *piano nobile*. The reception rooms were left unaltered along the garden front, but a 'prayer room' and a new study were added. The study was based around a single picture, a topographical view of the house which dated from the late 17th century. This was sold in 1986 for £110,000. Lanyon added a ballroom, the largest apartment in the house, whose ceiling was decorated with panels of French neoclassical grisaille wallpaper which tells the story of Cupid and Psyche. In the 1960s, Edward Heath is said to have accepted an invitation to address a Young Conservative conference in the house but, perhaps on hearing that the cook had fallen through a hole in the ceiling he cancelled his visit. It might be observed that cooks in Irish houses have had a hard time of it. The entire kitchen staff at Dunluce Castle fell to their deaths in 1639 when part of the castle fell into the Moyle Sea, while the cook at Castle Mac Garrett died in the fire of 1811 that destroyed the old house.

The fall in Colonel Cosby's rents during the 1880s did not prevent him keeping a coach and four, with a pair of footmen on the box, and the family kept a butler and a footman at the house until the outbreak of World War II. The aftermath of the 1916 rebellion brought much heart-searching among members of the Ascendancy, and to none more so than Colonel Robert Cosby, who stated to a Unionist gathering, in 1920 'I am a Unionist – as you know a life long Unionist – and now I have to pocket my feelings and to do what I can for the good and benefit of my beloved country.'

When the present owner of the estate, Adrian Cosby brought his bride Alison back to Stradbally in 1972, they were pulled by the local people in an open carriage to their home, much as the Duke of Richmond was pulled in his, by the inhabitants of Tullamore, when he visited Charleville Castle, almost two centuries before. Mr and Mrs Cosby were also presented with an illuminated address (as had been the custom in the late 19th and early 20th centuries). Despite the O'Mores, the Cromwellians, wild extravagance and a couple of Civil Wars, Mr and Mrs Cosby still live on and farm the land that their ancestor acquired four (or perhaps four and a half) centuries ago.

Notes

BALLYNEGALL

Irish Tatler and Sketch May 1962.

A WYATT WINDOW. A rectangular triple window of the late Georgian period, which has its two outer windows narrower than the central one. It is named after James Wyatt (1747–1813), a member of the prolific dynasty of architects.

FRANCIS JOHNSTON (1760–1829). The son of the architect William Johnston, he was born in Armagh (for which he later designed the Observatory). After moving to Dublin in 1793, he studied under THOMAS COOLEY and was appointed architect and inspector of civil buildings to the Board of Works in 1805. His principal buildings in Dublin include the General Post Office in O'Connell Street and the Chapel Royal in Dublin Castle. In his private practice, he designed Townley Hall in County Louth and Charleville Castle in County Offaly. One of the founders of the Royal Hibernian Academy, he served as its president from 1824 until his death in 1829.

MICHAEL STAPLETON (ff 1770–1801). A Dublin stuccodore who has been described as 'the Irish Adam'. His best work is the ceilings and staircase hall at Belvedere House, Dublin, the chapel at Trinity College, Dublin, and the plasterwork at Powerscourt House, in Dublin.

THE NORMAN INVASION OF IRELAND. In 1152, Diarmuid na nGall mac Murchadha (1110–71) became King of Uí Chinnsealaigh and of Leinster (from 1126) and abducted Dearbhorgaill (Dervorgilla) the wife of Tighearnán Ó Ruairc, King of Bréifne. Although she was returned to her husband a year later, Ó Ruairc never forgave the affront to his honour and in 1166 he destroyed Diarmuid's castle at Ferns after which the High King Ruaidhrí Ó Conchobhair expelled Diarmuid from Ireland. Diarmuid went to England to seek aid from King Henry II who (having obtained Diarmuid's promise that Leinster would become a vassal state of the English king) agreed to give his knights permission to assist Diarmuid in the recovery of his kingdom. These Normans, led by Richard fitz Gilbert de Clare, Earl of Pembroke, were promised large tracts of Leinster as their reward (while de Clare, who was known as 'Strongbow', was to receive the hand of Aoife, Diarmuid's daughter, and the kingdom of Leinster after his death). The Norman invasion of Ireland began in County Wexford in May 1169, 'Strongbow' following some months later. In 1170, he married Aoife, captured Dublin, and became King of Leinster when Diarmuid died in 1171 at Ferns. The *Annals of the Four Masters* record that Diarmuid mac Murchadha died 'without a will, without penance, without unction, as his evil deeds deserved'. Shortly afterwards, Henry II arrived to claim the whole island (the English Pope Adrian IV having generously given it to him some years previously). Some six and a half centuries would pass before King Henry's descendants agreed to return the sovereignty of at least a part of the country to its inhabitants.

HUGH DE LACY (1115–85). Lord of Meath. The son of Gilbert de Lacy, he accompanied Henry II to Ireland and was given some 900,000 acres of the country as his personal fief and, on that monarch's behalf, he received the submission of the High King Ruaidhrí in 1172 (and later married Ruaidhrí's daughter). He was murdered by a nephew of An Sionnach (known in English as 'The Fox') when he attempted to build a castle on holy ground at Durrow. De Lacy was described by the historian GIRALDUS CAMBRENSIS as being 'a swarthy man with small black deep set eyes, a flat nose, an ugly scar on his right cheek caused by a burn, a short neck, and a hairy, sinewy body.' His son, another Hugh de Lacy, was created Earl of Ulster by King John in 1205.

JAMES NORRIS BREWER. An English author who produced *The Beauties of Ireland: Being Original Delineations, Topographical, Historical, and Biographical of each county [with] engravings by J. and H. S. Storer after original drawings, chiefly by Mr. Petrie of Dublin* (who provided some 21 illustrations for the book).

BERMINGHAM HOUSE

Irish Tatler and Sketch June 1955

EDWARD BRUCE (d.1318). Earl of Carrick and the younger brother of Robert I, King of Scots (Robert the Bruce), Edward was offered the Crown of Ireland in 1315, by Domhnall Ó Néill and other Irish lords and arrived shortly afterwards with a force of some 6000 soldiers. Crowned King of Ireland at Dundalk in 1316, he soon conquered most of Ulster and later, with the aid of his brother, the Midlands were brought under his control. However, his attempt to carve out a kingdom for himself in Ireland came to a bloody end in 1318 when he was slain in battle by an English force led by John de Bermingham. As a direct result of his campaigning in the country, Ireland suffered three years of famine after his death, which led to a chronicle describing him as a 'destroyer of Ireland in general, both of English and of Gael.'

THE ANNALS OF CLONMACNOISE. These are an account of the history of Ireland 'from the earliest period to 1408'. The original Irish version is lost; but there is an English translation by Connell Mac Geoghegan of Westmeath, which he completed in 1627.

SIR HENRY SIDNEY (1529–86). A friend of Edward VI (who is said to have died in his arms), he married Lady Mary Dudley, the daughter of the Duke of Northumberland and was, consequently, the brother-in-law of the ill-fated Lady Jane Grey. He inherited Penshurst Place in Kent and in 1564, was made a Knight of the Most Noble Order of the Garter. Vice-Treasurer of Ireland from 1556 until 1569, he returned to that country as Lord Deputy in 1565 and remained in office until 1571, only to be reappointed in 1575. He established the boundaries of counties Clare and Roscommon and was instrumental in the submissions of Ruaidhrí Ó Mórdha (who was later executed) and of Toirdhealbhach Luineach Ó Néill. The brother-in-law of two other Lords Deputy of Ireland, the Earl of Sussex and Sir William Fitzwilliam, he was finally recalled in 1578. He declined the offer of a peerage and died at Ludlow in 1586 (the same year as his wife). His eldest son was Sir Philip Sidney, the soldier, statesman, courtier and poet.

LOUIS LE BROCQUY. Born in Dublin in 1916, he is Ireland's most distinguished living artist. In 1938 he left Ireland and went to London, Paris, Venice and Geneva to study art by himself, returning home in 1940. In 1947 he exhibited at the Gimpel Fils Gallery in London and became part of a group of artists that included Ben Nicholson, Graham Sutherland and Francis Bacon. In 1956, he won a major prize at the Venice Biennale with his painting *A Family*. Decorated by France and Belgium, awarded honorary doctorates by the National University of Ireland and other learned bodies, he is also the first living Irish artist whose work has sold for over a million pounds.

KCMG. The Most Distinguished Order of Saint Michael and Saint George was founded in August 1818 and is now awarded for services rendered by members of the Foreign Service or for administrative services to the Commonwealth. The Order is divided into three classes: Knight Grand Cross (GCMG), Knight Commander (KCMG) and Companion (CMG). There is a joke among members of the Foreign Service to the effect that CMG stands for 'Call Me God', KCMG is 'Kindly Call Me God', while those grand enough to be awarded the First Class of the Order (GCMG) are entitled to the appellation 'God Calls Me God.'

THE HONOURABLE DOCTOR DESMOND GUINNESS (b.1931). The second son of Bryan Guinness, 2nd Baron Moyne (1905–92) and Diana Mitford. His first wife was Princess Hermione Marie Gabrielle (d.1989) – the daughter of H.S.H. Prince Albrecht von Urach, Count of Wurtemburg) – by whom he had two children, Patrick (b.1956) and Marina (b.1957). He is now married to Penelope Cuthbertson, the daughter of Graham Cuthbertson. He was, with his first wife, the re-founder of the Irish Georgian Society and is one of the seminal figures in Irish Conservation today. His purchase of Castletown, near Cellbridge in County Kildare, the largest and most important Georgian mansion in Ireland, with most of its parkland, saved the building for the nation. His many publications, with those of Desmond FitzGerald, the Knight of Glin, awoke a generation to the necessity of preserving the domestic architecture of Ireland.

BLARNEY CASTLE

Irish Tatler and Sketch May 1955

THOMAS CROFTON CROKER (1798–1854). Born in Cork, the son of an army major whose ancestors had arrived from England during the 16th century, he developed an interest in the native folklore of Ireland. Between 1812 and 1815 he collected legends, folk songs and keens (laments for the dead), mostly from the south of the country. He described these activities as a sort of sport 'hunting up and bagging all the old "grey superstitions"'. He sent them to Thomas Moore who used some of them in his *Irish Melodies*. He was described by Sir Walter Scott as 'little as a dwarf, keen-eyed as a hawk, and of easy prepossessing manners'. His greatest work is *Fairy Legends and Traditions of the South of Ireland* (1825–28).

ANN (ANNABELLA) PLUMPTRE (1761–1838). Daughter of Robert Plumptre, who was the President of Queens' College Cambridge from 1760 until 1788. A novelist and dramatist, she was the author of

Something new: or, Adventures at Campbell-House (1801), which examined the life of a woman constrained by her time for no better reason than physical appearance and tackled her ability to evolve beyond such superficiality.

BARONS OF BLARNEY, VISCOUNTS MUSKERRY, EARLS OF CLANCARTY. Cormac Mac Carthaigh, the son of Sir Cormac Mac Carthaigh Mhúscraighe and his wife, the Honourable Mary Butler, daughter of Theobald Butler, 1st Viscount Caher, was created Baron of Blarney and Viscount Muskerry in 1628. He married Lady Margaret O'Brien, the daughter of Donnchadh Ó Briain, 4th Earl of Thomond, and was buried in Westminster Abbey in 1640. His son, Donnchadh Mac Carthaigh, the 2nd Viscount Muskerry was created Earl of Clancarty in 1658. His daughter-in-law (the daughter of Uilleag, Marquess of Clanrickarde) was described in Grammont's memoirs as having 'the shape of a woman big with child without being so; but had a very good reason for limping; for of two legs uncommonly short, one was much shorter than the other. A face suitable to this description gave the finishing stroke to this disagreeable woman.' The youngest son of the 1st Earl, the Honourable Justin MacCarthy (who was created Viscount Mountcashel by James II) went to France where he became the first Commander of the Irish Brigade. The 4th Earl (the last to own Blarney) escaped from the Tower of London, leaving his periwig block dressed up in his bed with the message attached to it 'this block must answer for me.' Lord Tyrawley, described the 5th Earl in 1734/35, as 'a brute that has been drunk the 24 hours round, now this week and more.' The earldom, viscountcy and barony are believed to have become extinct with the death of the last Earl's sons in about 1770. The current head of the family lives in Australia, although, at the turn of the last century, a French con-man, called Pol McCarthy, claimed to be the heir of this branch of the Clann Carthaigh and even took to calling himself by the bogus title of Duke of Clancarthy-Blarney.

RICHARD ALFRED MILLIKEN (1767–1815) was a member of the the 'Forty-Five Club' so called because each of its members was required to take part in that number of consecutive rounds of punch. He was ably assisted by his two friends, William Maginn (1793–1842) and Francis Sylvester Mahony (1804–66). The latter gentleman was born in Blarney, became a priest in Lucca in Tuscany in 1832, and, under the pseudonym 'Father Prout' produced a series of poems and jottings in 1837 under the title *The Reliques of Father Prout*.

COURT OF POETRY. In the 17th century, Blarney was well known as the seat of a Court of Poetry, where poets gathered on festive occasions to read their compositions, many of which have survived in the original Irish form and in English translations. There was also a bard in residence at Blarney Castle, serving the MacCarthys as poet, historian and musician. The Bardic School survived at Blarney until 1726.

JOHN LANYON (1840–1900). The eldest son of SIR CHARLES LANYON (1813–89), he entered his father's architectural practice in 1860 and ran the Dublin office until he returned to Belfast in 1867. In 1879, he designed additional buildings at Amiens Street Station in Dublin (now Connolly Station) and, in 1883, restored Belfast Castle for the Marquess of Donegall.

THE COLLEGE HISTORICAL SOCIETY ('The Hist'). The oldest surviving students' debating society in the world, this was founded in a pub on George's Street, Dublin in 1747, with HENRY GRATTAN among its founder members. First known as Burke's Club (after Edmund Burke), the name was changed in 1770 to The College Historical Society. In 1904 the Society moved into its present quarters in the Graduates' Memorial Building in Trinity College, and in 1969 women were allowed to become members (as the Society's condition that 'men will walk on the moon before women shall be admitted here' had been fulfilled).

THE IRISH PASSION FOR TREES is best exemplified by the story of an Englishman who suggested to the Irish parliamentarian, HENRY GRATTAN, that a beech tree in his demesne at Tinnehinch, in County Wicklow was uncomfortably close to his house. Grattan agreed and said that he had 'often thought of taking down the house'.

BORRIS HOUSE
Irish Tatler and Sketch November 1949

RICHARD DE CLARE, EARL OF PEMBROKE. The son of Gilbert fitz Gilbert (known as 'Strongbow'), who was created Earl of Pembroke in 1138, and his wife Isabel, the great-granddaughter of Henry I, King of France. His paternal uncle, Walter, was the lord of Nether Gwent and lived at his Castle of Strigoil (which was later called Chepstow). Round, in *Peerage Studies,* has suggested that it was the size and the strength of the bows used by the men of Gwent that gave the family their nickname. Certainly, the 1st Earl of Pembroke had an arrow on his counterseal. At the invitation of the Diarmuid, King of Leinster, Richard de Clare (who was also called 'Strongbow') landed at Waterford in 1170 and, with the assistance of his brother-in-law Raymond fitzWilliam (known as 'The Fat'), captured Dublin. He married King Diarmuid's daughter, Aoife, at Waterford in 1171. Henry II of England, jealous of Lord Pembroke's conquests, arrived in Ireland where Strongbow surrendered them all to his overlord and was given Leinster as his portion, to hold 'in fee'. He founded the Holy Trinity Hospital at Kilmainham and Christ Church Cathedral in Dublin.

SIR RICHARD MORRISON (1767–1849) and William Vitruvius Morrison (1794–1838). The son of the architect John Morrison, Richard Morrison married Eliza Ould and their second son, William, was born in 1794. By the age of 15, William was assisting his father in his architectural practice and together they had the most formidable partnership in Irish architecture until it was dissolved in the mid-1820s. Their *oeuvre* includes Ballyfin in County Laois, Castlegar in County Galway, Thomastown Castle in County Tipperary, Luggala Lodge, Castle Howard, Killruddery and Shelton Abbey, all in County Wicklow, as well as Borris House in County Carlow (the last three are featured in this book). William Morrison, who suffered from poor health died in 1838. In the following year, his father founded the Royal Institute of the Architects of Ireland and he was knighted by Queen Victoria in 1841. He died at his home Vaucluse, near Enniskerry in County Wicklow in 1849.

HERMAN, PRINCE VON PÜCKLER-MUSKAU (1785–1871). A Prussian officer and a German prince, he was the son of Count Pückler of Schloss Branitz and his wife, Countess Gallenberg, the heiress of the Muskau estates in Silesia. His parents divorced in 1797 and he entered the Saxon Army but gave up his commission in 1804. His father died in 1810, and in 1813 he enlisted in the Prussian army, where he served as an aide-de-camp to the Duke of Saxe-Weimar. In 1817, he married Lucie von Hardenberg (1776–1854), the daughter of Prince von Hardenberg, the Chancellor of Prussia, but their relationship ended in divorce in 1826. On the look-out for a rich wife, the prince (he had been raised to that rank in 1822 as compensation for Prussia's annexation of Silesia) travelled to London, where his attempts to catch an heiress were rebuffed. Despite his best endeavours, all the young ladies remained coy or, more probably, their parents were 'difficult'. He was accused of planning a sham marriage and returning to live with Lucie or even of contemplating matrimony with the Empress of Haiti (widow of King Henry Christophe), who was then on a trip to Europe). A distinguished landscape gardener, he designed the Babelsberg Gardens at Potsdam for the King of Prussia as well as the Muskau Park in Warsaw. He published '*Hints on Landscape Gardening*' and a series of letters to his former wife, which were later issued in English as *Tour of a German Prince in England, Ireland and France*. Goethe reviewed the book and stated that 'the writer appears to be a perfect and experienced man of the world, endowed with talents and quick apprehension; formed by a varied social existence, by travel and extensive connections'. In 1845, he sold Muskau and went to live at Schloss Branitz. When he died, he was buried in a tomb he had built for himself nearly 60 feet high in the form of a pyramid. Edgar Allen Poe mentioned him in '*The Domain of Arnheim*' (1850) and he appeared in 1932 as one in a collection of cigarette cards of Dandys issued by John Player & Sons (under the caption 'A Dandy's Entourage').

THE 19TH EARL OF ORMOND AND OSSORY. He served as Chief Butler of Ireland at the Coronation of George IV in 1821 and was one of the six extra Knights of Saint Patrick who were created on that occasion. In 1838 he was made Marquess of Ormonde. His daughter was the mother of Arthur MacMurrough Kavanagh. The 2nd Marquess died of apoplexy while sea bathing near Loftus Hall (one of the most haunted houses in Ireland) in County Wexford, in 1854. The Marquessate of Ormonde is now extinct.

SAINT MO LING (or Saint Mullins) 614–96. A pupil of Saint Kevin at Glendalough, he founded the monastery nine miles north of New Ross, County Carlow, that bears his name. The book of Saint Mo Ling (a 7th-century illuminated manuscript of the four Gospels) is now in the old library of Trinity College, Dublin. The Saint's feast day is 25 July.

FIGEEN. This is an annular brooch, synonymous with the term ring brooch and such objects have been a part of Celtic culture since the middle of the second millennium BC. The style of the Celtic brooch derives from that of the Roman cloak pin of the early Bronze Age, which was used as cloak fastener.

A TORC (OR MUINCE) is a neck ornament consisting of a circular tube that terminates in a pair of finials. The earliest torcs date from the late 2nd or early 1st millennium BC and continued to be made, or imported from Continental Europe, until the beginning of the Christian era.

CASTLE MAC GARRETT

Irish Tatler and Sketch August and September 1956

THE TRIBES OF GALWAY. This was used as a pejorative term by Cromwell's troops in Galway in 1652, to describe the old merchant families of the City. The 'Tribes' consisted of the following families: Athy, Blake, Bodkin, Browne, d'Arcy, Deane, Font, French, Joyce, Kirwan, Lynch, Martin, Morris and Skerret. Most were of Norman or Welsh ancestry (with a few native Irish among them). In 1652, Lord Clanrickarde described them as 'petty pedlars and bankrupt merchants'. His Lordship's bad opinion was a result of the merchants putting their own interests before those of the Crown during the Civil War.

THE EARLDOM OF ALTAMONT AND THE MARQUESSATE OF SLIGO. The Earldom was bestowed in 1771 on John Browne of Westport, County Mayo. The name of the title comes from the 'high mountain' (Croagh Patrick) that overlooks Westport. The 1st Earl married Anne, the daughter of Sir Arthur Gore, 1st Earl of Arran. The 3rd Earl was created Marquess of Sligo in the Union honours of 1800. William Hartpole Lecky wrote that he 'bargained for and obtained a Marquisate', while Thomas de Quincy described him as 'a very fat man, and so lame that he is obliged to have two servants to support him wherever he stirs'.

THE EARLDOM OF CLANRICKARDE. This was created in 1543 by Henry VIII for Uilleag na gCeann Bourke, lord of Upper Connacht. He died a few weeks after his ennoblement and the English made his son, Richard Bourke, the 2nd Earl, the Captain (or head) of the people of Clanrickarde against their wishes and the Brehon laws of TANISTRY. He divorced his first wife – the daughter of Murrough O'Brien, 1st Earl of Thomond by his wife Eleanor, a daughter of the Knight of Glin – complaining that she practised witchcraft against him, but he obviously harboured no grudge against the O'Briens, as his second wife was a daughter of Donough O'Brien, 2nd Earl of Thomond. Lord Clanrickarde's third wife was a daughter of Cormac Mac Carthaigh, Lord of Muskerry (he put her away after three or four years). He is also known to have kept a number of 'concubines' in his employment. Despite this, the English described him as 'a very comely and civil gentleman'. The 3rd Earl, Dominick Browne's patron, was a child of the 2nd Earl's first marriage.

THE EARLDOM OF KENMARE. James II created Valentine Browne of Killarney, a son of Sir Valentine Browne, 2nd Baronet, Baron Castlerosse and Viscount Kenmare in 1689. This was one of seven peerages bestowed in Ireland (where James was still legally king) after his flight from England. The 1st Viscount was attainted for his support of King James and the family estates were bought by Thomas Asgill, who had married one of his granddaughters. The 5th Viscount was created Viscount Castlerosse and Earl of Kenmare in 1801. He was a Roman Catholic who Lord Cornwallis described himself as 'obliged' to recommend for a peerage. Lecky wrote about the acceptance of the Earldom by Lord Kenmare that 'men who valued honour more than honours would not have so acted'.

THE BARONY OF KILMAINE. John Browne of the Neale, County Mayo, was the second son of Sir John Browne, 5th Baronet. He married the Honourable Alice Caulfield, the daughter of the 3rd Viscount Caulfield. There seems to have been no justifiable reason for the awarding of this Barony to Mr. Browne. Fitzpatrick in *The Secret Service under Pitt* states that it was sold to Mr. Browne for hard cash.

THE CASTLE OF CARRA BROWNE (Ceathramhadh Bruna). Situated at the southern end of a great plain, known as 'The Curragh', by the eastern shore of Lough Corrib, the castle was built by Sir David le Brun in 1316 and was in the possession of Daniel O'Hologan in 1574. Walter Blake, a cadet of the Blakes of Dunmacrine in County Mayo, had a lease on the castle, which he bequeathed to his brother, Dr Anthony Blake, Archbishop of Armagh who died there in 1784. In the 1830s it was back in the ownership of the Brownes, in the person of the 1st Lord Oranmore and Browne (the other families who lived there may also only have had leases on the property). The ruin of the castle collapsed in 1860.

Ó FLAITHBHEARTAIGH (O'FLAHERTY). The kings of Muintir Mhurchada, they claimed descent from Murchadh, the son of Maonach, a king of Magh Seola, who died in 891. Their original territories ran from Lough Corrib to Tuam, but after the Norman invasion of Connacht, Richard de Burgo and his ally Aodh Ó Conchobhair (Hugh O'Conor) deprived Aodh Ó Flaithbheartaigh of his lordship not of his lands. This was in 1232 and the new territory of the family, known as Iar Connacht, ran from Killarny harbour to Galway Bay (and included the Aran Islands), with a new castle at Ballynahinch. The family had split into two branches by the 1580s. The western one was under the command of Grace O'Malley's son, Murrough Mór, and the eastern branch under Murrough Dubh of Moycullen. The latter submitted to the Crown and signed the Composition of Connacht in 1585.

His reward was a re-grant of almost all of the O'Flaherty lands in 1588 (together with a knighthood), but the end of the 17th century, the O'Flaherties had lost pretty well all of their ancestral lands.

PRENDERGAST (OR MAC MUIRIS). An old CAMBRO-NORMAN family which arrived with Strongbow's friend, Maurice de Prendergast. They obtained grants of land in Tipperary, Waterford, Wexford, Limerick and Connacht. The branch that settled in the West of Ireland adapted to the native culture and after a few generations had been completely absorbed in Gaelic Ireland, altering their names from fitz Maurice to Mac Muiris.

THOMAS, LORD WENTWORTH (THE EARL OF STRAFFORD). Thomas Wentworth was the son of Sir William Wentworth, 1st Baronet, and was descended, in the female line, from the medieval Earls of Westmoreland. Charles I's chief minister, he was Lord Lieutenant of Ireland and was created Baron Wentworth in 1628 and Earl of Strafford in 1640 (Strafford is the name of the Wapentake in which the new Earl's home, Wentworth Woodhouse, was situated). Despised by the Puritans, he was tried for treason in 1641 and, when it looked as though he might be acquitted, an Act of Attainder was brought in and he was convicted and subsequently beheaded. In 1649, when Charles I was about to be executed, he acknowledged that his fate (from Heaven's point of view) was partly deserved because of Strafford's 'unjust sentence', which he had allowed to take effect. Lord Clarendon quoted Plutarch's epitaph on Sully to describe Lord Strafford, 'no man did ever pass him in doing good to his friends or in doing mischief to his enemies'. Strafford promised that 'landless I came hither and landless I shall go home'. Well, not exactly. Within seven years he had amassed some 27,000 acres of the kingdom. Having dispossessed the O'Byrnes from their ancestral lands in County Wicklow, he thought that it might be amusing to hunt 'these broken men as well as the deer.'

LORD TAAFE. Sir John Taafe, the son of Sir William Taafe of Ballymote, County Sligo, and described as a 'principal gentleman of an ancient English family', was created Baron of Ballymote and Viscount Taafe of Corren in 1628. Charles I appointed the 2nd Viscount, Theobald Taafe, as Governor of Munster. He lost the battle of Knocknanauss, near Kanturk in 1647 to the forces of Murrough O'Brien, Lord Inchiquin. It was Taafe's incompetence that cost the Royalist cause not only the battle but also the life of his second-in-command, Major General Sir Alasdair (macColla) MacDomhnaill, the son of Colla Ciotach Mac-Domhnaill (Colkitto), head of the Clann Iain Mhóir. Despite his failures in battle, Lord Taafe was created Earl of Carlingford in 1661, after the Restoration. The Earldom became extinct in 1738 and the family went to live abroad.

SIR HENRY LYNCH, 1ST BARONET. He was the fourth son of Nicholas FitzStephen Lynch, Mayor of Galway in 1584, and was created a Baronet in 1622. The 6th Baronet's wife, Elizabeth Baker, was the heiress of Tobias Blosse of Little Belstead in Suffolk and, in order to gain an inheritance, he added her surname to his. It was this Baronet's sister who married Dominick Browne of CASTLE MAC GARRETT. The present, and 17th, Baronet is Sir Richard Hely Lynch-Blosse.

EOGHAN RUADH Ó NÉILL (OWEN ROE O'NEILL) 1582–1649. The son of Art Ó Néill, who was the extra-marital son of Feardorcha (Mathew) Ó Néill, Lord Dungannon, who, in his turn, may (or may not) have been the extra-marital son of Conn Bacach, 1st EARL OF TYRONE. In any event, Eoghan Ruadh was the nephew of Aodh Ó Néill, 3rd Earl of Tyrone, who fled Ireland in 1607. Some four years before this event, Eoghan had taken up service with the Archduke in Flanders and he spent the next 30 years of his life fighting on the continent. In 1642, he returned to Ireland during the Confederate Wars, and was appointed Commander-in-Chief of the rebel forces in Ulster. In 1646, he defeated General Munro at the Battle of Benburb. Munro fled leaving 3000 of his men dead on the field and all of his arms and munitions behind. Ó Néill backed the Papal Nuncio, Rinuccini, and wanted to fight both Cromwell's men and the Royalist force under Lord Ormond. However, when Cromwell captured Drogheda, Ó Néill was forced to make common cause with the Royalists. He died at Cavan on 6 November, 1649 and is buried in Cavan Abbey.

CASTLE MAC GARRETT. This was named after Gerard fitz Maurice, the son of that Maurice de PRENDERGAST who came to Ireland with Strongbow. Gerard FitzMaurice accompanied Richard de Burgo to Connacht and the barony of Clanmorris (Clann Mhuiris) in County Mayo is named after him (as is the town of Claremorris – Clár Chloinne Mhuiris – which means the plain of the Prendergasts).

GENERAL GINKEL. Godard van Reede was the son of Godard, 1st Baron van Reede in Denmark. Although he is known to popular history as General Ginkel, this was never his surname; Ginkel was one of several Dutch lordships held by the family. William III appointed him Commander-in-Chief of the army in Ireland where he captured Athlone in 1691 and, in the same year, won the BATTLE OF AUGHRIM. He was naturalized as Baron de Ginkel in 1691/2 and created Earl of Athlone by a grateful sovereign, who also provided him with 26,481 acres of confiscated Irish land. Lord Athlone died of apoplexy in Utrecht in 1702/3. The title became extinct on the death of the 9th Earl who died in The Hague in 1844. His widow followed him to the grave in 1868.

THE PENAL LAWS. These were a series of laws passed by the Protestant Ascendancy in the years that followed the Battle of the Boyne. Although they also affected Dissenters in Ulster, they were principally aimed at the Catholic majority in the country. The Establishment felt that the only way that they could feel secure was to suppress the power of the Catholic Church and to deny Catholics any say in legal, military or political affairs. Contrary to popular propaganda, however, these laws were not really aimed at the ordinary Irishman. The vast majority of Catholics were illiterate and landless, and the chances in the 18th century of their being elected to Parliament, achieving a law degree or having the wherewithal to buy land was zero. The Penal Laws were really aimed against the Catholic gentry and, to a lesser extent, against the Church. Catholic priests were allowed into the country but had to register with the authorities. There was a fear of Catholic intentions; until 1766 the Pope recognized the Stuart claim to the throne of England, Scotland and Ireland, and his priests were seen as leaders among their co-religionists. It is true that the disabilities suffered by the Irish Catholics under the Penal Laws were nothing compared with those experienced by Protestants and Jews in Catholic Europe. But only in Ireland were the laws imposed by a minority on the majority of people.

GEORGE MONCK, 1ST DUKE OF ALBEMARLE. The second son of Sir Thomas Monck of Potheridge, he was created Duke of Albemarle for his part in securing the Restoration of Charles II in 1660. He married Anne, the daughter of John Clarges, a farrier who worked in the Savoy in the Strand in London. Lord Clarendon remarked that 'he was cursed, after long familiarity, to marry a woman of the lowest extraction, the least wit and less beauty', while Lord Ailesbury wrote that the Duke was 'naturally of heavy parts and illiterate'. He died in 1669/70 and the dukedom became extinct on the death of his son in 1688. The 1st Duchess's brother, Thomas Clarges, was knighted and the farrier's surname lives on today in a fashionable London street.

THE MARTINS. They claim to descend from Oliver Martin, a companion-in-arms of Strongbow. Richard Martin was granted almost all of the O'Flaherty lands as a result of the confiscations that took place under Cromwell and the redistribution of land that occurred after the Restoration. A prominent member of the family was Richard Martin (1754–1834), who was the largest landowner in Connacht, with an estate of over 200,000 acres (he boasted that he had a front drive 40 miles long). An energetic life that saw him leave his wife – she was alleged, among other things, to have had an affair with her children's tutor, Theobald Wolfe Tone – and acquired for him the nickname of 'Trigger Dick' because of his skills as a a duellist – culminated in the passing of the Martin Act in 1822, which prevented cruelty to large domestic animals. In 1824, he founded the Society for the Prevention of Cruelty to Animals, which good deed earned him the new nickname of 'Humanity Dick' from his friend King George IV. The Martin estates were centred on Ballynahinch Castle in County Galway, and were lost as a result of the great potato famine in the 1840s. Ballynahinch Castle, which is now an hotel, was bought in 1924 by Ranjit Singhji, His Highness the Maharaja Jam Sahib of Nawanagr. Known to millions as the almost legendary cricketer 'Ranji', several miles of the river on either side of the Castle are still known as 'Ranji's stretch'. His cousin Princess Purna of Morvi married GARECH BROWNE, son of the 4th Lord Oranmore and Browne.

THE GREAT FAMINE (An Gorta Mór). Despite previous food shortages in Ireland, nothing could have prepared the Irish people for the 'Great Hunger' of 1845–49. The Irish peasant survived on a diet of potatoes, which were easy to produce and provided the highest level of calories per acre of any food then grown in Europe. In 1845 the vegetable was hit by the fungus *Phytophthora infestans* that arrived from North America. The ensuing blight destroyed the entire crop for that year and three of the following four years. The spores of the fungus were wind borne and, within 24 hours of infection, reduced the tuber to an evil-smelling black sludge. Sir Robert Peel's Government failed to act, with Peel expressing the belief that the Irish always exaggerated reports of distress. The political and economic attitude of both Peel and his successor, Lord John Russell, was that if one gave the Irish anything gratis, they would be around one's neck forever asking for more free handouts. In order to justify giving money to the poor to buy food, they initiated work schemes such as canal and road building. Starvation was followed by epidemics of typhoid fever, cholera and dysentery as the poor took refuge in the towns and cities. In the end, more died from

these causes than from hunger. In September 1847 Russell's Government ended any attempts to provide relief and demanded that the Poor Law rate be paid to the Treasury before supplying any more aid. The potato crop failed again the next year, this time accompanied by Asiatic cholera. Some Irish landlords paid for their tenants to emigrate to America but many of the 'coffin ships' in which they travelled were barely seaworthy and nearly one-third of the passengers died during the Atlantic crossing. Despite the potato blight, Ireland was rich in food; the truth is that the people (who were described by an English visitor at this time as being 'worse fed and lodged than pigs are in England') starved not for lack of food, but for lack of food that they could afford. The British Association for the Relief of Distress in Ireland and Scotland was founded in London on 1 January 1847, and Queen Victoria gave the then great sum of £2000 to this fund. It did her no good in the eyes of the Irish who dubbed her the 'Famine Queen', and would later claim that she had only given £5! In 1841 there were 8.2 million people in Ireland; a decade later this had fallen to 6.1 million. It is now estimated that about one million people died of disease and starvation during those years and about one million emigrated to England and America. There is a saying that goes 'God sent the blight, but the English made the famine.'

FATHER VALENTINE BROWNE, another member of the family, became the Minister-Provincial of the Franciscan Order and wrote an extremely important letter, in 1632, to one of his brethren. It contained the following instructions 'Whereas with unremitting labour you have pored over the antiquities of our nation, and have endeavoured to rescue them from the almost Stygian darkness in which they were enshrouded…and now with the same endeavour and ardour you have purposed to compile from the ancient and almost obliterated Irish records whatever concerns the annals of our kings, and relates to the state, both ecclesiastical and civil, of this kingdom; lest we might not appear to second your work, which is so virtuous, and fills such a long-felt want, we command you by the merit of holy obedience to persevere until the end…in this laborious work of the Annals…and to submit all that you shall compile to the judgement of men skilful in the Irish tongue.' The recipient of this letter was Father Micheál Ó Cléirigh and the subject in hand was *The Annals of the Kingdom of Ireland* or, as it is better known, *The Annals of the Four Masters.*

COUNT GEORGE DE BROWNE of the Holy Roman Empire and Lieutenant General of the Armies of His Imperial and Catholic Majesty, was descended from the family of Browne of Camus. They were a cadet line of the Brownes of Moyne – themselves a junior branch of the Brownes of Galway. In 1726, James III (the 'Old Pretender') made him Earl of Browne. His son (the 2nd Earl) was born in Limerick in 1698 and rose to be a general in the Russian service. In 1738 he was captured by the Turks and was sold as a slave. He eventually obtained his freedom but remained in Constantinople, where he discovered some important State secrets which he brought back with him to Russia. For this deed the Empress Anna made him a Major General. Peter III later made him a Field Marshal and, from 1765 until his death in 1792, he served as Governor of Livonia (modern-day Latvia and Estonia) where he founded the city of Voru. When he presented his resignation to the Empress Catherine II – the 'Great' – she replied that nothing, except death, could separate them. He married the daughter of Field Marshal Count Lacy (1698–1751) and had two sons, who have possible descendants alive today. Ulysses von Browne, the 1st Earl's brother, was a Colonel in the Austrian Army and was made a Baron of the Holy Roman Empire by Charles VI. His son, Ulysses von Browne, Count of the Holy Roman Empire, Baron of Camus and Mountany, was an Austrian Field Marshal. Struck down by a cannon ball while heading a bayonet charge outside the city of Prague in 1757; he died a few weeks later of his wounds (a shattered leg).

DR PATRICK BROWNE, a great-great-great-grandson of Sir Dominick Mór, was born in 1720 near Crossboyne in County Mayo. He was one of the Brownes of Woodstock, who descended from Sir Dominick Mór's second son, Edward. His fame lies in his book of 1756, *The Civil and Natural History of Jamaica*, which was one of the most significant natural history books of the mid-18th century and second only to the early works of Carl Linnaeus, who on 19 October, 1756, wrote to Dr Patrick Browne: 'You ough(t) to be honoured by a Golden Statue'. Dr Browne's *Flora of County Mayo* was not published until 1995.

GARECH BROWNE founded Claddagh Records in 1962, and The Chieftains, for which activities – and others – he was rewarded with an Doctorate of Letters by Trinity College, Dublin, in 2000. In the citation he was praised for trouncing the scurrilous attempts by the Commissioners of Public Works to invade his 'agreeable solitude' in County Wicklow. Thanks to Mr. Browne's determined opposition, it continued, the Commissioners were forced to retire and admit their defeat.

CLONALIS

Irish Tatler and Sketch January and February 1951

FREDERICK PEPYS COCKERELL. The Cockerell family added the name of Pepys to their surname when John Cockerell married Francis, the grand-niece of the diarist, Samuel Pepys. They had three sons, John, Charles and Samuel, and a daughter. John entered the East India Company and, under Sir Robert Barker in Bengal, made his fortune. He returned home in 1795 and bought the estate of Sezincote in Gloucestershire; however, he died in 1798 before he could build himself a suitable residence. His heir was his next brother, Sir Charles Cockerell, who had also served in India from 1776 to 1790. Sir Charles bought out his sibling's shares in Sezincote and then requested his brother Samuel Pepys Cockerell (1754–1827), to design a house for him. What emerged was a rare example of the 'Hindoo' style of domestic architecture in England. Samuel Pepys Cockerell's son, Charles Robert Cockerell RA PRIBA (1788–1863) followed his father as an architect and designed, among other buildings, the Ashmolean Museum in Oxford. His eldest son was Frederick Pepys Cockerell, who designed Clonalis in County Roscommon and Blessingbourne in County Tyrone.

THE CROSS OF CONG. This is a processional cross, more properly called the Bachall Buidhe, now in the National Museum of Ireland, which was commissioned by Toirdhealbhach Ó Conchobhair, High King of Ireland. It is made of oak covered with copper plates, but much decoration has been added in the form of gold filigree work. It is 30 inches high, and 18 inches across the arms. In the centre is a boss of rock crystal, which formerly enshrined a relic of the True Cross brought back from Rome in 1123 by Toirdhealbhach Ó Conchobhair.

AODH RUADH Ó DOMHNAILL (Red Hugh O'Donel) (1571–1602). The son of Sir Aodh Ó Domhnaill, lord of Tír Chonaill, and Máire an Inghean Dubh Nic Dhomhnaill, the daughter of Séamus Mac Domhnaill, the lord of Dún Naomhaig agus na nGleann (Dunyvaig) and the Glens, he was fostered by Mac Suibhne na dTuath (a lord of the Clan Sweeney). In 1587 he was kidnapped by the Lord Deputy, SIR JOHN PERROTT, and held as a hostage for his family's good behaviour in Dublin Castle. He escaped four years later (with Énrí and Art Ó Néill, the sons of Seaán an Díomais Ó Néill) and they made for the safety of the Wicklow Mountains. It was bleak midwinter and Art Ó Néill died from exposure in the hills, but Aodh Ruadh Ó Domhnaill eventually reached his father's castle in County Donegal. Surgeons had to amputate one of his toes which had been damaged by frostbite. The next year his father abdicated his position as head of the O'Donels and Aodh was inaugurated in his place. He then overran Sligo and Connacht, joined forces with Aodh Ó Néill, EARL OF TYRONE and last King of Tír Éoghaín, and took part in the Gaelic victory at the battle of the Yellow Ford in August 1598. However, in 1601, following the Irish defeat at the Battle of Kinsale, he was sent to request more assistance from King Philip III of Spain. He died at Simancas on 10 September, 1602, almost certainly poisoned by James Blake of Galway, who may have been instigated to commit the murder by the English. He was buried, with Royal honours at the command of the Spanish King, in Valladolid.

THE EARLDOM OF TYRCONNELL. Ruaidhrí Ó Domhnaill, lord of Tír Chonaill was created Baron of Donegall and Earl of Tyrconnell in 1603. He was the second son of Sir Aodh Ó Domhnaill and his wife Máire an Inghean Dubh Nic Dhomhnaill, the daughter of Séamus Mac Domhnaill, the lord of Dún Naomhaig agus na nGleann (Dunyvaig and the Glens) and his wife Lady Agnes Campbell, the daughter of Colin Campbell, 3rd Earl of Argyll (Mac Cailean Mór). As a result, the 1st Earl of Tyrconnell had strong family connections on both sides of the Moyle Sea. He succeeded his brother, AODH RUADH ('RED HUGH') Ó DOMHNAILL as the head of the O'Donels of Tyrconnell. On 4/14 of September 1607, he left Ireland (from Rathmullan on Lough Swilly) in the company of The EARL OF TYRONE. This tragic event is known as the 'Flight of the Earls'. Lord Tyrconnell died in 1608 in Rome, where he is buried. His son assumed the title of Earl of Tyrconnell and was made the Commander of the Irish Brigade in Catalonia. He was killed (or drowned) on his ship, the *Santa Magdalena*, off Barcelona during a sea fight with the French in 1642.

ISAAC BUTT (1813–79). A member of the English and Irish Bar, he suffered from alcoholic and financial problems and spent 18 months in the County Debtors' Prison in Kilmainham. He defended participants in the abortive Young Ireland revolt (1848), and entered Parliament in 1852 as a Liberal-Conservative. He started the Home Government Association in 1870 to 'mobilise opinion behind the demand for an Irish Parliament with full control over domestic affairs' but, three years later, he felt strong enough to upgrade this organization into a fully-fledged political party, which had some 56 members in the House of Commons under his leadership. However, as he spoke in the House only when Irish questions were under discussion, his party seemed to some to be merely a lobby group, which was not to be taken seriously. The activities of two of its younger members, Biggar and Parnell, galvanized the members into action and Butt was more and more sidelined. In 1878, he praised the British Government and described the Westminster Parliament as the life of a 'Great United Nation'. This caused discontent in Ireland and his resignation as leader of the party (although, officially, this was stated to be on the grounds of his ill-health). He did, however, show the Irish people that democracy was a viable alternative to rebellion and terror as means to achieving political ends and, with his successor, Charles Stewart Parnell, this course was persued until it was distorted by the bloodshed of 1916 (and the 86 years of violence that have followed it so far).

THE IRISH NATIONAL PARTY re-formed in 1900 under the leadership of John Redmond, a decade after it split following the Parnell scandal. The party's aim was Home Rule for Ireland, which would have given an Irish Parliament control over Irish affairs (except for the armed forces, taxation and foreign policy which would be controlled from London). The Irish Volunteers, a movement that had 180,000 members, was organized to back the demands for this legislation. The Home Rule bill was passed in 1914 but its implementation was delayed until the end of the war (or for one year whichever might be longer). However, a section of the minority nationalist party, Sinn Féin, took matters into its own hands and launched a rebellion in Dublin during Easter week in 1916. The heavy-handed British response to this led to a complete reversal of Irish allegiances. In 1918, Sinn Féin won 73 of the 105 Irish seats in the House of Commons (but did not take their seats). John Redmond, who died in the same year aged 62, did not live to see the overthrow of his political party and its dreams.

DR DOUGLAS HYDE (Dubhglas de hIde) was born in Tibohine, Frenchpark, County Roscommon in 1860. The descendant of Elizabethan settlers, he was co-founder of the Gaelic League. He served as its President from 1893 until 1915, when he resigned from the organization, deeply unhappy with the stridently political, as opposed to cultural, tone that it was adopting. An author, he also wrote scholarly articles under the nom de plume of 'An Craoibhin Aoibhinn' ('the delightful little branch') and was the Professor of Modern Irish at University College, Dublin, from 1909 until 1932. On 25 June 1938, he was elected as the first President of Ireland. During his period in office he was expelled from the Gaelic Athletic Association (GAA) because he had attended a rugby match (rugby and soccer were seen by the GAA as 'foreign' games and even attending a match was enough for a member to be thrown out of the Association).

THE EARLDOM OF CLANCARE. Donnchadha Mac Carthaigh Mór, King of Desmond, was created Baron of Valentia and Earl of Clancare in 1565 by Queen Elizabeth.

DROMOLAND CASTLE

Irish Tatler and Sketch February and March 1949

JOHN DE COURCY, Lord of Ulster (d.1219). He arrived in Ireland from Stoke Courcy in Somerset in 1177 as part of the Norman force that came to assist Diarmuid mac Murchada, King of Leinster, regain his Kingdom. He then decided to press north and in a comparatively short time conquered a great deal of Ulster. In 1180 he married Affreca, the daughter of Godred, King of Man. In 1185, Henry II appointed him Justiciar of Ireland and he supported Richard I in his quarrels with his brother John. When the latter eventually became King of England, de Courcy was dismissed from office and in 1203 HUGH DE LACY, the son of the lord of Meath, was sent to capture him, but de Courcy escaped. He returned the next year with a force supplied by his brother-in-law, Ragnald, King of Man, but was again driven away by the de Lacys, whose leader, Hugh de Lacy, was created Earl of Ulster in 1205. John de Courcy was eventually reconciled with King John whom he outlived, dying sometime before September 1219.

THE 1ST DUKE OF ORMONDE. Ormond (Ermon or Urmhumhan) was the old name for the northern part of County Tipperary. The head of the Butler family had been created Earl of Ormond in 1328. The 11th Earl's grandson, James Butler, was born in 1610. He succeeded as the 12th Earl of Ormond and was created Marquess of Ormonde in 1642. He served as Lord Lieutenant of Ireland between 1643 and 1647. In this capacity he concluded peace with the Irish Roman Catholics in 1646 and again in 1648/9. He was defeated at Rathmines, outside Dublin, in 1648 by Colonel (later Lieutenant General) Michael Jones (the Governor of Dublin Castle for the Parliament) and fled to the continent. On the Restoration of Charles II, he was created Duke of Ormonde (in the peerage of Ireland) and, between 1662 and 1669 and again from

1677 until 1685, he served as Lord Lieutenant of Ireland. In 1660, he was created Duke of Ormonde (in the peerage of England). He died in 1688 and is buried in Westminster Abbey. The Dukedom and all of the other honours acquired by the 1st Duke became extinct on the death of the 3rd Duke in 1758, but the Earldom of Ormond survives to this day. (The Earldom was spelled 'Ormond' and the Marquessate and Dukedom 'Ormonde'.)

THE GLORIOUS REVOLUTION. When King Charles II died in 1685, he was followed by his brother, James II. The new King was the first Catholic to reign in England since Queen Mary I in the mid-16th century. The incumbent Tory party and many other sections of the country accepted him as their King because he was in his fifties and had a Protestant daughter to succeed him on the throne. When the Duke of Monmouth (Charles II's natural son) rose up against him, James put down the rebellion with great savagery in the 'Bloody Assizes'. He then demanded the repeal of the Test Act, which prohibited Catholics from holding high office. The Protestant majority felt threatened by these proceedings. Consequently, Parliament refused to repeal the measure, so James simply dissolved it and repealed the Act himself. As feared, he then gave prominent positions to Catholics. The Universities were purged and the King ordered his Protestant bishops to read a Declaration of Liberty of Conscience from their pulpits. When six bishops refused to comply they were put on trial for seditious libel but were acquitted, much to the King's fury. When Queen Mary gave birth to a son in June 1688, England was faced with the prospect of a line of Catholic sovereigns. Amid rumours that the baby had been smuggled in to the royal bedchamber in a warming pan, both the Whigs and Tories approached the King's son-in-law William of Orange, the Statholder of Holland, and invited him to come to England. When William landed in the country, King James panicked. His generals began to desert him and he fled from the country, dropping the Great Seal of England into the Thames as he went (it was recovered some months later). Parliament met and offered the Crown jointly to William and his wife, Princess Mary (King James's elder daughter), subject to their acceptance of a Bill of Rights. This guaranteed frequent Parliaments and an undertaking that the monarch would not alter the laws or maintain a standing army without Parliamentary consent. The revolution is called 'Glorious' because it was (initially) bloodless and because it was another step towards the sort of parliamentary democracy that England enjoys today.

THOMAS ROBERTS (c.1720). His father, a Welshman, also called Thomas Roberts and described as a man of 'property and beauty', had settled in Waterford in 1680. Young Thomas (the architect Lord Inchiquin considered for Dromoland) married Sarah Bowles and their son, John Roberts ('Honest John Roberts') of Roberts Mount, in the City of Waterford, was also an architect. 'Honest John' had three sons, Thomas Roberts, the talented artist, his brother, Thomas Sautelle Roberts (who was also a painter) and the Reverend John Roberts, whose son, Abraham, was knighted and whose grandson was the distinguished soldier, Lord Roberts of Kandahar.

JOHN AHERON (d.1761). He was born in Limerick and, apart from his work at Dromoland, he also had a hand in designs for Stradbally Hall in County Laois for the younger Pole Cosby in the 1740s, and Rockforrest in County Cork. In 1754, he published *A General Treatise on Architecture*, the first Irish book on the subject.

THE REVEREND DANIEL BEAUFORT was the father-in-law of Richard Lovell Edgeworth of Edgeworthstown, County Longford, whose daughter was the novelist Maria Edgeworth (1767–1849). Of Huguenot extraction, he had to flee to England on a number of occasions in order to escape from his creditors. In his accounts of a series of journeys throughout Ireland made between 1787 and 1808, he provided an invaluable account of the country as it was during those years

LEAMANEH CASTLE in County Clare is a four-storey building with many mullioned windows. It is basically a 17th-century house built on to a 15th-century tower. The house was probably built in 1639 when Conchobhair Ó Briain (Conor O'Brien) married Máire Ruadh ('Red' Mary), the daughter of Sir Toirdhealbhach Ruadh Mac Mathghamhna (MacMahon), lord of Clonderalaw. Conor was her second husband and was killed by Cromwellians at a fight in the pass of Inchicronan, in 1651. The story goes that his widow, a woman of strong character, refused to allow his body to be brought home to Leamaneh saying, 'We need no dead men here'. She decided that the best way to secure her son's inheritance would be to marry one of the enemy officers. Consequently, she took herself off to Limerick the next day and promptly married Cornet John Cooper. As she was no beauty (her portrait survives to prove the point), it must have been the prospect of the inheritance that tempted the Cornet. In any case, it did him no good for, when he made a disparaging comment about her late husband, she

allegedly killed him by throwing him out of a window at the castle. Nonetheless, she must have been married to him for at least seven years, because their son Henry was born eight years later. The poet and author Robert Graves descended from the child of this unlikely union. One possible side-effect of his mother's marriage to the Cornet was that her son by Colonel O'Brien was brought up as a Protestant.

LADY CHATTERTON. Henrietta Georgiana Iremonger was the daughter of Lascelles Iremonger, the Prebendary of Winchester Cathedral and his wife Harriet, the sister of Admiral Lord Gambier. She married Sir William Chatterton of Castle Mahon, County Cork. After he died in 1855, she married Edward Dering but continued to call herself Lady Chatterton. A romantic novelist, she was the author of *Rambles in the South of Ireland* (1839). THOMAS CROFTON CROKER dedicated *Fairy Legends and Traditions of the South of Ireland* (1828) to her.

SIR JOHN BERNARD BURKE (1814–92). The son of John Burke (1787–1848), a Londoner, who in 1826 published the *Peerage* that now bears his name. His son, John Bernard, a barrister-at-law, was the creator of *Burke's Landed Gentry* and in 1853 he was appointed ULSTER KING OF ARMS and Principal Herald of All Ireland, a position he held until his death. He was also Registrar of the Order of Saint Patrick, Keeper of the State Papers of Ireland from 1867–92, and a Governor and Trustee of the National Gallery of Ireland. Among his other published works were *Romance of the Aristocracy* (1855) and *Vicissitudes of Families* (1859–63). His son, Sir Henry Farnham Burke (1859–1930) was Garter King of Arms from 1918 until 1930.

THE EARLDOM OF THOMOND that had been forced on Murchadh Ó Briain in 1543 ended with the death of the 8th Earl in 1741. In his will, Lord Thomond left his estates (under a special remainder) to his wife's nephew, Henry Wyndham. As a result of this, the owners of the Dromoland estate still pay a head rent to Mr Wyndham's heirs, the Earls of Egremont. On the extinction of the Thomond branch of the O'Briens, the descendents of the eldest son of the Tanaiste, Murchadh, the Lords Inchiquin, became the senior line of the family. If King Brian Bóruma was the hero of the family pedigree, then Murrough, the 4th Baron Inchiquin was its villain. Educated as a Protestant, he had taken the Parliamentary shilling during the Civil War. His support for the Cromwellian cause reached its nadir when, in 1647, he burned the Cathedral of Cashel and slaughtered its inhabitants. For this act of genocide and vandalism he was thereafter known as Murchadh na dTíoiteán ('Murrough the Burner'). Like a true schizophrenic, he then not only turned his coat and went over to the King's side, but also converted to the Roman Catholic faith. Charles II, who like all the Stuarts, was better at rewarding his enemies (if he thought it would advance his cause) than remembering his friends, gave Murrough the Earldom of Inchiquin in 1654. In exile he was asked by Louis XIV to serve as Governor of Catalonia for the Spanish King. When he became a Catholic, his wife left him and got custody of their son in order to stop Lord Inchiquin from educating him as a papist. She was Elizabeth St Leger the daughter of Sir William St Leger, Elizabeth I's Governor of Munster. Later in his career, Lord Inchiquin was captured by pirates, together with his son, and taken to Salé in Morocco, but was eventually ransomed. He died in 1674 and was buried in Limerick Cathedral. The people, however, had not forgotten his atrocities at Cashel, for it was reported that his body was dug up and thrown into the river. His son, the 2nd Earl, was Governor and Vice Admiral of Tangier and, afterwards, he was sent to Jamaica as Captain General and Governor. He was taken with a fever and died there shortly after his arrival. The 5th Earl was a passionate supporter of the ACT OF UNION, for which assistance he was created a marquess in 1800. He revived the name of his kinsman's extinct Earldom when choosing his designation, becoming the Marquess of Thomond. His son was made a Knight of Saint Patrick and, with the death of the 3rd Marquess in 1855, the family titles became extinct except for the old Barony of Inchiquin, which devolved on the descendants of the 3rd son of Murchadh the Tanaiste, 1st Earl of Thomond, who were living at Dromoland in 1855. Apart from his Barony, the last marquess left a widow who was described by a family member as 'an old Cat & a Humbug!'

FRENCH PARK

Irish Tatler and Sketch January 1949

FATHER FRANK BROWNE SJ (1880–1960). He was born in Cork and was educated at Belvedere College, Dublin. He became a member of the Society of Jesus and served as an army chaplain with the Irish Guards during World War I, earning the Military Cross and Belgian Croix de Guerre. A keen photographer, by the time of his death he had accumulated over 42,000 negatives, which cover not only Ireland but also

England, Scotland, Australia, Spain, Italy, South Africa, Sri Lanka, Crete, Egypt and Aden (he had served as a missionary priest in some of these countries). His most famous photographs are those that he took in 1912, when he sailed from Southampton to Queenstown (now Cobh), in County Cork on board *Titanic*. When the ship docked at Queenstown to take on additional passengers, Father Browne disembarked.

PIETRO BOSSI. He first appeared in Wilson's *Dublin Directory* in 1785 with an address at 22 Fleet Street. By 1787 he had moved to 38 Fleet Street where he remained until his last appearance in the Directory in 1798. He worked in scagliola (*specchio d'asino*), a technique whereby small pieces of marble (*scaglia*) are reduced to a fine powder by fire and turned into a paste, which is then coloured and inlaid into a marble frame. This craft was used by the Romans and was revived in the 18th century. There are many stories told about Pietro Bossi and the lengths to which he went in order to protect the secret of his craft. It is reported that 'allegedly so while he was at work in Belvedere House, Lady Belvedere, with the curiosity of Eve, looked through the keyhole to try and see what was going on. Bossi, however sensed her presence and blew some powder through the keyhole which caused the lady a certain amount of physical discomfort.'

ISAAC WELD (1774–1856) He was born in Fleet Street, Dublin, and educated at Whyte's Academy in Grafton Street (now Bewley's Oriental Coffee House) and in England. In 1795, he went to Canada and America, 'for the purpose of examining with his own eyes into the truth of the various accounts which had been given of the flourishing and happy condition of the United States of America, and ascertaining whether, in case of future emergency, any part of those territories might be looked forward to, as an eligible and agreeable place of abode.' While there, he met George Washington. He returned in 1797 'without entertaining the slightest wish to revisit the American continent' and published *Travels through the States of North America, and the Provinces of Upper and Lower Canada, during the Years 1795, 1796 and 1797*. He compiled *A Statistical Survey of the County of Roscommon* (1838) for the Royal Dublin Society (of which he was the honorary secretary).

SIR WILLIAM BETHAM (1779–1853). He was appointed Deputy Ulster, King of Arms by 1815 and Ulster in 1820 (a position he held until his death). In this capacity, as Principal Herald of All Ireland, he oversaw the visit of King George IV to Ireland in 1821. He was the author of *Irish Antiquarian Researches* (1826), of *Etruria Celtica* (1842), of 30 volumes of abstracts from wills of the Prerogative Court, and of another 23 volumes of pedigrees, which are of extreme importance due to the destruction in 1922 of much of the original material on which they were based. These are today kept in the Genealogical Office in Kildare Street, Dublin. Sir William was a scholar of Irish history, within the standards of his own day, but later researches altered the validity of many of his conclusions. An example of his research concerns the 'wolf-dogs' that are mentioned in Irish poems and stories; Sir William wrote that he had 'heard from a very old person long since dead, of his having seen them at the Neale, in the County of Mayo, the seat of Sir John Browne, ancestor to Lord Kilmaine, I have no doubt they were gigantic greyhounds. My departed friend described them as very gentle, and that Sir John allowed them to come into his dining-room, where they put their heads over the shoulders of those who sat at table. They were not smooth-skinned, like our greyhounds, but rough and curly-haired. The Irish poets call the wolf-dog 'cu', signifying a champion.'

SIR JOHN PERROTT (1527–1592). Commonly reputed to be the natural son of Henry VIII, he was created a Knight of the Bath at the Coronation of Edward VI. In 1571, he was appointed by Elizabeth I to be the President of Munster and he was able to restore peace to that province after some two and a half years campaigning. In 1584, he was made Lord Deputy of Ireland in succession to Arthur Grey, 14th Lord Grey de Wilton. He failed in his attempt to destroy Somhairle Buidhe Mac Domhnaill (Sorley Boy MacDonnell), whose submission to the Crown he was forced to accept (as well as having to allow him to retain the Ulster lands that Somhairle had stolen from his nephew, Lord of Dunyvaig and The Glens and Lord of The Route). Perrott quarrelled with the Lord Chancellor of Ireland, Archbishop Adam Loftus, and in 1588 he was ordered back to England to be succeeded in Ireland by Sir William Fitzwilliam. In 1591, Sir John was committed to the Tower of London on a charge of High Treason. One of the charges against him was that, annoyed from being alternatively reprimanded and praised by the Queen, he publicly said of her, 'Lo, now she is ready to piss herself for fear of the Spaniard and I am again one of her white haired boys.' A year later, he was convicted of encouraging the rebellion of Sir Brian Ó Ruairc and of treasonable correspondence with the King of Spain and was condemned to death, but he died in the Tower before the sentence could be carried out. He seems to have had an obsession with dress and made an attempt to persuade Toirdhealbhach Luineach Ó Néill to dispense with the native Irish costume and to adopt that of the English Court. As Ó Néill and his followers complained that their new trousers 'embraced' them 'like fetters', this effort to 'civilize' the Gaels came to nothing.

TANISTRY. As used by the English, the word meant the system under the Brehon laws that regulated the succession to 'Gaelic lordships'. Under this arrangement, it was not necessary to be the senior male of a family to inherit (as it would have been in the case of a peerage) but rather the most suitable candidate. Consequently, Sir Aodh Ó Domhnaill followed his brother (who had sons) as the head of the Clann Dalaigh and was able to renounce his position in favour of his son, AODH RUADH. Seaán an Díomais Ó Néill was followed by his cousin, Toirdhealbhach Luineach Ó Néill, who then surrendered 'his lordship' to another cousin, Aodh Ó Néill, the 3rd EARL OF TYRONE, while, in the Clann Aodh Buidhe branch of the Clann Néill, the second half of the 16th century saw the lordship pass from one brother to a second and then on to a third. It then went to the son of the third brother who was followed by the son of the first and then back to the third brother's second son. It came to rest with the son of the second brother just as the English were making an end of the Gaelic Order and forcing primogeniture on the native lords. The system of tanistry in Brehon Law meant the naming of a successor in the lifetime of a Gaelic lord.

THE BATTLE OF AUGHRIM. This engagement was fought on 12 July 1691 at the insistence of King James II's General, Charles Chalmont, Marquis de Saint-Ruth, and against the advice of his comrade-in-arms, Patrick Sarsfield (Earl of Lucan in the Jacobite Peerage). About 20,000 men took part on each side and the field was won by GENERAL GINKEL for William III. Some 9000 died that day, 7000 of them Jacobites, including the Marquis de Saint-Ruth. Aughrim is a village in County Galway; the name means 'horse hill' (Each Dhruim).

SIR EDWARD CROFTON, 2nd Baronet. He was the son of Sir Marcus Crofton, 1st Baronet, (who had changed his surname from Lowther) and his wife Catherine Crofton, the daughter of Sir Edward Crofton 3rd Baronet (of a previous creation). The 2nd Baronet was the Member of Parliament for Roscommon. He died before he could be made a peer and so his widow, Armida Croker of Boxtown, County Kildare, was created Baroness Crofton of Mote, County Roscommon (with remainder to the heirs male of the body of her late husband) on 8 March 1798. She died in 1817 and was succeeded in her peerage by her grandson – her son, Sir Edward Crofton, the 3rd Baronet, had committed suicide at the family seat, Mote Park, in 1816.

GLANANEA
Irish Tatler and Sketch November 1952

SAMUEL WOOLEY. He is reputed to be the architect of the Glananea gates. However, all he left is a watercolour of the entrance (dated 1796) and, as he is best known simply as a watercolourist, it may be that he did not design them at all but only recorded what he saw, as he did with such pictures as his view of the House of Lords entrance to the Irish Parliament (dated 1797).

LADY HARRIET MONCK. She was the sister of Lady Cecily Monck, the daughter of the 2nd Viscount Monck of Ballytrammon (he was also the 1st, and last, Earl of Rathdowne), who married William Barlow Smyth of Barbavilla. The Moncks were collateral relations of George Monck, 1st Duke of Albemarle.

BEAN SÍ (Banshee). A being of the Celtic Otherworld, the name translates as 'fairy woman'. The unearthly eerie and high-pitched shriek of these creatures announced the death of a member of prominent Irish families. The sound would usually be heard near the doomed person's house, even if they were far away at the time. In the North of Ireland, death was foretold by three ghostly knocks on the front door.

GORMANSTON CASTLE
Irish Tatler and Sketch May 1947

LORD ST ARMAND held a Barony by Writ (a summons requiring the named person to come to parliament as a peer – as opposed to those peers whose titles were created by Patent). The first Lord St Armand was summoned in 1299, but this dignity became extinct on his death in 1310. It was revived (again by Writ) for his brother in 1313. Amauri St Armand fought at Crécy in 1346, and was Justiciar of Ireland between 1357 and 1359. He died in 1381.

SIR GEOFFREY FENTON (1539/40–1608). The principal Secretary of State for Ireland, he played a major part in defeating the EARL OF TYRONE's rebellion in Ulster. His sister's five sons, by the name of

Parsons, followed their uncle to Ireland, where he promoted their careers. The Earl of Rosse, a descendant of one of them, Sir Laurence Parsons, still lives at Birr Castle in County Offaly.

THE EARL OF DESMOND'S REBELLION. Gerald Fitzgerald, 14th Earl of Desmond, rose up against Queen Elizabeth I in 1579. Attainted in 1582, he was slain in 1583 at Gelnagintigha, near Tralee, and some 600,000 acres were declared forfeit to the Crown (his murderer, Daniel Kelly was later executed at Tyburn). The Earl's head was sent to London and was spiked on London Bridge as a warning to all other potential traitors. This 'Rebel Earl' only succeeded to the title because his father had declared that all of his children by an earlier marriage were illegitimate (on the grounds of consanguinity with his wife). Despite his 'bastardization', the 13th Earl's eldest son, Thomas Ruadh (the 'Red') FitzGerald refused to accept that he was illegitimate and assumed the Earldom when his father died. His son, the '15th' Earl, James FitzGerald was known as the 'Súgán' Earl (or 'Earl of Straw'). On the death of the '17th' Earl in 1632, the male line descendants of the 7th Earl (who was beheaded in 1467/8) died out and no one has attempted to assume the title since. The 14th Earl of Desmond's rebellion was put down savagely, the *Annals of the Four Masters* reporting that 'the lowing of a cow or the voice of a ploughman could scarcely be heard from Cashel to the furthermost point of Kerry.'

THE EARL OF TYRONE. Conn Bacach Ó Néill (Conn The Lame), King of Tír Éoghaín (1484–1559), submitted to Henry VIII in 1542 and was created Earl of Tyrone, with remainder to his son, Feardorcha (Mathew) and his heirs male. Feardorcha was created Baron of Dungannon at the same time. Conn Bacach had already made a show of obedience some years before when he carried the Sword of State at the installation of his cousin, Gerald FitzGerald, 9th Earl of Kildare, as Lord Deputy of Ireland in 1524. The State papers record that Ó Néill became so humble as to 'bear the sword before my lord of Kildare covering his shorn poll with a coif, which was a monstrous sight to behold.' His legitimate son, Seaán an Díomais (Shane the Proud), went to war with his father in 1551 over control of the Ó Néill lands and subsequently became King of Tír Éoghaín. In 1558, Feardorcha was murdered by his half-brother and Conn Bacach fled into the English Pale for protection. On his death, the earldom passed to Feardorcha's elder son, Brian, who was murdered in 1562 by Seaán an Díomais's cousin and tánaiste (heir), Sir Toirdhealbhach Luineach Ó Néill. The earldom then came to Feardorcha's younger son, Aodh (Hugh), who became the 3rd Earl. In 1591, he succeeded Sir Toirdhealbhach Luineach (d.1595), King of Tír Éoghaín, who had resigned from the dignity, as Ó Néill. In 1593, Aodh began the Nine Years War against the English, inflicting defeats on them at Clontibret (1593) and the Yellow Ford (1598). Defeated by Lord Mountjoy at Kinsale in 1601, he submitted again to Queen Elizabeth in 1602/3 and was restored to his honours. However, in 1607, fearing that he was about to be accused of treason, he fled from Ireland from Rathmullen, on Lough Swilly, taking with him his wife, three of his sons, the Earl of Tyrconnell and about 90 others. They arrived at Rouen and made their way to Rome, where they settled. The Archbishop of Canterbury wrote about him at this time that 'he is poor, old and drunken.' But other evidence contradicts this which is probably English propaganda. Lord Tyrone, who became almost blind, died in Rome in 1616. The earldom was claimed by his sons and, on the death of the last of them without male heirs in 1640/1, it was used by the descendants of Feardorcha's illegitimate offspring, the last of whom used the title Conde Tiron in about 1670. Today, the nearest male-line relation of the O'Neill, kings of Tír Éoghaín and earls of Tyrone, is the Spanish Marqués de la Granja y del Norte. He is Ó Néill an Fheadha (O'Neill of the Fews) and descends from Art Ó Néill, King of Tír Éoghaín from 1509 to 1513. Hugo O'Neill, Mac Uí Néill Buidhe (Ó Néill of Clanaboy), descends from Énrí Ó Néill, King of Tír Éoghaín (1325–45) and is the senior line of the family.

AS THE EARLS LEFT IRELAND, they were harassed by the galley of the MacSweeney of Doe (MacSuibhne na dTuath). His direct descendant is Tom Sweeney, MacSuibhne na dTuath, who lives in Donegal and Dublin.

OWEN 'THE POPE' O'MAHONY (1904–70). A genealogist and raconteur, he was a Knight of Malta and an active member of the Irish Georgian Society. He toured the USA and Canada in an effort to save Georgian buildings in Dublin, which were threatened with demolition. He also broadcast a series of programmes on the Irish radio station, Radio Éireann, entitled 'Meet the Clans' and, between 1966 and 1968, was a visiting professor at the University of South Illinois, where he annotated the university's large collection of Irish writings. He was known as 'The Pope' O'Mahony and the reasons given for this range from an alleged desire to be Pontiff (expressed while still at school) to the story that he removed several generations of spurious ancestors from the pedigrees of a fair proportion of the Irish landed gentry and, when asked how he could justify tampering with information which had at least a couple of centuries of tradition (if not of fact) to back it up, stated that, in such matters, he was infallible. What is certain is that with the author's father, he went to a Mass that was given in the early 1960s for the Papal Legate to Ireland at Croke Park in Dublin. O'Mahony, whose white beard was identical to the Legate's, was wearing the full dress uniform of a Knight of Malta and, in this resplendent uniform, he was approached by a crowd of Dublin urchins, who gathered around him shouting 'Hey Mister! Are you the Papal Legate?' 'No' he replied firmly 'I am the Pope!' Perhaps appropriately, he never married.

A MEMBER OF THE PRESTON FAMILY said that the new menservants' wing in the Castle was so large that 'a footman could rear a large family there without anyone in the house knowing a thing about it.'

HEADFORT
Irish Tatler and Sketch October 1948

SIR WILLIAM PETTY (1623–87). The son of a clothier, he arrived in Ireland as physician to Cromwell's troops and eventually grabbed some 270,000 acres in the kingdom for himself. He cut down a great deal of ancient forest and, although he never built a great house for himself in Ireland (being content to contrive 'many noble places on paper'), his widow was created Baroness Shelburne after his death. This peerage was bestowed on her only for her lifetime, but it was regranted in turn to each of her two sons (the second of whom was created Earl of Shelburne). As both of her sons died without heirs, the family estates passed to her daughter Anne, who married John FitzMaurice (the 5th son of the 19th Baron, and 1st Earl, of Kerry), who adopted his wife's surname in 1751 and was created Earl of Shelburne in 1754. The second Earl of this creation was made Marquess of Landsdowne, County Somerset, in 1784, and the present Marquess is the 8th (the family's surname is now Petty-FitzMaurice). Their titles are remembered in Ireland (though with different spelling) in the name of a hotel in Dublin – The Shelbourne – as well as a road in Balls' Bridge and the Landsdowne sports stadium where international rugby is played.

JOHN ENSOR (d.1787). He came to Ireland from Coventry in the 1730s and became Richard Castle's assistant. He laid out the north side of Merrion Square from 1762 onwards for the Earl Fitzwilliam and designed the great round room beside Dr Mosse's hospital, which gave the building its name – The Rotunda. Appointed as the Clerk of Works to the Surveyor General in 1744, he married the heiress of Ardress House, County Armagh, and enlarged the house.

THOMAS COOLEY (1740–84). A Londoner, he came to Ireland having won the competition to design the Royal Exchange (now the City Hall) and was appointed as architect to the Board of Works (Inspector of Civil Buildings) in 1775. He designed Rokeby Hall, the Archbishop's palace in Armagh, Caledon in County Tyrone (for Lord Caledon), Mount Kennedy in County Wicklow (for the future Lord Rossmore), part of Ardbracken in County Meath and the Public Record Office (which was afterwards incorporated in James Gandon's design for the Four Courts).

ARTHUR YOUNG (1741–1820). The son of the prebendary at Canterbury Cathedral, he became the agent to Lord Kingsborough in 1777 and published *A Tour in Ireland* in 1780. This was followed by a series of famous tours through France (before and during the Revolution) entitled *Travels in France* (1792). In 1793, he was appointed as the 1st Secretary of the Board of Agriculture and is regarded as the father of modern agriculture. He went blind at the end of his life.

THE MOST ILLUSTRIOUS ORDER OF SAINT PATRICK. This was created in 1783 by King George III to be a National Order of Chivalry for Ireland – as the Most Noble Order of the Garter was for England and the Most Ancient Order of the Thistle was for Scotland. The Irish Order consisted originally of a Grand Master and 13 Knights (later increased to 22). Of the heads of the families whose seats are featured in this book, 4 of the 13 founder Knights and 14 others were members of this Order (the 2nd Viscount Lismore – from Shanbally Castle – refused the honour in 1864 and the 1st Viscount French, afterwards the 1st Earl of Ypres (from the French Park family), was made a Knight in 1917). The ribband and the mantle of the Order were of sky-blue silk, which is consequently known as 'Saint Patrick's Blue'; however, although blue is the heraldic colour of Ireland, it is a royal or dark shade of azure in its earliest depictions. The Knights whose seats are in this book were:
William Robert Fitzgerald, 2nd Duke of Leinster 1783 (a Founder Knight)

Thomas Taylour, 1st Earl of Bective 1783 (a Founder Knight)
Charles Moore, 6th Earl of Drogheda (created in 1800 1st Marquess of Drogheda) 1783 (a Founder Knight)
Murrough O'Brien, 5th Earl of Inchiquin (afterwards, 1800, 1st Marquess of Thomond) 1783 (a Founder Knight)
Thomas Taylour, 1st Marquess of Headfort 1809
William O'Brien, 2nd Marquess of Thomond 1809
John Chambré Brabazon, 10th Earl of Meath 1821
Arthur James Plunkett, 8th Earl of Fingall 1821
John Hely-Hutchinson, 3rd Earl of Donoughmore 1834
Thomas Taylour, 2nd Marquess of Headfort 1839
William Forward Howard, 4th Earl of Wicklow 1842
Arthur James Plunkett, 9th Earl of Fingall 1846
Henry Francis Seymour Moore, 3rd Marquess of Drogheda 1868
Thomas Taylour, 3rd Marquess of Headfort 1885
Edward Donough O'Brien, 14th Baron Inchiquin 1892
Reginald Brabazon, 12th Earl of Meath 1905
Richard Walter John Hely-Hutchinson, 6th Earl of Donoughmore 1916
Geoffrey Henry Browne, 3rd Baron Oranmore and Browne 1918.

JOHN PHILPOT CURRAN (1750–1817). A King's Counsel, he first achieved notice when he successfully defended a Catholic priest who had been whipped by Viscount Doneraile. A gregarious man, he was the 'Prior' of the 'Monks of the Screw' a literary and drinking club which also included HENRY GRATTAN and Lord Charlemont among its members. He was a Member of the Irish Parliament from 1783 until 1797. A strong advocate for Catholic Emancipation, he defended Hamilton Rowan and Theobald Wolfe Tone during their trials for High Treason. A distinguished orator, he is probably best remembered for his pronouncement, during a speech in 1808, that 'Eternal vigilance is the price of liberty'. It was at his home, The Priory, near Rathfarnham, in County Dublin, that his youngest daughter, Sarah (1782–1808) met and fell in love with Robert Emmet (1778–1803). This engagement was to prove the greatest tragedy of John Curran's life and, after Emmet's failed and messy rebellion of 1803, he turned on his daughter who was forced to leave his house and seek refuge with friends in County Cork. Sarah's attachment to Emmet led to her father being examined by the Privy Council, but he was soon cleared of any suspicions of disloyalty. Appointed Master of the Rolls in 1806 and made a Privy Councillor for Ireland, he retired in 1814 .

JAMES FRANKLIN FULLER (1835–1924). A Kerryman, he worked in England under Alfred Waterhouse before returning to Ireland as the architect to the Representative Church Body in Ireland. He designed the Great Southern and Western Hotels at Kenmare and Parknasilla in County Kerry, Kylemore Castle (with Samuel Ussher Roberts) in County Galway, Coolavin in County Sligo (for The MacDermot), Harristown in County Kildare (for the La Touche family).

FAMINE ARRIVED IN IRELAND IN THE 1840s and County Meath was not spared. *The Meath Herald*, which was published in Kells, gives an indication of the poverty in 1845 in the following court case: Matt Smith, wood ranger to the Marquess of Headfort, found the defendant, also named Smith, lying in a ditch with a small amount of ash, which he had stolen. Even the magistrate pointed out that it was a trifling amount involved – worth a shilling. The unfortunate defendant was fined two and six, plus costs, or one week in jail.

KILKEA CASTLE

Irish Tatler and Sketch August and September 1957

SIR WALTER DE RIDDLESFORD (d.1226). He married Amabilis, daughter of Henry fitz Henry, a natural son of King Henry I of England. Apart from Kilkea Castle, Sir Walter was granted the lands of Bray in County Wicklow, where he built a wooden castle beside the Dargle river. He died of a surfeit of lampreys.

GIRALDUS CAMBRENSIS (Gerald de Barry) 1147–1216/20. A writer, historian and ecclesiastic, he was born in Wales into a noble family, his uncle being the Bishop of Saint David's. After studies in Paris, he was appointed Archdeacon of Brecknock. When his uncle died, he was chosen by the chapter to succeed him but Henry II vetoed this. Giraldus then went to Paris and in 1184 accompanied Prince John on his Irish expedition. While there, he wrote *Topographia Hibernica*, which purports to give a description of the country. He left Ireland two years later and preached the crusade throughout Wales. In 1198, the chapter of Saint David's again chose him to be their bishop, but this time it was the Archbishop of Canterbury who objected. Giraldus went to Rome to plead with Pope Innocent III, but the Pontiff took the side of Canterbury and he had to return to Wales. In the following years Giraldus, who had fled to Rome a second time, was reconciled with the

King and accepted a small pension. His works are important – although he was obsessed with superstitions and the practice of witchcraft – and a good deal of their content, as with Geoffrey Keating's *History of Ireland* four centuries later, was made up of what Giraldus himself describes as, 'the popular rumours of the land'.

CROM-A-BOO. The motto and war cry of the FitzGeralds. It comes from the name of their stronghold in Limerick and translates as 'Crom For Ever!' Its utterance was once prohibited by an Act of Parliament. There is a Cromaboo bridge over the River Barrow at Athy, in County Kildare.

SILKEN THOMAS. Thomas FitzGerald, 10th Earl of Kildare (1513–1536/7). His father, the 9th Earl, had spent quite a few periods as a State prisoner in the Tower of London for suspected treason. There was a rumour in 1534 that Lord Kildare was to be beheaded and, on 11 June in that year, his son and heir, Thomas FitzGerald, renounced his family's loyalty to the English Crown. His nickname of 'Silken Thomas' comes from the fact that on that day his bodyguard of 140 horsemen wore coats of mail with silken fringes. A month later, he murdered John Allen, the Archbishop of Dublin, and was excommunicated. He petitioned his uncle, the Lord Lieutenant, Lord Leonard Grey, for mercy and agreed to surrender if he was shown clemency. Although this was promised by the Crown, Thomas, together with his five uncles, was hung, drawn and quartered at Tyburn in 1536/7. His father had died in 1534 and he had succeeded to the earldom, which was attainted on account of his treason but was restored to his brother in the reign of Queen Elizabeth I. It remains one of the junior titles of the present Duke of Leinster.

THOMAS REYNOLDS was the Treasurer of the Leinster Directory of the SOCIETY OF UNITED IRISHMEN, an organization dedicated to bringing about Ireland's independence. Reynolds's son claimed that his father became an informer only because he was alarmed by the Society's bloody plan of action to achieve its aims. It was Reynolds's decision to give evidence for the Crown in open court, which made his information so valuable to the Government. As a result of his betrayal, the authorities arrested all but three members of the Leinster Directory on 12 March 1798. Loyalty, or a twinge of conscience, caused him to alert Lord Edward Fitzgerald, the Duke of Leinster's son, who remained at liberty for another two months. Reynolds was rewarded with a pension of £1000 a year and was allowed to settle in England. After an extravagant sojourn in Cumberland and Monmouth, he was given a salaried position as packet agent in Lisbon. In 1817, he was appointed British consul in Iceland, with the understanding that he did not have to live there. When his patron, Lord Castlereagh, committed suicide in 1822, Reynolds was disowned by the Government. He later settled in Paris.

THE SOCIETY OF UNITED IRISHMEN was founded on 14 October 1791 in Belfast, to lobby for parliamentary reform, Catholic Emancipation, and, as Wolfe Tone said, for the unity of all the people – Catholic, Protestant and Dissenter – under the common name of Irishmen. Although in 1793 the Government extended the franchise to Catholics with a minimum freehold of 40 shillings, and allowed them to hold minor military rank, the United Irishmen pressed for the full repeal of the PENAL LAWS, and by 1798 they had thrown in their lot with Revolutionary France from whom they expected military assistance. In March of that year, however, almost the entire Leinster Directory of the Society was arrested, on the information of THOMAS REYNOLDS, while planning a rising for 23 May. Their leader, Lord Edward Fitzgerald, was later taken and died of his wounds in gaol. Those members who had not been taken then decided to proceed with the rebellion, even if the French did not arrive. Their efforts failed, as they were unable to take Dublin, were defeated in Wicklow and Kildare, and received no assistance for the Northern Directory, which failed to mobilize. In County Wexford a 'Wexford Republic' was set up, but the atrocities perpetrated upon Protestant captives tarnished this part of the rebellion. The 'Wexford Republic' was defeated at the battle of Vinegar Hill on 21 June. Two weeks earlier, Henry Joy McCracken led a belated rising in Ulster, but was defeated at Antrim and, six days later, Crown forces beat his colleague, Henry Munro, at the battle of Ballynahinch. After this, the Ulster part of the rebellion collapsed and McCracken and Munro were executed. Eight weeks later the French, under GENERAL HUMBERT, finally arrived on the west coast of Ireland, with 1019 men. After an initial success at Castlebar, they were also defeated, so when another French army, with Wolfe Tone in attendance, arrived on 12 October, the rebellion was all but over. The British captured the French flagship, *La Hoche*, and Tone was taken prisoner; sentenced to death, he committed suicide in prison. The Government reaction to the uprising was severe; several of the Society's leaders were executed and hangings took place all over Ireland. The rebels in County Wicklow under Michael Dwyer held out in the mountains until 1803, when Dwyer surrendered and was transported, but by then the Government had arranged for the dissolution of the Irish Parliament and for the political Union of Great Britain and Ireland.

KILLEEN CASTLE
Irish Tatler and Sketch October 1950

LORD FALKLAND. Henry Carey (1575–1633) was created Lord Carey and Viscount of Falkland in the Peerage of Scotland in 1620 and served as Lord Deputy of Ireland between 1622 and 1629. He died as a result of the amputation of his leg, which he broke when he fell from his horse.

BERWICK'S REGIMENT. James Fitz James was born in France in 1670. He was the natural son of James Stuart, Duke of York (afterwards King James II). He was created Duke of Berwick in 1687. After the dissolution of his Troop of Irish Horse in 1698, he obtained an Irish Infantry Regiment, which was named after his senior English title. This regiment was made up from what remained of the Regiment of Athlone, the King's Dismounted Dragoons, and the three Independent Companies of King James II's army. His first wife, Lady Honora Bourke, was the widow of Patrick Sarsfield (Earl of Lucan in the Jacobite peerage). He was naturalized as a French subject in 1703 and created a Marshal of France in 1706. In the course of a distinguished military career, he was created Duke of FitzJames (in France) and Duke of Liria (in Spain). His life ended on 12 June 1734, when a cannonball at the battle of Philipsbourg blew his head off. The Regiment of Berwick was disbanded by an order of the National Assembly on 21 July 1791.

JAMES SHEIL (1790–1867) He worked at Killeen Castle for the Earl of Fingall and at Pakenham Hall (now Tullynally Castle) for the 2nd Earl of Longford. He also redesigned Rathaldron in County Meath, a gothicized house with a vaulted hall, and Corke Lodge at Shankill, County Dublin, in 1840. Corke Lodge is now the home of Alfred Cochran, the architect and designer, brother of Sir Marc Cochran, Bart.

SAINT OLIVER PLUNKETT. He was born in 1625 at Loughcrew, County Meath. Ordained a priest in 1647, he went to study in Rome in 1650 and was made Archbishop of Armagh and Primate of All Ireland in 1657. The 'Popish Plot' of 1673 (which was the invention of a monster named Titus Oates) led to a renewal of anti-Catholic feeling and forced Plunkett into hiding. The Privy Council in London were informed that the Archbishop had planned a French invasion and in 1679 he was imprisoned in Dublin Castle. In June 1681, he was found guilty of High Treason in London (on the evidence of two Franciscans) and on 1 July 1681 he was executed at Tyburn. Beatified in 1920, he was proclaimed a Saint by the Catholic Church in 1975.

JEREMY WILLIAMS. An illustrator and architect, he was educated at Glenstal, County Limerick, and University College, Dublin. Formerly a partner in the firm of Williams, Cochrane and Flynn-Rogers, he is also the author of *A Companion Guide to Architecture in Ireland, 1837–1921* (1994) and has illustrated several books including *The Irish Chateaux, in search of the Wild Geese* by Renagh Holohan (1999). He is the greatest living authority on Irish Victorian architecture.

JOHN DILLON (1851–1927). His father was John Blake Dillon (1816–66), a barrister and one of the 'Young Ireland' leaders. The younger Dillon was educated at the Catholic University of Dublin. A Member of Parliament, he supported the 'boycotting' of landlords but, a passionate supporter of Home Rule, he opposed the 1916 Rising. Once the uprising had been put down, he argued in the House of Commons for the executions to stop. He said that the authorities were 'letting loose a river of blood' that would destroy his Party's efforts to end centuries of 'hatred and strife' and would drive the ordinary Irish people more and more towards the rebels' cause. His reward was to see his party trounced in the 1918 elections by Sinn Féin. His son, James Dillon (1902–86), was the leader of the Fine Gael Party in Dáil Éireann from 1959 until 1965.

KILLRUDDERY
Irish Tatler and Sketch December 1947

LORD CROMWELL. A Barony by Writ called George Cromwell (son and heir of Thomas Cromwell, KG, (1485–1540) Earl of Essex and Henry VIII's Vicar General) to Parliament as a peer in 1540. As a personal honour (not a courtesy title) it was not included in the Act of Attainder that led to Lord Essex's execution in 1540. When the Brabazons acquired Killruddery, the Lord Cromwell was Thomas Cromwell, 5th Baron (1594–1653). He was created Viscount Lecale in 1624 and Earl of Ardglass in 1644/5, which earldom became extinct in 1687.

SIR GEORGE HODSON, BART. His family's title had been created in 1789 and he was the 3rd Baronet. He engaged William Vitruvius Morrison to design a new mansion for him on his property near Bray in County Wicklow. This is Holybrooke Hall, today the home of Scott MacMillan of Rathdown and his wife, Katherine (the best-selling novelist Katherine Kurtz). Sir George Hodson died in 1888.

EUGENE O'CURRY (1794–1862). A member of the Ordnance Survey in Dublin, he was the greatest expert of his time on ancient Irish manuscripts and, with his brother-in-law John O'Donovan, he set up the Brehon Law Commission. He was appointed Professor of Archaeology and Irish History in the new Catholic University in 1854 and his lectures on 'The Manners and Customs of the Ancient Irish' were published in 1873.

VOTA VITA MEA (Prayers are my Life). This is the motto of the Earls of Meath. Considering how well they have prospered, it might not be unfair to suggest that their prayers have indeed been answered.

GASPARE GABRIELLI (ff. 1790–1833). An Italian artist who lived in Dublin, he specialized in landscapes and painted the series of canvases at Lyons, County Kildare, for Lord Cloncurry. Lyons has been splendidly restored by its current owner, Tony Ryan of Ryanair.

WILLIAM BURN (1789–1870). Born in Edinburgh, the son of the architect Robert Burn, he was the pioneer of the Victorian version of the Scottish Baronial style. In Ireland, he designed Muckross House in County Kerry, Bangor Castle in Clandeboye and Castlewellan (all in County Down), Dartrey in County Monaghan and Lough Rynn in County Leitrim.

GBE. The Most Excellent Order of the British Empire was founded by George V on 4 June 1917 as the Order of British Democracy. It has five classes; Knight or Dame Grand Cross (GBE), Knight or Dame Commander (KBE) – Bob Geldof, the musician was awarded this class for his services to charity, Commander (CBE), Officer (OBE) and Member (MBE). This is the decoration that was given to the Beatles on the recommendation of Prime Minister Harold Wilson.

GCVO. The Royal Victorian Order was founded in 1896 by Queen Victoria. As a Family Order, it is outside the power of Government to make recommendations for appointments to it. There are five classes: Knight or Dame Grand Cross (GCVO), Knight or Dame Commander (KCVO or DCVO), Commander (CVO), Member 4th Class (MVO) and Member 5th Class (MVO).

THE HONOURABLE CLAUD PHILLIMORE (1911–94). The son of the 2nd Baron Phillimore, he was an architect who specialized in a reduced form of the neo-Georgian style. In Ireland, apart from his work at Killruddery, he designed Killarney House, County Kerry. He eventually succeeded his brother in the peerage as the 4th Lord Phillimore, and was, in his turn, followed as the 5th Baron by his son.

KILMURRY
Irish Tatler and Sketch February 1952

THERE IS AN EFFIGY AT KILFANE, County Kilkenny, of Sir Thomas Cantwell, who died in 1319. Eight feet high, it provided the knight with his nickname Cantwell Fada or Long Cantwell.

GENERAL JEAN-JOSEPH HUMBERT (1767–1821) rose through the army ranks as a protégé of General Lazare Hoche (1768–97), with whom he fought during the latter's ill-fated attempt to land French troops at Bantry Bay in 1796. On 22 August 1798, Humbert landed at Cill Chuimín, County Mayo, and captured Killala and Ballina. Four days later he engaged the British Militia under General Gerard Lake at Castlebar. It was General Lake's policy of terror that drove many apolitical Irishmen to revolt, and provoked the rebellion of 1798. After a short, sharp battle, Lake's men turned tail and fled in disarray to Tuam. This engagement was known thereafter as 'the races of Castlebar'. Humbert established a 'Republic of Connacht', with John Moore of Moore Hall as president and Randal MacDonnell as vice-president, and moved from Castlebar but was defeated at the Battle of Ballinamuck by General Lord Cornwallis. The French were taken prisoner of war, but the Irish were massacred. This badly planned expedition is known as 'Bliain na bhFrancach' ('The Year of the French'). After his release, Humbert led an adventurous life in America. He taught French and fencing and when he died was given what amounted to a State funeral, but today he lies in an unmarked grave. The General Humbert Summer School is now held in his memory each year in County Mayo.

SIR JONAH BARRINGTON. A barrister, he was elected to the Irish House of Commons in 1790 and (with only one year's exception) sat there until the ACT OF UNION dissolved that body forever in 1800. Curiously, although he voted against the Act (and claimed to have been offered the post of Solicitor General for Ireland had he done so), he acted as an agent for Mr. Pitt's Government in persuading other members of the House to vote in favour of the measure. He received a knighthood in 1807 but was later accused of financial improprieties and was removed from his judicial office in 1830. He was the author of *Personal Sketches of His Own Time* (1827–32; 3 volumes).

SIR PHILIP CRAMPTON, 1ST BARONET (1777–1854). At the age of 14, he was indentured to Surgeon Richards and entered the Royal College of Surgeons, of which he would be four times President. He was also the founder and first President of the Zoological Society and was instrumental in obtaining for them a site in Phoenix Park for the Dublin Zoo. In 1821, with two colleagues, he founded the first teaching hospital for children in the British Isles. John Gibson Lockhart (1794–1854) wrote about Sir Walter Scott's visit to Ireland 'from Dublin, we made an excursion of some days into Wicklow, halting for a night at the villa of the Surgeon-General, Sir Philip Crampton, who kindly did the honours of Lough Breagh and the Dargle.' His companion during Scott's visit was Maria Edgeworth who wrote a poem in his honour in 1821 (another companion on that occasion was Mr Jephson of Mallow Castle). Because of his love of clothes and the good life, he was known as 'Flourishing Phil' and boasted that he could swim in his lake at Lough Bray, ride 15 miles into Dublin and amputate a leg – all before breakfast. Surgeon General to the Forces and Surgeon in Ordinary to George IV and Queen Victoria, Webb's *Irish Biography* said of him that 'his fame was almost European, and he enjoyed an immense practice. The brilliancy of his conversational powers was remarkable, and the amenity of his manners made his company universally desired.' Fitzpatrick, in his *Life of Lever* tells of a 'practical joke played late one night, when a messenger aroused Sir Philip from his bed to inform him that a great personage had fallen from his horse in Dublin'. When he arrived, he found King William III's statue blown by gunpowder from his charger. One of his medical advances, in about 1834, was a procedure to remove bladder stones. He was created a baronet in 1839 and four years after his death a memorial, complete with a drinking fountain, was unveiled in Dublin. This attracted the attention of James Joyce who mentions it in *The Portrait of an Artist as a Young Man*, where Stephen Dedalus asks 'is the bust of Sir Philip Crampton lyrical, epical or dramatic?', and in *Ulysses* where Leopold Bloom asks for a communal ('incorporated') drinking cup 'Like Sir Philip Crampton's fountain.'

11TH VISCOUNT MOUNTGARRETT (1745–93). The son of the 10th Viscount, he married Lady Henrietta Butler, a daughter of Somerset Butler, 1st Earl of Carrick. She died in 1788 at Mount Juliet, the house that was named after her mother. Lord Mountgarrett died at his house in Saint Stephen's Green, Dublin after three days of sickness caused by eating a meal of strawberries and cider. On hearing the news, Lord Clonmell wrote in his diary 'Died Lord Mountgarrett, as wicked a malignant selfish monster as I ever knew, a victim to brutal appetites and thirst for blood; a lesson to vice, and a caution to be civil to all, obliging to many, to serve few, and offend none, as the safest, wisest, pleasantest mode of going through life.'

KNOCKLOFTY
Irish Tatler and Sketch April 1949

WILLIAM TINSLEY. Born in 1804, he initially worked as an architect in Ireland (with a preference for the Gothic style). Apart from his work at Knocklofty, he remodelled the entire town of Cahir for the Earl of Glengall. In 1851 he moved with his family to the USA and settled in Cincinnati. He designed several university buildings in Indiana and Wisconsin, as well as the Tyler-Davidson fountain in Cincinnati. He built the Christ Church at the Quarry to designs that are very similar to a church which he had built in Clogheen, County Tipperary, years before (to plans supplied by George PAIN). He died in 1885 and a stained glass window in Old Saint Mary's Church, in his native Clonmel, commemorates his family.

THE HUTCHINSON FAMILY (four brothers, a sister and their widowed mother) emigrated from England to America in 1633. One brother, William Hutchinson, married Ann Marbury ('a woman of a haughty and fierce carriage, of a nimble wit and a very voluble tongue'). It probably helped that she also owned the whole of Rhode Island, but her prosperity failed to impress the Native Americans, who slaughtered her and her children in 1643. The grandson of another brother was Thomas Hutchinson, the first Governor of Massachusetts Bay, while yet another brother, Richard Hutchinson, returned to England in 1648, joined Oliver Cromwell in his Irish campaigns, and was rewarded with the grant of Knocklofty. He died in London in 1688 and was succeeded by his son, Ezekiel, who died at Knocklofty in 1699.

SIR JOHN DE BLACQUIERE (1732–1812). A member of successive Irish

Parliaments from 1773 until 1800, he was also, between 1772 and 1777, the Chief Secretary to Lord Harcourt, the Lord Lieutenant of Ireland. Created a Knight of the Bath and a baronet in 1774, he became a peer as Baron de Blacquiere in the Union honours of 1800. He died at his home in Bray, County Wicklow, in 1812. Horace Walpole described him as 'a weak and conceited man', while Lord Charlemont thought him 'a man of low birth, no property and weak genius, yet possessing in an eminent degree those inferior abilities which are more prized by, and perhaps more useful to, an evil Government...cajoling and jobbing were this Secretary's talents.' J. Swift McNeill in *Titled Corruption* wrote that he was 'one of the most shamelessly corrupt self-seekers in the Irish House of Commons' and Lord Camden recorded that de Blacquiere's elevation to the peerage was 'almost intolerable'.

LORD NORTH. This was a Barony by Writ that was created in 1554 for Edward North, the son of Roger North, a London merchant. The 4th Baron's great-grandson was created Earl of Guildford in 1752. His son, Frederick North, the 2nd Earl, was Prime Minister and First Lord of the Treasury between 1770 and 1782, and it was his Government that presided over the loss of the British Colonies in North America. Edward Gibbon wrote that the ministry of Lord North (his courtesy title at the time) was a 'lazy, stormy, and at length unfortunate administration.'

THE ACT OF UNION. After the 1798 rebellion, the government of William Pitt decided that the best way of dealing with the Irish problem was to bring about a legislative Union of the two Kingdoms. Pitt's agents then proceeded to bribe and coerce the members of the Irish Parliament to vote themselves out of existence. They did so in August 1800, and the Act of Union became law on 1 January 1801. The proffer of titles was one of the weapons in the British Government's armoury. The Lord Lieutenant, Lord Cornwallis, complained to the Prime Minister about his involvement in 'this dirty business....my occupation is now of the most unpleasant nature, negotiating and jobbing with the most corrupt people under heaven.' Not all Irishmen were so venal. Charles Vereker refused the offer of a peerage, saying that 'having defended my country with my sword (against GENERAL HUMBERT) I will not betray her with my vote.' When a government agent offered Lord Powerscourt an earldom in exchange for his vote, the gouty lord rose from his sickbed and kicked the offending messenger downstairs.

MALLOW CASTLE
Irish Tatler and Sketch May 1949

BARON NORREYS OF RYCOTE (1525–1601). He married Margaret, a daughter of John Williams, Lord Williams of Thame, and was the Member of Parliament for Berkshire between 1547 and 1552 and for Oxford between 1571 and 1572, in which year he was created a peer. His grandson was created Earl of Berkshire in 1620/21 and killed himself in the same year with a crossbow. The earldom became extinct on his death but the Barony of Norreys passed through his daughter to the Earls of Abingdon, who hold it to the present day. The family surname is variously spelled Norreys and Norris but is pronounced Norris.

SIR HENRY BEDINGFIELD (1509–83). The grandson of Sir Edmund Bedingfield of Oxburgh, in Norfolk, who had fought on the Yorkist side during the Wars of the Roses. On the death of King Edward VI, it was Sir Henry who, with Sir Edward Jerningham, was principally responsible for securing the throne for Mary I (Mary Tudor). In 1554, during Mary's reign, Bedingfield, who was the Lieutenant of the Tower of London, acted as Princess Elizabeth's gaoler; when she became Queen, she dismissed him from court saying that 'whenever she had a state prisoner who required to be hardly handled and strictly kept she would send for him'.

THE GERALDINES. This is the collective name given to the family and followers of the Fitz Geralds, the Earls of Kildare and Desmond and the three Palatine Knights: the Black Knight (of Glin), the Green Knight (of Kerry), and the WHITE KNIGHT (FitzGibbon).

THE PLANTATION OF MUNSTER. The concept of settling English colonists in the south of Ireland took concrete shape in the 1580s after the crushing of the DESMOND REBELLION and the confiscation of the earl's vast estates. Sir John Perrott arrived in Ireland as Lord Deputy in 1584 and quickly set to work. A quarter of a million acres was to be divided in 20 seigniories (or estates), which could be then subdivided. The land was to be given to gentlemen who would each agree to bring 91 English tenants and their servants to settle the land. All the native Irish would be expelled and each undertaker was to provide mounted soldiers and 105 foot soldiers (a total force of 60 cavalry and 2100 foot soldiers under arms). Unfair treatment of the natives led even a loyal Englishmen like Sir William Herbert to protest that 'Our pretence in this enterprise of plantation was to establish...piety, justice, inhabitation and civility...

Our drift now is, being here possessed of land, to extort, make the state of things turbulent and live by prey and pay.' The land had been badly mapped and the incomers in many cases permitted the Irish to remain as their tenants. Throughout these years, the English settlers made the fatal error of assuming that they were secure. Edmund Spenser, who had an estate in County Cork, wrote in 1598 'that more care was taken for profit and utility than for strength and safety'. The Irish had not welcomed these foreigners who had stolen their land and mocked their religion and, when the Aodh Ó Néill, EARL OF TYRONE, rose up against the English Crown, Munster rebelled against the colonists. After Ó Néill's flight from Ireland in 1607, it was his territories in the Northern province of Ulster that were successfully colonized. In Munster only the very great English landowners remained, as the ordinary colonists returned to England, disillusioned with the whole enterprise.

THE ANNALS OF THE FOUR MASTERS (ANNALA RIOGHACHTA ÉIREANN). These are the most comprehensive of all of the ancient histories of Ireland and cover the period 'from the earliest times' (c 2242 BC) until AD 1616. Compiled between 1632 and 1636 by Father Micheál Ó Cléirigh, a Franciscan from Donegal, who had previously written an account of many of the lives of the Irish Saints, the Annals were under- taken under the patronage of Fearghal Ó Gara, Lord of Magh Gara and Coolavin in County Sligo. Father John Colgan, the author of the Acta Sanctorum Hiberniae, who knew Ó Cléirigh, gave the Annals their name by adding to Ó Cléirigh's own, the names of three of his co-workers, Fearfeasa Ó Maolchonaire, Peregrine Ó Cléirigh and Peregrine Ó Duibhgeannain. Later, the name of Muiris Ó Maolchon- aire was added, but the title was not changed to the Annals of the Five Masters. The best translation of the work is by John O'Donovan and was published in 1851.

LORD CASTLEHAVEN. James Tuchet, 3rd Earl of Castlehaven (1617–84). His grandfather, George Tuchet, 11th Baron Audley, was wounded at the Battle of Kinsale in 1601 and was created Earl of Castlehaven in 1616. The 2nd Earl was beheaded in 1631 for sodomizing his page, Laurence Fitzpatrick (who was later executed at Tyburn for the same offence). The Earl's wife, a notorious adulteress, was the principal mover in securing her husband's fate. The 3rd Earl joined with the Confederate Roman Catholic Irish in 1641 and remained one of their number until 1643. He fought under General Preston 9Lord Gormanston's brother, but in 1652 he fled Ireland and fought under the Prince de Condé during the Fronde rebellion against the French king. Lord Castlehaven was succeeded in his title by his youngest brother. George, his next brother and rightful heir, was passed over in an Act of Parliament of 1678 because he was a Benedictine monk.

SIR JOHN AUBREY, 2nd Baronet. The title was created in 1660 and, in 1678/1679, the 2nd Baronet married Margaret Lowther, the 15th child of Sir William Lowther (a collateral relation of SIR EDWARD CROFTON). Sir Thomas died of injuries caused by a fall from his horse and the baronetcy became extinct on the death of the 7th Baronet in 1856.

MOORE ABBEY

Irish Tatler and Sketch September 1962

O'DEMPSEY (Ó DÍOMUSAIGH). This family (who take their surname from a forebear named Díomusach) claim descent from Rus Failghe, son of Cathaoir Mór, quasi-historical King of Leinster and, in consequence, have the same ancestry as Ó Conchobhair Failghe, Lord of Offaly. The Ó Dempseys were also known as the Clann Mhaolughra (Clan Maliere). Diarmuid Ó Díomusaigh (who was among the few Leinster leaders who refused to answer King Henry II's summons to meet him at Dublin in 1171) established a monastery for the Cistercians at Monasterevin in 1178. Their territory comprised the baronies of Portnalinch in County Laois and Upper Phillipstown in County Offaly, where their principal stronghold was at Ballykean. They remained loyal to the crown during the reign of Queen Elizabeth I, and their lands were untouched. In 1599, Toirdhealbhach Ó Díomusaigh (Terence O'Dempsey) was knighted by the Earl of Essex, and his grandson and successor was created VISCOUNT CLANMALIER. They lost their lands as a consequence of their support for James II, Séamus a'Cacha ('James the Shit').

MITRED ABBEY. This refers to a monastic foundation where the abbot has been given the privilege of wearing a mitre (usually reserved for bishops and archbishops), of wearing the Papal ring and carrying the Papal cross. It also allowed the abbot, by virtue of his office, to sit in the great councils of state. Another mitred abbey in Ireland was Baltinglass in County Wicklow, while in England, Westminster Abbey was raised to the status of a mitred abbey in 1216.

VISCOUNT CLANMALIER. Toirdhealbhach Ó Díomusaigh (Terence O'Dempsey) was created Baron of Phillipstown and Viscount

Clanmalier in 1631. The area from which the title derives its name extends on both side of the River Barrow into counties Laois and Offaly. The 1st Viscount died in 1637 and was followed by his grand- son, Lewis, whose father, Owny Ó Díomusaigh had already lost two- thirds of his property to Henry Bennet (later created Earl of Arlington) who built the town of Portarlington on the former Ó Díomusaigh lands. Lewis, the 2nd Viscount Clanmalier, was attainted for his part in the 1641 rebellion but was restored in 1662 after Charles II returned to the throne. He married Anne, the maternal granddaughter of Thomas Fitz Maurice, Lord Kerry, but died childless. No one came forward to claim his peerages, but as he had six uncles and two great-uncles (all of whom were potential heirs to the viscountcy under its patent of creation), it may be reasonably assumed that the title is dormant rather than extinct.

CAPTAIN WARHAM ST LEGER (1579–1632). He was the brother of Sir William St Leger (d.1658), the son of Sir Anthony St Leger (d.1602) and the grandson of Sir Warham St Leger (1525–1600) and his wife the Honourable Ursula Neville, daughter of the 3rd Lord Abergavenny. Consequently, through his grandmother he was a descendant of John of Gaunt and Edward III. He lost a large amount of money as a result of his involvement with Sir Walter Raleigh and his expedition to Guiana in 1618, during which St Leger commanded his own ship.

LORD DEPUTY RUSSELL. He was youngest son of Francis Russell, Earl of Bedford, and had campaigned in the Netherlands before coming to Ireland, where he replaced the Lord Deputy Sir William FitzWilliam. One of his first tasks was to visit Connacht and, as a consequence of what he heard in Galway, he removed the local Governor, SIR RICHARD BINGHAM, from office. While in the town he built up the fortifications and provided 'great guns' for the town's defence. He then had to con- front Aodh Ó Néill, King of Tír Eóghain and EARL OF TYRONE, who had been accused of treason by members of the council. Ó Néill, 'came unto him beyond all men's' expectation, and falling on his knees, most humbled, craved pardon in writing for that he had not come unto the former Lord Deputy, being commanded'. Ó Néill offered to assist in raising the siege then taking place at Enniskillen and promised that 'would he never take arms against the Queen's Majesty'. This was an undertaking that he would shortly break. Russell went on to raise the siege of Enniskillen and then turned his attention to the rebel leader, FIACHA (MAC AOIDH) Ó BROIN, in County Wicklow. He executed the rebel leader and took his wife, Róis Ní Thuathail (O'Toole), captive.

THE 1ST EARL OF BESSBOROUGH. The grandson of John Ponsonby, a Cromwellian Colonel of Horse, Brabazon Ponsonby, 2nd Baron Bess- borough and 2nd Viscount Duncannon (1679–1758), was created Earl of Bessborough in 1724. He served as Marshal of the Admiralty in Ireland from 1751 until 1752, and was made Vice Admiral of Munster in 1755.

MRS DELANEY (1700–88). Born Mary Granville, she was first married to a Mr Pendarves and was a key figure in literary London. Her second husband was Dr Patrick Delaney (1685–1768), the Chancellor of Saint Patrick's Cathedral in Dublin. A friend of King George III and Queen Charlotte, she left a diary, which gives one of the best insights into life in aristocratic and artistic circles in the 18th century.

COUNT JOHN MACCORMACK. He studied with Vincenzo Sabatini and between 1907, when he made his debut at Covent Garden, and 1923, he appeared in all the great opera houses in Europe and America. The first of the 'super tenors', he would give concerts for over 5000. He was created a Papal Count in 1928 in recognition of his services to Catholic charities and died in 1945. The present Count MacCormack is the tenor's grandson, John, who is a successful restaurateur in Dublin.

MOUNT JULIET

Irish Tatler and Sketch December 1957 and January 1958

RAYMOND LE GROS 'the Fat' fitz Gerald was the son of William fitz Gerald, and the grandson of Gerald FitzWalter and Nesta, the daugh- ter of Rhys ap Tewdwr Mawr (King of Deheubarth). He took part in the captures of Dublin and Limerick, built the choir in the Cathedral of the Holy Trinity (Christ Church) in Dublin and died childless, despite which the Grace family claim descent from him. Described as 'big- bodied and strong-set', he died in 1182 and is buried in the Abbey of Saint Molanfide, now part of the demesne of Ballynatray House, County Waterford.

JERPOINT ABBEY, County Kilkenny. This is located by the River Arrigle and was founded in 1158/60 by Domhnall Mac Giolla Phádraig, King of Ossory, for the Benedictine Order, but it was taken over in 1180 by Cistercian monks from Baltinglas Abbey in County Wicklow. The oldest parts of the abbey are the Irish-Romanesque transepts and chancel, but building continued after the Cistercians had taken control; the east window dates from the 14th century and the central tower from the 15th. In 1540 the Crown granted it to James Butler, Earl of Ormond.

PATRICK OSBORNE. An Irish stuccodore from Waterford whose delicate style may be seen in Castletown (Cox), County Kilkenny and the Mayoralty House (now the Mercy Hospital) in Cork, as well as the Chamber of Commerce, George's Street, Waterford. Osborne's work is typified by wall panels and plasterwork ceilings enriched with garlands, swags and eagles.

ROCKFLEET
Irish Tatler and Sketch May 1954

IN THE BOOK OF RIGHTS (Leabhar na gCeart), which dates from the 10th century, the O'Malleys are listed as being tributary kings to the provincial Kings of Connaught.

GRÁINNE NÍ MHÁILLE (GRACE O'MALLEY). It is a moot pint as to whether or not Grace O'Malley was actually the head of the O'Malley clan. She never was, nor could be, a Gaelic lord or head of a Gaelic family. The 'Composition of Connacht' of 1585 was signed among others by Maoilsheachlainn Ó Mháille of Belclare. One of the items that the signatories to this document agreed was that the names, titles, captainships, tanaistships, and other Irish jurisdictions, with all other elections and customary division of lands, 'shall henceforth be utterly abolished'. However, 22 years later, in the Inquisition of 1607, Owen O'Malley of Cahernamart (Westport) is described as Chief of his Name and it is stated that some of his rights have come to him by way of tanistry. It is worth noting that an Owen O'Malley of Cahernamart was one of the signatories to the 1585 'Composition of Connacht'. It would seem that the lordship passed from Maoilsheachlainn O'Malley to Eoghan O'Malley (despite whatever might have gone on in the family around Clew Bay during those years).

CAMBRO-NORMAN. Used to describe those Normans who took possession of estates in Wales following the Norman Conquest of England in 1066.

SIR RICHARD BINGHAM. He was appointed Governor of Connacht by Queen Elizabeth I. In 1586, the Bourkes rose up against the Crown, and Bingham (who was known as 'the Devil's Sickle') defeated them at the battle of Berna na Gaoithe. The prisoners, men, women and children were taken to an island in Lough Conn (where they were all probably slaughtered). Shortly afterwards some 2000 MacDonnells arrived to assist the Bourkes, but Bingham (who lost six horses from under him during the fight) and his troops killed all but a few of them at Ard na Riadh (Ardnaree). Sir Richard was later removed from office when Sir JOHN PERROTT, the Lord Deputy, complained to the Queen about his severity and insubordination. He was imprisoned in the Fleet prison but was afterwards returned to office and in 1598, with 5000 troops, he was appointed Marshal of Ireland. He died in Dublin in 1598/9 before he could take up his command. His relations stayed on in Ireland, however, and from his brother, Sir John Bingham, descended Field Marshal the Earl of Lucan who commanded the Heavy Brigade during the Crimean War, as well as the unfortunate Lord Lucan, who having allegedly murdered his children's nanny, fled England and has not been seen since.

MACWILLIAM ÍOCHTAR. This was the patronymic given to the head of the Mayo Bourkes, as opposed to the head of the Clanricarde Bourkes who was MacWilliam Uachtar.

LORD HOWTH (1590s). Nicholas St Laurence, 8th Baron Howth (1555–1607). He inherited the title at the age of 34 in 1589.

LORD HOWTH (1469–79). Robert St Laurence (1437–89), 2nd (or possibly 1st) Baron Howth – the date of the creation is unclear. A supporter of the House of York during the Wars of the Roses, he married Lady Joan Beaufort, a daughter of Edmund Beaufort, Duke of Somerset and became Lord Chancellor of Ireland in 1483. Lord Howth was made a Knight of Saint George, which was a military fraternity, established by Edward IV in 1472, in order to defend the Pale against the native Irish. Among the 13 Knights of this Order were Lord Gormanston, the Earl of Kildare, Sir John Plunkett and Alexander and Edmund Plunkett (all of whose seats feature in this book). The Knights of Saint George were abolished by a clause of Poynings Act in 1494, their Order having lasted for a mere 22 years.

THE O'DONELS OF NEWPORT. Neale O'Donel, who descended from Sir Niall Garbh Ó Domhnaill, the head of the senior branch of Clann Dalaigh, was created a Baronet of Ireland in 1780. The title became extinct in 1889 on the death of the 5th baronet but was claimed in 1893 by an Australian convict who asserted that he was the grandson of Connell O'Donel, a younger brother of the 4th baronet. The real Connell had, however, died unmarried in Dublin lunatic asylum.

ROCKINGHAM
Irish Tatler and Sketch November 1948

CASTLE – OR ROCK – ISLAND in the demesne was one of their seats and there Tadgh MacDermot once entertained all of the poets of Ireland to a great feast. W.B. Yeats wanted to use it as a meeting place for a mystical Order of initiates.

THE ANNALS OF LOUGH CÉ were written in the Abbey on Trinity Island by the White Canons in, about, 1589.

THE MACDERMOT. (Mac Diarmada) This family shares a common ancestor with Ó Conchobhair Donn, O'Conor Don. The Kings of Moylurg, their lands were in the counties of Roscommon and Sligo (as well as parts of Mayo). Brian Mac Diarmada married Sarah, the daughter of O'Conor Sligo, and it was their grandson who went to live at Coolavin on the shores of Lough Gara in County Sligo. What little remained of the great estates of the family was lost in the next generation, when his son was captured after the Battle of Aughrim fighting for King James II. Two distinguished heads of this family were the Right Honourable Hugh MacDermot PC, who styled himself Prince of Coolavin in the 19th century, and, in the 20th century, Sir Dermot MacDermot KCMG, who served as the British Ambassador to Indonesia and Thailand. The present head, Niall MacDermot, was born in 1935.

THE EARL FERRERS. Laurence Shirley, Earl Ferrers, was described in a contemporary report as 'when sober....not such as to be remarkable, yet his faculties were so much impaired by drink that, when under the influence of intoxication, he acted with all the wildness and brutality of a madman'. In January 1760 he murdered his steward, a Mr Johnson, and was executed four months later at Tyburn. What makes this event singular is that it was, allegedly, the first time that a drop was used during a hanging. As a peer, Lord Ferrers was strung up with a silken, instead of a hempen, rope. The present Earl Ferrers was a Minister of State at the Home Office (under Douglas Hurd) during Margaret Thatcher's Premiership.

EDWARD KING drowned while returning to Ireland. This melancholy event prompted John Milton (1608–74) to compose *Lycidas*, (1645) which was written as 'A lament for a friend drowned in his passage from Chester on the Irish Seas. 1637'.

THE WHITE KNIGHT. (FitzGibbon or Mac Giobúin). One of three Palatine Knighthoods (the others being the Green Knight of Kerry and the Black Knight of Glin) bestowed on his sons by John Fitz Thomas Fitz Gerald of Shanid, Lord of Decies and Desmond. The eldest son, Gerald Fitz Gerald (the ancestor of the White Knights) was fostered by Giobúin Ó Coinín of Thomond, and, on this account, the family surname became FitzGibbon. Maurice FitzGibbon, the last White Knight, died in the reign of Charles I and his descendants today in the female line are the Earls of Kingston. The White Knight's lands extended from southeast Limerick into County Cork. The origin of these knights is obscure, for instance the so-called white Knight is actually called An Ridire Fionn (fair-haired knight). A Giobún FitzGerald had a liaison with Ó Coinín's wife and the result was the White Knight.

JOHN NASH (1752–1835). The architect of Regent's Park and Regent Street, London, Nash was also the personal architect of the Prince Regent and designed Buckingham Palace (since altered) for him. He also remodelled Brighton Pavilion between 1815 and 1821 and laid out Carlton House Terrace on the site of the Regent's short-lived Palace of Carlton House; its entrance portico survives around the corner at the National Gallery in Trafalgar Square. His architectural practice was enormous and his Irish buildings included Gracefield Lodge (altered) in County Laois, Rockingham in County Roscommon (demolished), Shanbally Castle in County Tipperary (demolished), Killwaughter Castle in County Antrim (in ruins), Killymoon Castle in County Tyrone and Lough Cutra Castle in County Galway.

THE BROTHERS PAIN. James Pain (1779–1877) and George Richard Pain (1793–1838) were the sons of James Pain (the elder) who designed both Kew Bridge (rebuilt in 1913) and Richmond Bridge (1780) in London. He was also the Director of the Society of Architects (1771). His father, William Pain (1730–90), was a distinguished architect and the author of many standard works on the subject. The brothers Pain arrived in Ireland in 1816 to oversee the construction of Lough Cutra Castle in County Galway to the designs of JOHN NASH (to whose practice they were apprenticed) and they decided to settle in the country. Their country house practice became quite extensive and included (separately or in tandem) Dromoland and Knappogue Castle (both in County Clare), Blackrock Castle in Cork, Castle Bernard and Laughton (both in County Offaly), Strancally Castle in County Waterford, Mitchelstown Castle in County Cork and Adare Manor in County Limerick.

SHANBALLY CASTLE
Irish Tatler and Sketch November 1957

HENRY GRATTAN (1746–1820). He became a Member of Parliament in 1775 and soon became the leader of the opposition. Having removed the restrictions of Irish trade then in force, he campaigned for legislative independence from England, which led to a breach with his colleague Henry Flood (1732–91). Henry Grattan left Parliament in 1797 due to increasing ill health and went to live at his country house, Tinnehinch in County Wicklow. He returned to Parliament as a Member for that county after the rebellion of 1798 and fought, unsuccessfully, against the proposed ACT OF UNION between Great Britain and Ireland. When that measure was passed, he returned to Tinnehinch but re-entered politics in 1805 as a Member in the English House of Commons, where he supported the cause of Catholic Emancipation. His health finally gave way in 1819 and he died in London on 4 June 1820. He is buried in Westminster Abbey.

LORD SACKVILLE. Edward (Eddie) Sackville-West, 5th Lord Sackville of Knole (1901–65). He was the friend of the author Elizabeth Bowen and a collateral descendant of the Duke of Dorset, who gave the family's surname to the principal street in Dublin (although the name of the thoroughfare was later changed to that of Daniel O'Connell).

SHELTON ABBEY
Irish Tatler and Sketch January 1947 and March 1951

SIR GEORGE GILBERT SCOTT (1811–78) PRIBA. The architect of the Albert Memorial (1863 onwards), the Midland Railway Terminus Hotel, St Pancras (1867–74), the Foreign Office, Whitehall (1861–68), the Home and Colonial Offices (from 1858 onwards) and the opulent India Office (1867), the Martyrs' Memorial, St John's College Chapel and Exeter College Chapel (all in Oxford). He also designed the General Infirmary in Leeds and the Episcopal Cathedral of Saint Mary's Edinburgh, as well as Glasgow University (1866–1871). He was the Professor of Architecture at the Royal Academy from 1866 until 1873 and, during the course of his career, he restored over 500 churches and 39 Cathedrals. He was knighted in 1872.

JOHN PRESTON NEALE (1780–1847). After an inauspicious beginning as a post office clerk, he became friends with the distinguished watercolourist John Varley (1778–1842), who persuaded him to become a painter. Exhibiting 74 times at the Royal Academy between 1804 and 1844, he was principally a landscape artist working in both oils and watercolours. As such, he provided the illustrations for a number of publications including *Views of the Seats of Noblemen and Gentlemen* (1822–24, with a second series in 1829), *Graphical Illustrations of Fonthill Abbey* (1823) and *An Account of the Deep-Dene in Surrey* (1826), He had one son, Edward Pote Neale (1801–71).

HUGH HOWARD (1675–1737). Son of Dr Ralph Howard, he went to Rome from Ireland in 1697 in the company of Thomas, 8th Earl of Pembroke, who was the English Ambassador to the Treaty of Ryswyck. Howard worked in Carlo Maratta's studio until 1700 when he went to London, where William, 2nd Duke of Devonshire, employed him as his artistic advisor. Howard married, in 1714, Thomasina Langston, a daughter of General Thomas Langston. He was buried at Richmond beside his wife. George Vertue described him as being a 'sober sparing man', so much so that he is reported to have left between £40,000 and £100,000 on his death.

ULSTER KING OF ARMS. The first Herald appointed in Ireland was John Chandos in 1382 as 'Ireland King of Arms'; the last to hold this office was Thomas Ashwell in the reign of King Edward IV. In 1552, King Edward VI wrote in his diary 'There was a King of Arms made for Ireland, whose name was Ulster, and his province was all Ireland; and he was fourth Herald of Arms and first Herald of Ireland.' The last Herald to be called Ulster was Sir Nevile Wilkinson who died in 1941. His deputy, Thomas Sadlier, continued as Deputy Ulster until 1943, and at that time the Irish Government took over the office and appointed Dr Edward MacLysaght to be Chief Herald of Ireland (with all of the prerogatives of that office, except those concerning the MOST ILLUSTRIOUS ORDER OF SAINT PATRICK). Thus the old office continues to this day, but under a new name. It is, incidentally, the oldest office in the Irish State (the name of Ulster was then attached to the English Heraldic Office of Norroy King of Arms and today has jurisdiction over the six counties of Northern Ireland, and not the whole island as Ulster's authority was in the past).

SIR NEVILE RODWELL WILKINSON KCVO (1869–1940). Ulster King of Arms and Principal Herald of All Ireland from 1908 until his death, he was the last Chief Herald of Ireland to use the designation Ulster. In 1903 he married Lady Beatrix Herbert, the daughter of Sidney Herbert, 14th Earl of Pembroke and 11th Earl of Montgomery (1853–1913). He founded the State Heraldic Museum in 1909 and built a famous doll's house, 'Titania's Palace', which is now at Legoland in Denmark.

SIR HAROLD ACTON CBE (1904–94). An historian and aesthete, he was descended from a Prime Minister of Ferdinand IV of the Two Sicilies. After Oxford, where he knew Evelyn Waugh and Cyril Connolly, Harold Acton became acquainted with the Bloomsbury Group and with T.S. Eliot and Aldous Huxley. He wrote *Peonies and Ponies* (1941), *The Last Médicis* (1984), *The Bourbons of Naples 1731–1825* (1986), *Memoirs of an Aesthete* (1948), *More Memoirs of an Aesthete* (1970) and a memoir on Nancy Mitford.

THE CONTENTS OF SHELTON ABBEY were sold in a 13-day sale held by Allen and Townsend in 1950. There were special train and bus services from Dublin to Arklow and coaches ferried the prospective purchasers up and down the avenue to the Abbey. There were pictures by Reynolds (bought in at £500), Rubens (£1500) and whole series painted by Richard Wilson. A Saxon jewel, known as the Sutton brooch, part of a hoard that was recovered at Sutton on the Isle of Ely in 1694 was sold, together with a powder horn and other items, as a lot for ten shillings. It is now in the British Museum. Sotheby's also held a two-day sale of a selection of books from the library at Shelton Abbey that yielded a total of £4317 in December of the same year.

STRADBALLY HALL
Irish Tatler and Sketch February 1947

THE Ó MORDHA (O'MORES), LORDS OF LAOIS (Leix). This family claim descent from Laoighseach, a son of Conall Cearnach, an Ulster Hero of the Heroic Age. As a reward for defending Leinster from the men of Munster, he and his descendants were given the lands of Laois (named after Laoighseach) and they continued to rule this territory until the reign of Queen Elizabeth. They were the leading dynasty in a group of seven septs in Laois, which also included the O'Kellys, O'Lalors, O'Dorans, O'Dowlings, O'Devoys and the MacEvoys. The last O'More, lord of Laois, was Eoghan mac Ruaidhrí Ó Mórdha, who was killed in 1600 during the Nine Years' war between Aodh Ó Néill, EARL OF TYRONE (and Aodh Ruadh (Red Hugh) Ó Domhnaill) and the English.

THE 1ST (AND LAST) LORD SYDNEY OF LEIX, Baron of Stradbally married Lady Isabella St Laurence, the daughter of the 1st Earl of Howth by his wife Isabella King, the daughter of Sir Henry King (of Rockingham), 3rd Baronet and the sister of Edward King, 1st Earl of Kingston.

FIACHA (MAC AOIDH) Ó BROIN (O'Byrne) (1544–97). Lord of Gabhal Raghnaill, he was constantly in rebellion against the Government in Dublin Castle. From his base at Ballinacor, he raided the Pale in 1571 with Ruaidhrí Ó Mórdha, attacked the queen's seneschal and was involved with the murder of Robert Browne. He was pardoned for all of this in 1573, but seven years later he attacked seneschal Masterson in Wexford, joined Lord Baltinglas's rebellion and advanced to within ten miles of Dublin. When the Lord Deputy, Lord Grey de Wilton, attempted to capture Ó Broin, he was routed at Glenmalure by the men of Wicklow. Once again, in the next year, Ó Broin was pardoned, but in 1595, his sons burnt the house of the sheriff of Kildare and he was again proclaimed a traitor. This time, the new Lord Deputy, Sir William Russell, captured Ballinacor and Ó Broin fled. He appealed to Queen Elizabeth for pardon but then joined the EARL OF TYRONE in his rebellion. Ó Broin was captured by the Lord Deputy after a fierce fight in Glenmalure and was immediately beheaded.

WILLIAM COSBY. Cosby arrived in New York in 1731 (he had just been the controversial Governor of the Leeward Islands). Almost his first official action was to remove Mr Morris as Chief Justice of New York because he decided against him in a lawsuit. He then followed this up by a course of ballot rigging and, when he wrote an editorial attacking the Governor, the printer of the *Journal*, John Peter Zenger, was promptly arrested and put on trial. Cosby, who died in New York in 1736, has been described as 'spiteful, mean-spirited, quick-tempered, greedy, jealous, dull, and a petty tyrant.' That he achieved the position of Governor of New York has been explained by one historian, who wrote that such positions came to be occupied 'most often of members of aristocratic families whose personal morals, or whose incompetence, were such that it was impossible to employ them nearer home.'

SIR CHARLES LANYON (1813–89). An Englishman, he was articled to Jacob Owen, the architect of the Board of Works in Dublin, whose daughter he married in 1832. Appointed as the County Surveyor of Antrim, he designed Drenagh, County Londonderry, Dunderave, County Antrim and, his masterpiece, Ballywalter, County Down (as well as Killyleagh Castle in the same county).

Index

FitzGibbon family 28, 185
Fitzmaurice, Lady Charlotte 29
Fitzpatrick Mac Lochlainn, King
   of Aileach 66
Flaithbheartaigh *see* O'Flaherty
Flanagan, Donal O'Neill 74, 175
Fleming, David, Lord Slane 101
Follett, Rosina 193
Forward family 199, 200
Fox, Lucy 106
Fox, Michael and Katherine 147
French family 45, 75–84
French Park 75–84, 219–20
Freyne, de, family 83–4
   see also French
Fuller, James Franklin 113, 222
Fytton, Sir Edward 59–60

GABRIELLI, Gaspare 140, 223
Gaelic League 84
Galway Blazers 18, 20, 21
Gay, John 87, 89
Gaybrook 14, 85–90
GBE 141, 223
GCVO 141, 223
General Post Office, Dublin 12
Geraldines 157, 179, 224
Gibbons, James 12
Gilbert de Kentewell 144
Gilligan, Simon 140
Ginditz, Brian Kavanagh, Baron
   34
Ginkel, General (later 1st Earl of
   Athlone) 48, 216
Giraldus Cambrensis 117, 222
Gladstone, W.E. 141
Glananea 14, 91–6, 220
Glencairn Abbey (Castle Richard)
   146
Glorious Revolution 68, 80, 139,
   145, 211, 219
Gore, Sir Arthur 81
Gore-Booth, Sir Josslyn 188–9
Gorges, Lt-Gen. Richard 139
Gormanston, Viscounts (Preston)
   17, 97, 101–6
Gormanston Castle 95–106, 220–1
Gortnalea 65
Gosford Castle 70
Goulding, Sir Lingard 114
Grattan, Henry 193, 215, 221, 227
Gray, Sally *see* Stevens, Constance
Gregory, Sir William 6
The Guild of the Blessed Virgin
   125
Guinness, Sir Benjamin Lee 52, 53
Guinness, the Hon. Desmond 21,
   110, 214
Guinness, Oonagh 53
Gurney, Mr 51
Gurteen le Poer 57
Guthrie, Christina 52
Gwynn, Professor Denis 194, 195

HACKET, Mr 199
Hamilton, Lucy 68
Hare, Lady Louisa 147
Harman *see* King-Harman
Hayter, Sir George 44
Hazells, Mrs 199
Headfort, Marquesses (Taylor)
   110, 112–14
Headfort 107–14, 221–2
Hely-Hutchinson family
   (Donoughmore) 151–4
Herbert, Lady Beatrix 204
Herman, Prince von Pückler-
   Muskau 215

Hickman, Colonel 68
Hicks of Dublin 52, 130
Hillyard, Major Jack 30
Hodges, William 176
Hodson, Sir George 137, 223
Hollow Sword Blades Company 27
Home Rule 40, 132, 193
Hone, Evie 18
Hopkins, Gerard Manley 163
Hopper, Thomas 70
Hoskyn, Dr 145
Howard, Lady Anne 160
Howard family (Clonmore;
   Wicklow) 197–206
Howard, Hugh 200, 227
Howth family 180, 226
Howth Castle 137, 180
Humbert, General Jean-Joseph
   151, 223
Hume, Sir Gustavus 77
Humewood Castle 29
Huston, John 21
Hutchinson family 151–2, 224
Hyde, Ann 70
Hyde, Dr Douglas 62, 84, 218

IKERRIN, Viscount (Butler) 173
Inchiquin, Barons (O'Brien) 47,
   62, 63
IRA 132, 194
Irish names 8
Irish National Party 62, 218

JEFFERYES FAMILY 25–9
Jephson family 158–62
Jerpoint Abbey 173, 225
John, Augustus 18
John, King 43, 157, 158
Johnston, Francis 9–12, 102, 112,
   126–30, 214
Joyce family 179

KAVANAGH FAMILY 33–4, 37–40,
   122
   see also MacMurrough
   Kavanagh
KCMG 19, 214
Keightley, Catherine 67, 68
Keightley, Lady Frances 70
Kells-in-Ossory, Barons 101
Kendall, Mr 174
Kenlis, Barons (Taylor) 113
Kenmare, Earls 43, 216
Kenmare 43
Kensington, Louisa 160, 161
Kerry, 1st Earl 29
Kiely family 93
Kildare, Earls (Fitzgerald) 101,
   115–22, 118, 222
Kilfane 146, 223
Kilkea Castle 115–22, 222
Kilkenny 84
Killeen, Barons (Plunkett) 124,
   125, 134
Killeen Castle 123–34, 126, 223
Killeen House, Dublin 126
Killruddery 36, 135–42, 202, 223
Kilmaine, Barons (Browne) 43, 216
Kilmurry 143–8, 223–4
Kilshannig 36
Kincora 58, 65, 66
King family (Erris of Boyle;
   Kingston; Lorton) 70, 185–90
King, Edward 226
King, Mary 92
King-Harman, Laurence 187, 188
Kingsale, Lord 17
Kingsborough, Lord 82

Kingston, Earls (King) 70, 185,
   187–8, 190
Kneller, Sir Geoffrey 70
Knockdrin Castle 12
Knocklofty 149–54, 224
Kraft, David Von 30
Kruger, B.J. 114
Kylemore Castle 113

LA FELDE, Nicholas de 137–8
la Touche family 28, 29
Lacy, Hugh de 12, 59, 109, 117,
   125, 173, 214
The Ladies of Llangollen 34
Land League 93
Lane, Sir Hugh 129–30
Lanesborough, James Butler, 1st
   Viscount 87
Lanfranc, Archbishop of
   Canterbury 65
Langford House 110, 111
Langford, Sir Charles 212, 227
Lanyon, John 29, 215
Lapière, Gabriel 18
Lavalette, General Count 152
le Brocquy, Louis 18
le Brun family 43
   see also Browne
Leamaneh 219
Leathley, Frances 39
Leinster, Dukes (Fitzgerald)
   115–22
Leinster House, Dublin 44, 47, 52
Lemanagh Castle 70, 73
Lewis, Samuel 71
Limerick 65
Lismore, Barons; Viscounts
   (O'Callaghan) 193
Loftus family 166–8
Lorton, Viscounts (King) 185, 187
Lough Bray Cottage 146
Lough Cutra Castle 70
Louth, Earls (de Bermingham) 17
Lovett, John 139
Luggala Lodge 27, 53
Lynch, Henrietta 50
Lynch, Sir Henry 50, 216

MAC CARTHAIGH *see* MacCarthy
Mac Colman (Mac Giola-
   Maholmock) 138
Mac Diarmada Mhaighe Luirg *see*
   MacDermot
Mac Feorais family 17
Mac Giola-Maholmock, (Mac
   Colman) Dermait 138
Mac Giolla Phádraig *see*
   Fitzpatrick
Mac Lochlainn, King of Aileach 66
Mac Muiris (Prendergast) family
   45
Mac Murchadha Caomhánach
   family *see* MacMurrough
   Kavanagh
Mac Thoirdealbhaigh *see* Curley
McCalmont family 171, 174–6
MacCarthy family (Blarney;
   Carignavar; Clancar; Clancarty;
   Mountcashel; Muskerry)
   23–30, 48, 65, 125, 215
MacCormack, John 170, 225
McCullagh, John 110
MacDermot family 184, 226
MacDonald, Michael 14
MacDonnell family 98
McDonough, Bernard P. 74
McLeish, Alexander 12
MacLochlainn, Domhnall 58

MacMurrough Kavanagh family
   (Mac Murchadha
   (Caomhánach)) 8, 31, 33
MacSweeneys of Doe 221
MacWilliam family 179, 180
MacWilliam Íochtar 226
Malaspina, Marchese 53, 54
Mallow Castle 155–62, 224–5
Marconi, Gugliemo 73
Martin family 6, 217
Martyn, Edward 50
Massey, Revd Charles 112
Máire Ruadh 67
Maynooth Castle 117, 119
Mayo, Viscounts (Bourke) 179
Meade, Lady Melosina 140
Meath, William Brabazon, Earl 137
Meath, Manor of 125
Mee, Ann 44, 52
Meissen porcelain 52
Mellefont Abbey 167
Mereworth Castle, Kent 52–3
Miller, Gertie 121
Milliken, Richard 27, 28, 215
Millner, John 140
Mitchelstown Castle 70, 71, 187,
   188
mitred abbey 165, 225
Mo Ling (Mullins), St 215
Mon-a-beallin 208
Monasterevin 165–8
Monck family 6
Monck, Catherine and Henry 50
Monck, George, 1st Duke of
   Albemarle 50, 217, 220
Monck, Lady Harriet 95–6, 220
Montefiore, Sir Moses 51
Moore family 166–8
Moore Abbey 163–70, 226
Morrison, Sir Richard 31, 34, 36,
   37, 42, 50, 70, 135, 140, 143,
   146, 197, 200, 201–3, 215
Morrison, William Vitruvius 31,
   34, 36, 37, 146, 197, 200, 201–3,
   215
Mount Juliet 145, 171–6, 225
Mountcashel, Viscounts
   (MacCarthy) 26
Mountgarrett, Viscounts (Butler)
   158, 160, 224
Mountjoy, Lord 166
Moylug Tower 190
Muircheartach, Brian 58
Munster 64, 158, 224
Murphy, Frank 154
Muskerry, Viscounts (MacCarthy)
   26, 215

NASH, John 70, 185, 186, 187, 191,
   192, 193, 226
Nash, Piers O'Connor 62
The Neale 43
Neale, John Preston 34, 201, 227
Nevins, Thomas 132
Nicklaus, Jack 176
Nickson, Christina 151
Norbury, Mary 193
Normans 8, 12, 58–9, 142, 184
Norris (Norreys) family 156–62,
   224
North, Edward, Baron North 151,
   224
Nugent, Father Robert 119

O
Ó Hámsaigh, Donnchadh (Dennis
   Hempson) 6
Ó Néill, Art 6

O'Brien family (Clanrickarde; Inchiquin) 8, 43, 47, 62, 63–74, 120, 128
Ó Broin, Fiacha MacAoidh (O'Byrne) 227
O'Callaghan family (Lismore) 192–4
O'Carolan, Turlough 6, 57
Ockwells Manor 161
Ó Conchobhair Donn see O'Conor
O'Connell, Daniel 19, 50, 126, 152, 161
O'Connor, Maurice 104
O'Conor family 8, 55–62, 65, 78–81
O'Conor Roe family 59
O'Curry, Eugene 137, 223
O'Daly, Cormac 34
O'Dempsey family 165, 225
O'Dempsey, James 170
Ó Diomusaigh, Diarmuid see O'Dempsey
Ó Domhnall, Aodh Ruadh 158, 218
O'Donel family (Tyrconnell) 125, 180–1
O'Donovan, John 61
O'Flaherty family (Ó Flaithbheartaigh) 8, 44, 179, 216
Óg, Thomas 17
Oilioll Olum, king of Munster 64
O'Keefe, Paddy 154
O'Mahony, Owen 'The Pope' 221
O'Mahony, Tim 176
O'Malley family 8, 178–81
O'Malley, Grace (Gráinne Uaille or Ní Mháille) 178–80, 225–6
O'Mara 208
O'More family 208, 209, 213, 227
O'Neill family (Tyrone) 8, 47, 101, 167
Ó Néill, Eoghan Ruadh 47, 101, 216
Oranmore, Barons (Browne) 42–5, 48, 51–4
Ormond, Earls (Butler) 34, 215, 218
Ormond, Lord 45, 48, 125, 138
Ormonde, Dukes; Marquesses (Butler) 47, 68, 199, 218
O'Rorke family 8, 15, 18–22, 60, 61
O'Rorke, Mollie 18, 20–1
Orpen, Richard Caulfield 52
Ó Ruairc see O'Rorke
Osborne, Patrick 174, 226
Osler (lighting) 52
O'Toole, St Laurence 58, 116

Pain, George Richard 70, 187, 226
Pain, James 70, 187, 226
Pakenham-Mahon, Olive 189
Panini 110
Parnell, Charles Stuart 40
Pearce, Sir Edward Lovett 77
Pearse, Patrick 72
Peel, Sir Robert 81
Pembroke, Earls 33, 39, 43
    see also Clare, Richard de
Penal Laws 50, 104, 216
Pepusch, Dr John 89
Perrott, Sir John 78, 220
Petty, Sir William 108, 221
Phillimore, the Hon. Claude 141, 223
Plantation of Munster 158, 224
Plumptre, Ann 25, 27, 215
Plunkett family (Fingall; Killeen) 123–34
Plunkett, St Oliver 130, 223

Plunkett, Sir Nicholas 48
Pole-Carew, Lady Beatrice 194
Polmonty 33
Ponsonby family 34, 47, 52
Ponsonby, Frances 193
Ponsonby, Lady Sarah 168
Popje, Henry 140
Povey, Sir John 87
Powerscourt 77
Prendergast Castle 48
Prendergast family (Mac Muiris) 45, 216
Prendergast, Judith 139–40
Preston family (Gormanston; Tara) 17, 98–106, 126
Prout, Father 24
Purcell, Sgt Major 158
Pyne, Sir Richard 27

Quinn, Ian (mason) 126

R
'The Races of Castlebar' 151
Ralphsdale see Glananea
Rathcrogan 57
Rathmines, Battle of 125
Rathmore 117
Ravensworth 192
Raymond le Gros 173, 225
Redman, Elinor 174
Reilly, John 70
Reynell family 12
Reynolds, Thomas 120–1, 222
Riddlesford, Sir Walter de 117, 222
Riggs, Richard 93
Rinnuncini, Cardinal 47, 119
Roberts, Arthur 212
Roberts, Thomas 69, 219
Robertson, Daniel 141, 147–8
Rockfleet (Rossyvera) 177–82, 226
Rockingham 183–90, 226
Rosmead 93
Rossyvera (Rockfleet) 177–82, 225–6
Rowley, Hercules Langford 110
Ruaidhrí Ó Conchobhair 8
Russborough 77
Russell, Sir William, Lord Deputy 45, 166, 225
Ryan family 33

Sackville, Edward Sackville-West, Lord 195, 227
St Armand, Lord 100, 220
St Lawrence, Isabella 212
St Leger, Captain Warham 166, 225
Saint Patrick, Order of 52, 112, 113, 128, 140, 141, 154, 168, 193, 202, 221
St Valery 146
Sassoon, Sir Victor 132, 133, 134
Saunders, Mary 181
Schreiber, Lady Charlotte 52
Scott, Sir George Gilbert 198, 227
Scott, Michael 54
Semple, George 110
Seymour, James 65
Shanbally Castle 191–6, 227
Shannon, Mr (builder) 120
Sheil, James 129, 223
Shelton Abbey 36, 197–206, 226–7
Sheridan, Rev. Thomas 49
Sidney, Sir Henry 179, 214
Sisters of Charity of Jesus and Mary 170
Slane, David Fleming, Lord 101
Slane Castle 70

Slater, William 141
Slattery, Chris 134
Sligo, Marquessate 43, 216
Smith family 14, 19, 87–90, 91–6
Smith, Barney 18
Smith, Charlotte 72
Smyth family 14, 85–90, 91–6
Snow, Carmel 182
Society of United Irishmen 120, 222
Somerville, Admiral the 17th Baron 90
Somerville, Edith 147
South Sea Bubble 87
Southwell, Lord 126
Sovereign Military Order of Malta 204, 227
Stafford, Dr Thomas 188
Stafford-King-Harman family 188–90
Staples, Sir Robert 89
Stapleton family, stuccodores 11, 36, 37, 174, 214
Starkey family 67
Stephens, James 28
Stephens, Richard 109
Stevens, Constance (Sally Gray) 54
Stoney family 181
Stopford, Dorothea 139
Stradbally Hall 207–13, 227
Straffan House 14
Strancally Castle 70, 93
Strokestown Park 77
Strongbow see Clare, Richard de
Suirdale, Viscount 152
Summerhill 77, 109, 134
Sweet, Mr 174
Swift, Jonathan 7, 139
Sydney of Leix, Baron 212, 227

Taafe, Lord 48, 216
tanistry 220
Tara, Viscount (Preston) 101, 103
Taylor family (Bective; Headfort; Kenlis) 108–14
Taylour see Taylor
Thomastown Castle 37, 202
Thomond, Kings 8, 59, 64, 66
Thomond, Earls (O'Brien) 67, 219
Thomond House 74
Thomson, John 106
Tilden, Philip 190
Tilson, Sir Robert, 1st Lord Muskerry 6
Tinsley, William 150, 224
Tír Chonaill (Tyrconnell) see O'Donel
Tochar Mona Coinneadha, Battle of (Athenry) 17
Toirdhealbhach Ó Briain 65
Toirdhealbhach Ó Conchobhair, King of Connacht 58
Toirdhealbhach Ruadh 59
Toirdhealbhach Óg Ó Conchobhair Donn 59
Tone, Theobald Wolfe 120, 145
torc (muince) 215
Townley Hall 12
Treaty of Windsor 58
Trench, Lady Harriet 37
Tribes of Galway 43, 78, 215–16
Trollope, Anthony 18
'The Troubles' 189
Truffet, June 77
Tuite family 12
Tullamore 213
Tyrconnell, Earls (O'Donel; O'Donnell) 61, 218

Tyrell family 90
Tyrone, Earls (Ó Néill) 167, 221

Ufford, Robert d' 59
Uí Maine, King of 59
Ulster King of Arms (Sir J.B. Burke) 71, 78, 199, 204, 219, 227
Upper Dromore House 6

Vanvitelli 110
Vauxhall 111
Veale, John and Margaret 154
Vesey (de Vesci) family 83
Virginia Park Lodge 113
Vota Vita Mea 140, 223

Walter de Riddlesford 117
Wandesford, Eleanor 145
Waton family 174
Waton's Grove 173, 174
Waugh, Evelyn 104–6
Weld, Isaac 78, 186, 220
Wentworth, Thomas, 1st Earl of Strafford, Lord Deputy 46, 47, 167, 216
West, Robert 6
Westport House 43, 50
White Knight 185, 226
Wicklow, Earls (Howard) 197–206
Wild, David 114
Wildenstein, Daniel 133
Wilkinson, Sir Nevile Rodwell 227
William of Orange (later William III) 48
Williams, Jeremy 121, 204, 223
Williamson, Lt Richard 158
Wogan family 117
Wood, Mr (tutor to Kavanaghs) 38
Wooley, Samuel 92, 93, 220
Wyatt, James 86, 87, 92
Wyatt, Mathew 141
Wyatt windows 11, 86, 87, 145, 147, 214

Yeats, Jack B. 18
Young, Arthur 62, 93, 111–12, 221

Zucchi, Antonio 110, 111
Zuchelia, Roberto 110

Selected Bibliography

Many manuscripts, books, magazines and other publications have been consulted during the writing of this book. For those who have an interest in the topic and would like to read other books on the subject, the following are the volumes that have been of most assistance to me.

BENCE-JONES, MARK: *Burke's Guide to Country Houses, Volume I, Ireland* (London 1977) and revised as *A Guide to Irish Country Houses* (London 1988).

BENCE-JONES, MARK: *The Twilight of the Ascendancy* (London 1987).

BREWER, J.N.: *The Beauties of Ireland* 2 volumes (London 1825–1826).

BURKE, SIR BERNARD: '*A Visitation of the Seats and Arms of the Noblemen and Gentlemen of Great Britain and Ireland* 2 volumes (London 1852–1853); 2nd series, 2 volumes (London 1854–1855).

Burke's Landed Gentry of Ireland: 1912 edition.

Burke's Peerage: 1936 and Millennium editions.

COKAYNE, GEORGE EDWARD (edited by Gibbs, Vicary): *The Complete Peerage of England, Scotland, Ireland, Great Britain, and the United Kingdom* 13 volumes (London 1910–1959) and HAMMOND, PETER: *The Complete Peerage: Addenda and Corrigenda* vol. 14 (London 1998).

Country Life (London, various issues to date)

CRAIG, MAURICE: *Classic Irish Houses of the Middle Size.* (London 1976)

DE BREFFNY, BRIAN AND FFOLLIOTT, ROSEMARY: *The Houses of Ireland* (London 1975).

DE BREFFNY, BRIAN: *Castles of Ireland* (London 1977).

The Dictionary of National Biography (London 1885–1990)

GRIFFIN, DAVID J., ROBINSON, NICHOLAS K. & GLIN, THE KNIGHT OF: VANISHING COUNTRY HOUSES OF IRELAND. (Dublin 1988)

GUINNESS, THE HONOURABLE DESMOND AND RYAN, WILLIAM: *Irish Houses and Castles* (London 1971).

GUINNESS, THE HONOURABLE DESMOND AND O'BRIEN, JACQUELINE: *Great Irish Houses and Castles* (London 1994).

HALL, SAMUEL CARTER AND HALL, MRS (Anna Maria Fielding): *Ireland, its Scenery, Character, etc.* 3 volumes (1841–1843)

HARBISON, P.: *Guide to the National Monuments of Ireland* (Dublin 1975)

HOWLEY, J.: *The Follies and Garden Buildings of Ireland* (Yale University Press and London 1993)

THE IRISH ARCHITECTURAL ARCHIVE (Rowan, Ann Martha, Rowan, Alastair and McParland, Edward): *The Architecture of Richard Morrison and William Vitruvius Morrison* (Dublin 1989).

The Irish Tatler and Sketch (1947–1961)

KILLANIN, THE LORD. & DUIGNAN, M.V.: *The Shell Guide to Ireland* (London 1976).

LEWIS, SAMUEL: *Topographical Dictionary of Ireland* 2 Vols (London 1837).

MALINS, EDWARD AND GLIN, THE KNIGHT OF: *Lost Demesnes: Irish Landscape gardening 1660–1845* (London 1976).

MALINS, EDWARD AND BOWE, PATRICK: *Irish Gardens and Demesnes from 1830* (London 1980).

MILTON, THOMAS: *A Collection of select views from different seats of the nobility and gentry….in Ireland* (London 1783 – 1793).

MORRIS, THE REVEREND F.O.: *A Series of Picturesque Views of the Seats of the Noblemen and Gentlemen of Great Britain and Ireland* 6 volumes (London 1866–1880).

NEALE, J.P.: *Views of the Seats of Noblemen and Gentlemen in England, Wales, Scotland and Ireland* 6 volumes (London 1818 – 1823); 2nd series, 5 volumes (London 1824–1829).

A New History of Ireland, under the auspices of the Royal Irish Academy: Volume IX - Maps, Genealogies. Lists (Oxford at the Clarendon Press 1984)

PAKENHAM, VALERIE: *The Big House in Ireland* (London 2001).

SOMERVILLE-LARGE, PETER: *Life in the Irish Country House: A Social History* (London 1995)

WILLIAMS, JEREMY: *A Companion Guide to Architecture in Ireland, 1837–1921* (Dublin 1994).

This book was prompted by a love for Irish domestic architecture, a passion that was awakened by Desmond Guinness' 1971 book on Irish Country Houses. In its wake came important books and articles written by Brian de Breffny, Maurice Craig, Dr Mark Girouard, Alastair Rowan, Edward McParland and Desmond Fitzgerald, The Knight of Glin (Ridire An Gleanna). However, the most invaluable (and essential) volume was written for Burke's Peerage by Mark Bence-Jones (who followed it up with a superb account of the final days of the old order in *Twilight of the Ascendancy*). The witty and scholarly *Companion to Victorian Architecture* by Jeremy Williams fittingly (and chronologically) rounds off this field of thoroughbred authors and volumes.

ACKNOWLEDGEMENTS

This book may have a single name on the title page but it is the work of many hands. With this in mind, I should like to thank my mother, Kathleen Dolan MacDonnell, for her love and encouragement, without which I could not have written this book; those members of my family who have gone but who believed that I had the ability to write, my father, Robert, my grandmother, Maud Dolan, and my grandaunts, Ethel, Rita and Clare Reid, are in my heart and my thanks goes out to them. Garech Browne, whose assistance with the whole concept was, literally, invaluable, and the great kindness and encouragement of Susan Haynes, which turned the notion of this book into a reality; my editor, Jinny Johnson, who helped to fashion a real book out of a plethora of words, and Michael Dover, who generously commissioned it, are owed a debt I cannot repay. Special gratitude is also owed to John Mitchinson.

My family and friends have kept me sane during this period (I am not at all sure that it has been reciprocal). Accordingly, I would like to thank my brother, Count Peter MacDonnell, and Kieran Conroy; David Swift, Tom McDonald, Sam Durrant, Jack Hagenaars; my sister, Joan MacDonnell-Alexander, her husband, Edmund and their children, Peter-Randal, Michael and Siobhan (as well as their families); my cousin, Dr Alasdair McDonnell; Toby Borland, Stephen O'Dea and my old friends, John Moulder-Brown, Michael Cochran and Leonard Whiting (not forgetting Arthur, Gigi, Sidonie, Honey and Harvey).

I have had the assistance of some of the best experts on the subjects of genealogy, architecture, history and Gaelic as I wrote this tome. The help given by the Chief Herald of Ireland, Brendan O'Donoghue; the Deputy Chief Herald, Fergus Gillespie (for his advice, scholarship and knowledge of the Irish language), and his wife Conchita; Mícheál Ó Comáin and his wife Morita; the former Chief Herald, Donal Begley; David Griffin, Director of the Irish Architectural Archive, and Hugh Doran and Ann Henderson; Dr W. Simpson, the Librarian of Trinity College, Dublin and Charles Benson, the Keeper of Early Printed Books, Trinity College, Dublin; Muriel Allison, who organised everything with great good humour and flawless efficiency; the staff of the National Library of Ireland, especially Kevin Browne, Bernard Devaney and Sandra MacDermot; as well as Scott MacMillan of Rathdown and his wife, Katherine Kurtz, has made this book possible.

Special mention should be made of the people who copied the photos, Helfried Prünster, Jeannette Müller and Harald Longo. I wish to thank Jonathan Dalton and Paddy Lyons who showed me how to use a computer and patiently put up with my mistakes until I became the expert (!) that I am today. I also had invaluable advice and encouragement from the irrepressible Susan Chenery, Jeremy Williams, Dr John Gilmartin, Camille Souter, Baron Thierry Terrier, David Mlinaric, the Stafford-Northcote family, The Honourable Desmond Guinness, Patrick Guinness, Jerry Scanlan, Gordon Campbell, Philip Bryan, Aidan Corcoran, Hugh Dunn, Aidan Kelly, Brendan Wrafter, Jamie Murphy, Trevor McDowell, Gráinne Ni Cormac (Mrs Grace Pym), Frank Stanley, Danny, Paula and Christina Hughes, Seamus Hosey, Paul Sinnot and Duncan Stewart. Also Michael O'Sullivan (who provided both friendship and encouragement) and Brendan Ward (who went so far as to buy me a typewriter several years ago to enable me to write), Tony Boylan (who had to listen to chapter after chapter) and the staff at Luggala, whose support has been nothing less than phenomenal – Nicholas Meyers, Frances Gillespie, John M. Welsby, Noleen Webster, Tom Clinton, Mary O'Leary and Margaret Tracey, and Michael de Cozar, hall porter at the Ritz in London. There are those whose friendship has supported me during the past few years. I wish to thank Princess Purna of Morvi, her sister, Princess Uma of Morvi and their mother, Her Highness The Maharani of Morvi; for the information he gave to me about his family home, I wish to thank Lord Oranmore and Browne; and Michael Houlihan, who opened up the gates of Shelton Abbey for me and whose kindness will not be forgotten.

The list of those who have helped and encouraged me would be utterly incomplete if it did not include Miss Catherine Carney and her sister, Dr Claire Carney, (whose father Michael J. Carney owned the The Bray Printing Company which printed the *Irish Tatler and Sketch*), Anne, Lady Crofton, Jonathan Dawson, Lord Inchiquin (Ó Briain), Alfred Cochran, Hugo O'Neill of Clanaboy, Valerie, Lady Goulding, Marcus Clements and his wife, Amanda Douglas, Rudra Kapoor, Sasha, Freiherr von Hoyningen-Huene, Seamus Heaney, John Montague and Elizabeth Wassell, Sean Galvin, Louis le Brocquy and Anne Madden, Ben and Frances Kiely, Peter and Dorothy Berresford-Ellis, John Hurt and Sarah Owens, my friend Tom, Mac Suibhne na dTuath and Barbara, Madam MacSweeney (for so much kindness both), Frank McDonald (who read the text even when he had a deadline to make), Oliver and Maureen Nulty and Noelle Campbell-Sharp (who first asked me to write professionally) and Mark Nixon (who took my photograph for the jacket). A last thank you to two little Burmese ladies in London, Claudia and Lily.

DEDICATION

*To my father Robert (Robin)
and my mother, Kathleen
For all of their love
and care*

*To my grandmother,
Maud (Mimi)
and my grandaunts, Ethel,
Rita and Clare
For their love, gentleness
and generosity*

*To Peter
For being the best brother
in the world*

*To Kieran
For simply being there*

*To Garech
For his friendship and
his generosity*

*To Purna
For her friendship
and kindness*

*To Susan
For her goodness and her
patience (if she does not
qualify for canonisation
after this, she never will!)*

*To Fergus
For his advice, scholarship
and knowledge of the
Irish language*

First published in the
United Kingdom in 2002 by
Weidenfeld & Nicolson

Text copyright
© Randal MacDonnell, 2002

Design and layout copyright
© Weidenfeld & Nicolson, 2002

The moral right of
Randal MacDonnell to be
identified as the author of this work
has been asserted in accordance
with the Copyright, Designs
and Patents Act of 1988

The photographs in this book are from *Irish Tatler & Sketch*, and are reproduced with the kind permission of the National Library of Ireland, Kildare Street, Dublin 4, Ireland.

In some instances the author found rejects from the photographer's original commissioned shoot and, where possible, these have been included in the book with the kind permission of Trinity College, Dublin, the Office of Public Works, Dublin, the Architectural Archive, Dublin, The Hon Garech Browne, and Viscount Gormanston.

A CIP catalogue record for this book is available from the British Library

ISBN 0 297 84301 X

Design director David Rowley

Editorial director Susan Haynes

Designed by Ken Wilson

Edited by Jinny Johnson

Proofreader Gwen Rigby

Indexer Elizabeth Wiggans

Typeset in Monotype Imprint
Printed and bound in Italy

Weidenfeld & Nicolson
Wellington House
125 Strand
London
WC2R 0BB